Mind Your Faith

Essays in Apologetics

2nd Edition
Revised and Expanded

Doy Moyer

ISBN-10: 1890119571
ISBN-13: 9781890119577

Contents

Dedication

For family

Laurie, my wife of over 31 years
Caleb, Caitlin, and Eliana Moyer
Luke, Sarah, Joshua, Elizabeth, Abigail, and Nathan Moyer
Audrey Moyer

Preface: Readings in Apologetics

Apologetics is a formal term for the discipline that rationally seeks to defend the Bible and Christianity. It derives from the Greek *apologia* (cf. 1 Pet 3:15) and means to give a reason or defense of something (it does not mean to be sorry in this context). We call this Biblical Apologetics because here we are seeking to give a rational defense of God, Jesus, the Bible, and all that goes with our faith.

Why do we engage in apologetics? First, because those who do accept the Bible believe that God desires for us to engage in some level of apologetics: "always ready to make a defense to everyone who asks you to give an account for the hope that is in you" (1 Pet 3:15). We try to do this with gentleness and respect. As Christians, we have a firm conviction that what we believe and accept is the truth, and we will try to persuade others to accept it also.

Involved in the study of apologetics is the presentation of both evidence and reason. Christians believe that faith is reasonable, not contrary to the evidence that exists. Faith and reason work together and help provide a solid foundation upon which faith can grow stronger.

Yet the study of Apologetics does not, in itself, create saving faith. Saving faith comes from hearing the word of God (Rom 10:17). What the study of apologetics does is to help remove stumbling blocks that sometimes get in the way of faith. Ultimately, our goal in presenting apologetics is to help people come to Christ. If we can help remove a few stumbling blocks along the way, then by God's grace we have been successful in our efforts. This is explained further in the readings.

These readings were designed for an introductory course in evidences. Each reading was purposefully kept brief in order to help reinforce the material covered in class. However, they can stand on their own as an introduction to the various fields covered by apologetics. Even then, not everything that can be covered is here. Those who have studied evidences already know that the subject areas and available materials are vast. Further, I make no claim that the material in these readings is completely original to me. In some cases, I have summarized what many others have written in lengthy books and articles. The idea here is to facilitate an introductory understanding and urge deeper study in areas that interest the reader.

If you already believe in God and the Bible, then perhaps we can say a few things that will aid you in your efforts to talk to others. If you are a skeptic, then we ask that you keep an open mind and carefully weigh what is said. I realize that issues in apologetics are argued in different ways. Some arguments are better than others. I continually modify my approach because growth and argumentation is never static. I do not suspect that all will agree with the way I present everything. That is to be expected. But I do think that the dialogue is important. I do not pretend to have all the answers to every question that might be asked. But I will offer up my thoughts as one who is convinced of the truth of God and the Bible as His word. It is to this end that I may strive to glorify Him.

The 2nd edition

Because of various needs and issues that need to be addressed, adding extra material to Mind Your Faith was deemed expedient. Clarification of some materials is also helpful, and this, too, has been part of this revision for some chapters. Some chapters have also been rearranged in an effort to keep general topics together. While the first edition was written as an aid to an introductory course in evidences, the 2nd edition is the result of further reflection and the desire to be more thorough, while still keeping most of it at an introductory level. No doubt more can be added.

Introduction to Apologetic Methods

How shall we approach the study of evidences? What is the best method for approaching people? How can we be the most effective in reaching out with the message of Jesus Christ in a world so full of skepticism?

Apologetics (the defense of God, Jesus, and Scripture) is a multi-faceted discipline. There are several approaches that may be used, but there are disagreements among apologists as to what methods are the most biblical and which work the best. Some are quite critical of other approaches for a variety of reasons, but the purpose here is not one of critique. I will give a brief overview of the some of the major approaches, using the classification system presented in the book *Five Views on Apologetics*.[1] I recommend a reading of this book for a good overview of various methods, including the pros and cons.

In a general sense, three of the methods can fall under the classification of *evidentialism*. This means that they are focused more upon the use of evidences to make the case, and they generally agree on the relationship between faith and reason. These methods are often eclectic, overlapping with each other at various points and arguments. These classifications are given simply as a starting point for understanding the issues involved.

The Classical Method starts with natural theology (arguing for God's existence from nature) in order to establish theism as the proper worldview. Only after theism is established through natural theology do the proponents move to historical evidences to show the truth of Jesus. In other words, they first want to show that theism is true generally, then demonstrate that the biblical view is the best view of theism (making this a two-step approach: God first

---

[1] Steven B. Cowan, ed., *Five Views on Apologetics* (Grand Rapids, MI: Zondervan, 2000).

(generic), then the God of Scripture (specific). Examples of arguments from natural theology include the Cosmological Argument (i.e., first cause) and the Teleological Argument (design of the universe, etc.). Sometimes it is argued that this two-step approach is necessary as a foundation for arguing historical evidences. The idea is that, without a theistic base, one could not show historically that miracles occurred. Biblically, natural theology is supported by passages like Psalm 19: "the heavens are telling of the glory of God; and their expanse is declaring the work of His hands" (v. 1). Natural theology is biblical, but the question is whether or not it is the best starting point.

The Evidentialist Method (i.e., Historical Method). If the classical method is seen as a two-step approach, the historical method is more of a one-step approach. Proponents would disagree with the classical approach in that they do not think that one must begin with natural theology, even if the person they are trying to persuade is an atheist. Miracles are stressed as being historical, which, in turn demonstrated God and His activity in the world. In other words, historical miracles, particularly the resurrection, can be used as evidence for both the existence of God and the truth of Jesus Christ all in one step. If the resurrection of Jesus is historically real, then the event would show that there is a God and that Jesus is the Lord. This method is focused on the nature of history and how God has empirically revealed Himself in history through the life, death, and resurrection of Jesus.

The Cumulative Case Method argues that the case for Christianity is not a strict formal argument (which more characterizes natural theology and historical evidences), but is, instead, informal, like a lawyer would present a courtroom brief before a jury. The argument is that the biblical view is the best explanation of all of the data taken together. Proponents do not seek to rely upon one or two major arguments, but instead take all of the evidence as a whole to argue that biblical theism best explains everything. The strength of this approach would be that even if one or two particulars can be explained away by skeptics (e.g., the problem of evil), they must explain all of the evidence taken together. This approach uses the arguments from natural theology and historical evidences, but is more concerned with everything taken together for a total explanation. Critics argue that this approach can look as though one is simply trying to make up for lost ground by adding together several weaker arguments instead of focusing positively on the solid, strong historical evidences at our disposal.

Presuppositionalism. In this view, believers and unbelievers do not have enough common ground between each other to allow the evidentialists (any of the above approaches) to accomplish their goals. No assumptions are neutral enough to reason with unbelievers. "The presuppositionalist emphasizes the way all human belief systems depend on unprovable basic assumptions, arguing that biblical faith or its lack thereof crucially shapes our presuppositions." Believers and unbelievers will not agree on the fundamentals needed for evidentialists to establish their position. Thus, one must presuppose Christianity as the beginning point in apologetics. All meaning and thought presupposes the existence of the God of Scripture. Presuppositionalists try to demonstrate that unbelievers cannot argue, think, or live properly without first presupposing the biblical God. Only biblical theism can make sense of the world, and all other worldviews are inherently flawed. Further, a Christian simply cannot believe in God and Scripture and at the same time try to entertain the idea that God may not exist or that the Bible may not be God's revelation. Neutrality is not possible, and no Christian should ever attempt to be neutral. Presuppositionalists often focus on the inherent inconsistencies of non-biblical worldviews.

---

[2] C. Stephen Evans, *Pocket Dictionary of Apologetics and Philosophy of Religion* (Downers Grove, IL: InterVarsity Press, 2002), 96.

Reformed Epistemology. Proponents of reformed epistemology hold that it is perfectly reasonable to believe many things without evidence. Belief in God does not require the support of evidence or argument in order for it to be rational. Advocates would argue that God has given us an awareness of Himself that can be awakened in many ways (e.g., a sense of awe at nature). In this way, people can be "taken" with belief in God, not argued into belief. Belief in God is not dependent upon theistic arguments. The natural knowledge we all have of God simply needs to be roused, which requires our humility and awareness. Rational people can believe without evidence.

Personal remarks. This short overview hardly does justice to the positions described. I encourage readers to consider detailed explanations and defenses of these positions from their own advocates. These are methods that may help, but they are not catch-all methods for every occasion. As Os Guinness writes, "Every single person is unique and individual and deserves an approach that respects that uniqueness," and, "Creative persuasion is a matter of being biblical, not of being either modern or postmodern."[3]

I find myself agreeing with all of these at some points, and disagreeing (sometimes strongly) at other points. The argument I appeal to most often is the historical resurrection of Jesus. I believe that miracles can be established on historical grounds, which, in turn, argues for God. I make use of natural theology, but do not think it is a necessary first step. I find a cumulative case can be helpful, as long as it is not about pooling a bunch of weak arguments (several weak arguments do not make for one strong one); most arguments I would employ in this realm are about defending against attacks and showing the reasonableness of faith in God so as to remove stumbling blocks to faith. Further, the recognition of presuppositions is vital (see the chapter on this), but

---

[3] Guinness, Os, *Fool's Talk: Recovering the Art of Christian Persuasion* (Downer's Grove, IL: InterVarsity Press, 2015), 33-34.

this does not rule out the use of evidence. All people have presuppositions, but can we recognize them for what they are and keep an open mind about reality? If so, then we can have some common beginning ground with unbelievers.

These methods are useful depending on the circumstances and the objections being raised. We should try to start where people are (e.g., Paul in Acts 17 at Athens), and then use valid arguments that address people where they need to be addressed. In the end, however, the only real positive argument that demonstrates the truth of Jesus must necessarily be about the resurrection (1 Cor 15). No apologetic system will ever be complete apart from the most basic and foremost facts of the gospel: Christ died, was buried, rose again, and appeared to many people. Based upon these facts, we can confidently serve the Lord, knowing that our labor is not in vain (v. 58). May God bless us as we seek to better understand our role in getting the message of the Gospel out to a world so much in need of God's grace.

Discussion Questions

1. How does a little understand of how people approach evidences help us make a better case for Christ?

2. What are the basic differences between natural theology, the historical approach, and the cumulative approach? How do these differ from presuppositionalism and reformed epistemology?

3. How do you think you can use these approaches in a positive way?

4. Do you think there is an approach we should avoid? Why or why not?

Made to Think

Man is obviously made to think. It is his whole dignity and his whole merit; and his whole duty is to think as he ought.

Blaise Pascal, Pensées, 46

Faith and Evidence

1

Faith is a key component of conviction. If we are convinced that something is true, then we trust 1) that our evidence or reason for believing is solid, and 2) that our reasoning abilities are sufficient to properly interpret the evidence so that our conclusion is true (agrees with reality). If either the evidence or the reasoning process is faulty, then our faith has been misplaced and our worldview will not accurately reflect reality. A sound worldview must be based upon truth, and this means that Christians, who are especially concerned with truth, are also concerned about both the evidence and how they reason about that evidence.

The Bible teaches that faith is the "assurance of things hoped for, the conviction of things not seen" (Heb 11:1). Faith stands under hope as a foundation. Without faith, we cannot please God (v. 6). In this passage, we are told that we must believe 1) God is, and 2) God rewards those who diligently seek Him. This provides the basis for hope of the unseen. To be assured of what we hope for, we must be convicted about that which we cannot physically see—namely God and the reward He has promised. This also means that we must use our reasoning abilities in order to have some kind of conviction about these unseen matters. In order to do this properly, we need a little better understanding of what we mean by "evidence." We also need better understanding of the term "faith."

Sometimes people disconnect faith from evidence. That is, if we ask for evidence, then we are somehow indicating a lack of faith because faith should be able to stand on its own apart from any evidence. But this misunderstands the nature of faith and its relationship to evidence and reason. God expects us to use the reasoning abilities that He created in us. Faith and reason go hand in hand because the reason and evidence that promotes faith all come from the hand of God.

Faith and Evidence Tied Together

In order to see how the Bible ties faith and evidence together, consider the following passages:

1. John 20:30-31. In the context, Jesus has been raised from the dead and is appearing to His disciples. Thomas was missing on the first occasion and would not believe the other disciples when they told Thomas that they had seen Jesus alive. Thomas' attitude is seen in his reply: "Unless I see ... I will not believe" (see v. 25). Jesus later appeared and told Thomas to see and touch: "do not be unbelieving, but believing" (v. 27). Thomas responded, "My Lord and My God!" (v. 28). The next three verses tell us the purpose of the Gospel of John. Jesus told Thomas, "Because you have seen Me, have you believed? Blessed are they who did not see, and yet believed" (v. 29). The question is, how do we believe if we have not seen? John answers: "Therefore many other signs Jesus also performed in the presence of the disciples, which are not written in this book; but these have been written so that you may believe that Jesus is the Christ, the Son of God; and that believing you may have life in His name" (vv. 30-31).

Just because we have not seen something does not mean that no evidence exists for it. Most of us have not seen atoms (and then can only do so with help), yet we accept that they exist. In a court of law, jurors listen to testimony in order to ascertain the truth of the case. They were not witnesses themselves to the alleged crime (they wouldn't be on the jury if they were), but they consider the evidence and the testimony (often from eyewitnesses), then use their reasoning abilities to evaluate and determine whether or not the defendant is guilty. They did not have to see the events to be able to say, beyond a reasonable doubt, that the events did or not happen a certain way. That is how evidence works in a court of law, with evaluating history, and with respect to the Bible and Jesus Christ.

John said that Jesus performed "signs" that lead to belief, even for those who have not actually witnessed them firsthand. When we consider that evidence refers to the facts or signs upon which a conclusion can be based, then we can see how the Bible itself points to evidence on behalf of Jesus. Based upon that evidence, there is an expectation of a response of belief. If we can trust the testimony, then faith has been engaged and it is founded upon proper evidence.

2. Matthew 11:2-6. John was in prison and he sent disciples to Jesus and asked, "Are You the Expected One, or shall we look for someone else?" Jesus' answer gives some insight into the nature of faith and evidence: "Go and report to John what you hear and see" (v. 4). Notice that Jesus did not say, "You just have to believe," as if it did not matter what evidence He had given. Instead, Jesus pointed to what they could see and hear. This is evidence. They could hear the teachings of Jesus and they could see what He was doing, and based upon that they had all they needed in order to know who Jesus was.

Even though we do not "see and hear" Jesus in the same way they could, we have the testimony of those who did see and hear Him. When that testimony is passed along, even in written form, then we still have evidence upon which we can draw conclusions (much like a historian would draw conclusions based upon ancient documents and testimony). Evidence is not lacking at all on behalf of Jesus. Digging deeper will show that evidence is plentiful, and it both informs and encourages our faith.

What is Biblical Faith?

The common idea about faith is that it is "belief without evidence" or "believing something in spite of the evidence." This makes faith sound unreasonable, blind, and gullible. If the world can represent faith like that, then no wonder people want to avoid "faith." No one wants to be unreasonable and gullible. Sadly, the world has been able to abuse the concept of "faith" in this way and it has resulted in serious misunderstandings about God, Jesus, the Scriptures, and the overall nature of faith.

Everyone exercises faith in something. No one is exempt from having faith, and that includes atheists who believe that nature alone is capable of producing the universe and the living conditions of the earth. This philosophy of naturalism is not, by any stretch of the imagination, a proven, scientific fact. It is a faith. People exercise faith daily and constantly. The basic idea of faith is trust, and we trust people and circumstances every day. Any time we use our hands to feel, our eyes to see, and our minds to think, we have faith that our senses accurately perceive reality. We trust that our parents are who they say they are. We trust that gravity (of which we only see effects) will keep us on the ground. Juries trust that the evidence leads them to a conclusion "beyond a reasonable doubt." Faith is as much a part of our lives as breathing. We cannot function without it. No one can, and those who would deny this are fooling none but themselves.

There is nothing inherently gullible or blind about faith, and when we consider the fact that the Bible warns against being gullible (see 1 John 4:1; Acts 17:11), we learn that biblical faith is neither blind nor unreasonable. Proper faith rests securely upon the evidence God has provided for us. In the situation of Thomas in John 20:24-31, the irony is that he was not being the most reasonable when he refused to believe the witnesses who saw Jesus alive again. "I will not believe" is not in itself a reasonable statement, especially if our worldview has shut the door to the possibility that there might be greater forces at work than what our limited sight can envision.

What is necessary in order to have a reasonable, saving faith? What does the Bible show us with respect to faith? First, reasonable faith has some level of understanding (Acts 17:22-31). When Paul went into the city of Athens, he began where they were with their gods.

He then proceeded to explain to them the true God of heaven and earth. If we are going to have proper faith, we must believe that God is (Heb 11:6), but this implies that we have some level of understanding about who God is. Second, reasonable faith requires that we have a reason for accepting what we believe. In other words, faith is not just some willy-nilly "think whatever you wish" whim, but is grounded on objective evidence and testimony. Peter wrote that we must sanctify Christ as Lord and always be ready to give a defense of our hope (1 Pet 3:15). We cannot offer a defense or a reason for the hope within if we have no reason for it to begin with. Third, biblical faith requires a willingness to act (Jas 2). James informs us that faith involves the mind or intellect, the emotions, and the will to act. Even the demons believed (intellectual acceptance), and shuddered (emotional reaction), but who will argue that they were saved? James argued that a person of faith must act, and that takes an act of the will.

Also important is understanding what faith does *not* require. Faith involves making a conscious decision about what we cannot see (2 Cor 4:18). We can do this with evidence and reason, and even though we need some level of understanding, faith does not require that we know all there is to know about the subject, or that we understand all the "why's and wherefore's" about it. Most of us will not understand everything there is to know about cars or computers, but that does not stop us from using them. We need some understanding of God, but this does not suggest that we can know or understanding all there is to know about God (see Job 38; Rom 11:33-34), especially since He is capable of doing far more than we can even think (Eph 3:20). We are finite, necessarily limited by time and space, so faith does not mean that we have figured everything out that is possible. Faith requires humility, an acknowledgement that we are not the final authority on life and reality. Someone much greater exists upon whom we must rely.

On the Nature of Evidence

We have already illustrated the nature of evidence by appealing to a courtroom setting where the jury assesses the evidence and makes a decision. Whatever they decide will necessarily involve faith. The point, though, is that the nature of evidence conforms to the nature of reason. Virtually any idea that we hold as a conviction is, at least in our minds, beyond a reasonable doubt. What that means is that we begin to consider doubt to be unreasonable along the way of our acceptance of a position. Most accept that their parents really are their parents without feeling the need to scientifically verify it. Is it reasonable to trust that our parents are who they say they are? Must we have further proof in order for this to be reasonable?

How do we know that anything has happened in history? How do we know that we didn't just pop into existence five minutes ago complete with a false memory? Really. How do we know? Silly, one may think, but the fact is that whatever we believe about the past is going to be based upon faith. How do we know that George Washington was the first President of the United States? Or that Julius Caesar was assassinated in Rome? Or that Alexander the Great pushed his forces to the edge of India? We accept these matters on faith, and for the most part believe it would be unreasonable to doubt them because the evidence leads us to that conclusion. But do we realize that there is as much or more evidence for the resurrection of Jesus than there is for other ancient historical people?

Typically, apologetics (a system of defense) breaks down into three primary categories: scientific, philosophical, and historical. We will be considering evidences in all of these categories. Scientific evidences appeal to what we can learn from the nature of our world and universe (for example, the cosmological argument for God's existence). Philosophical evidence appeals to logic and reason, recognizing that God gave us rational minds to think and reason on matters that cannot be empirically verified (for example, the problem of evil and suffering). Historical evidence appeals to the objective testimony that is open to investigation, the ancient documents and eyewitness accounts (that tell us, for example, about the resurrection of Jesus). Together, these areas of evidence give us the warrant to confidently assert our faith in Jesus as Lord and the Bible as His word.

Faith has consequences for eternity. We don't give up our intellect when we choose to believe. Rather, we use our intellect to inform our faith so that, in the final analysis, God will be glorified.

Discussion Questions

1. Why is faith necessary to live life?

2. How is faith tied to evidence? Discuss John 20 and Matthew 11.

3. What is biblical faith? Why is this sometimes misunderstood?

4. What is necessary for reasonable faith?

5. What is not necessary for reasonable faith?

6. What does "beyond a reasonable doubt" mean? Why is the principle significant?

7. How do you know anything historically? Why is this type of evidence important?

Why Study Logic?

First, a study of logic helps apologists to think and present their position objectively and accurately. Second, a large number of rational objections brought against the Bible and the Christian faith stem from logically faulty deductions.

Johnson C. Philip and Saneesh Cherian,
Logic and Apologetics

The Need for Apologetics 2

Christians in the first century lived in a dangerous world. To become a Christian, one needed a mindset of being willing to suffer and, if called upon to do so, die for Jesus Christ. "Be faithful until death, and I will give you the crown of life," said Jesus (Rev 2:10). This did not mean simply to stay faithful until growing old and dying, but to stay faithful even to the point of dying for the cause of Christ.

Peter told his readers that, as Christ suffered in the flesh, they needed to arm themselves with that same purpose (1 Pet 4:1-2). To do so meant that a Christian was genuinely convinced and convicted about the truth concerning God, Jesus as Lord, and His divine word. The great temptation was to give up so that they did not suffer at the hands of the enemies of the cross (see 1 Pet 4:12-19).

Because of those trials that they were ready to suffer, God's people had to be prepared to face the world in such a way that they were unashamed to be called Christians (1 Pet 4:16). Not only were they to be ready to suffer, they needed to have the tools in hand to try to persuade others of the truth of Jesus Christ. Peter wrote:

> Who is there to harm you if you prove zealous for what is good? But even if you should suffer for the sake of righteousness, you are blessed. And do not fear their intimidation, and do not be troubled, but sanctify Christ as Lord in your hearts, always *being* ready to make a defense to everyone who asks you to give an account for the hope that is in you, yet with gentleness and reverence; and keep a good conscience so that in the thing in which you are slandered, those who revile your good behavior in Christ will be put to shame. For it is better, if God should will it so,

that you suffer for doing what is right rather than for doing what is wrong. (1 Pet 3:13-17)

Today we face similar challenges. Though we may not be suffering physical persecution at the present, that possibility is always there. Even more, we face practical and academic challenges from a world that more and more ridicules faith and Scripture. We cannot bury our heads and think that these challenges will just go away. We must be prepared to meet them head on. In order to do that, we must do exactly what the Christians in the first century were told to do. Note 1 Peter 3:15: "but sanctify Christ as Lord in your hearts, always *being* ready to make a defense to everyone who asks you to give an account for the hope that is in you, yet with gentleness and reverence." In order to be effective in the world, Christians must set aside Christ in their hearts as the Lord, ready to "make a defense" to everyone who asks a reason for our hope, and with an attitude of respect and gentleness.

What is Apologetics?

The term used for "make a defense" in 1 Peter 3:15 is the word *apologia*. From this word we get "apology." Today, "apology" carries the idea of being sorry for something, but that is not the meaning of the term in Scripture. We are certainly not to be sorry for being Christians! Rather, in Scripture, the *apologia* means *a verbal defense* or a *speech in defense*. Peter was telling Christians that they needed to be ready to speak up in defense of their hope in Christ in the face of persecution. Paul used the same word in Philippians 1:7, where he wrote of the Philippians participating with him in the "defense and confirmation of the gospel." He also used the word in Philippians 1:16-17, where he said that he was "appointed for the defense" of the gospel. From *apologia*, we get *apologetics*, a term that is now used to refer to the comprehensive defense of faith in God, Jesus Christ, and the Scriptures as the inspired word of God.

Apologetics is its own field of study, incorporating many facets of evidences. It is the discipline that teaches Christians how they can defend the reason for their hope in Christ. Generally, there are three aspects of apologetics that are intertwined. *First* is the offering of *positive argumentation and proof* on behalf of Christianity. This is the rational presentation of the truth of Christianity. "Proof," used in the same sense that might be used in a court of law, is the evidence that helps establish the validity of something, persuading or compelling us to accept its object as true. "Evidence" refers to the facts or signs on which a conclusion can be properly based. Christians need to take on the burden of proof and be able to point to the evidence that will help others to make an informed decision about Christ. *Second* is providing a *defense* to the objections made against Christianity. Once the evidence is presented, we will face further questions and objections that need to be considered and answered to the best of our ability. *Third*, there will be appropriate times to go on the *offense*, demonstrating the folly of unbiblical worldviews so that people can see worldly and unbelieving philosophy for what it really is (see 1 Cor 1:18ff). The truth will destroy speculations and "every lofty thing raised up against the knowledge of God, and taking every thought captive to the obedience of Christ" (2 Cor 10:5). This must be done with respect and gentleness, for the purpose is not merely to win temporary arguments, but to win souls for eternity.

This brings us to a vital aspect of the nature of apologetics. Apologetics is a part of *evangelism*. It is an intellectual side of evangelism in which we try to deal with the difficulties that keep people from coming to Christ. Sometimes there are hurdles in the form of doubts and questions, and people need to get over these if they will embrace Jesus as their Lord. Evangelism includes apologetics because part of teaching people will often involve providing answers to their questions and helping them overcome doubts.

Some have likened apologetics to "foreign evangelism." It is as if we are entering a foreign situation (the culture of the world) to become all things to all men (1 Cor 9:22), as Paul did when he went into Athens (Acts 17). We learn about the language and the ideas of the culture around us so that we can properly apply the gospel to the situation of the world. While we do this, we are careful not to be conformed to the world (Rom 12:1-2). Evangelism requires that we understand the culture, not become absorbed in the culture.

Paul is a good example of one who regularly used apologetics in evangelism. He explained and gave evidence in Thessalonica (Acts 17:2-3). He reasoned in the synagogue at Corinth (Acts 18:4), and reasoned with the Jews at Ephesus (v. 19). He reasoned with the governor Felix (Acts 24:25). Everywhere Paul went, he was set for the defense of the gospel and gave his all trying to convince and persuade others that Jesus is the Son of God. In Paul we see a strong biblical example of being an apologist for Christ.

Why is Apologetics so Important?

We discussed the nature of faith, showing that biblical faith is not blind or gullible. God Himself provided evidence through the signs Jesus performed (John 20:30-31). Faith and evidence are compatible, and God has given us minds to think and reason. Faith is a choice that can be reasonably made. Apologetics is important because it helps to shore up our own faith and give us more confidence to speak with others about Jesus.

The importance of apologetics comes to light in the face of the many challenges that are directly related to biblical faith. For example, there is a new atheism that is aggressively trying to undermine God and Scripture. Darwinian evolution, with its underlying philosophy of naturalism, is still being taught as the default theory of how human beings and other creatures came to their present state. Postmodern concepts have taken hold in society, essentially denying biblical moral standards in favor of relativism and tolerance of virtually any lifestyle that fits the "politically correct" agenda. One does not need to look far to see how biblical ideals are ridiculed and believers are scoffed at as being bankrupt of intelligence. Widespread immorality challenges believers to stay true to biblical ethics, while we strive to persuade the world that there is a better way. In short, the world offers many worldview alternatives. Why should people choose to be Christians over all of these other worldviews? We must be able to answer this.

Additionally, personal doubts occasionally arise in our minds. Apologetics can help us gain confidence and remove the stumbling blocks that might keep us from fully devoting ourselves to the Lord. We are striving to know that our labor is not in vain in the Lord (1 Cor 15:58), so instead of just dangerously pushing doubts aside only to have them eat at us later, we should use these questions to pursue truth. In the end, we can become stronger in our faith.

God gave us minds to think, and apologetics can help us deal intelligently with the questions that are honestly asked by others. Sometimes people may raise questions so that they can evade the real need to change their lives. But many have legitimate questions, and we should always give the benefit of the doubt and try to help them by providing reasonable responses. Once again, evidences and apologetics become a powerful tool for evangelism.

On the Cultural Situation

We mentioned that there are many challenges that we face in the world, and we will be studying some of these in more detail. In more general terms, though, we find ourselves facing a cultural situation that can be described as pluralistic and secular. Pluralism (or multiculturalism) is the idea that all diverse views about truth and morality should be considered equally valid. No one view should be considered right for everyone. No standard of moral behavior should be considered universal. Instead, we must tolerate all views equally. Now we live in a "post-truth" world. Truth is created in the mind of each person, and ethics are merely a cultural construct (in this view), so no one has a right to pronounce a universal standard for everyone. Ironically (and inconsistently), this pluralistic concept is found everywhere around the globe and is considered to be a universal standard by many who won't tolerate absolutes!

To say that the world is "secular" is to say that people do not generally think or act with spiritual motivation today. Today's modes of thinking have been set by the media, movies, sports, and even video games (which often use inappropriate dress and language for entertainment purposes). When we speak of the Bible in this culture we risk being seen as right-wing religious fanatics who are unintelligent and superstitious. We risk being the punch line of late-night television jokes. The world just does not think in biblical terms, and they hold people suspect who do think that way. This is consistent with Paul's point to the Romans. The world will suppress the truth in unrighteousness (Rom 1:18). In other words, don't expect the world to play fair. The world has its own agenda, and it is not an agenda aligned with what God desires. Interestingly enough, the culture of today is not all that different from the 1st century culture in which the gospel was first preached.

There was a time when more people thought and talked in religious and biblical terms. Over the years, the Bible has been taken less and less seriously, however. Historical Jesus scholars began to separate the Christ of the Gospels from what they considered to be the real Jesus of history. The truth of Scripture was doubted and the Gospels were not credited with the authority they once held. Consequently, the God of the Bible was no longer considered sovereign in the minds of many. Once the value of Scripture and the power of God has been downplayed in culture, the value of human beings and human life also gets questioned. The wars of the twentieth century, the startling number of abortions, and the glorification of immorality demonstrate a general lack of desire to pay attention to God or to human value. Today, in spite of technological and scientific advances, virtually anything goes morally. There is little respect for God and His word in a culture that accepts almost anything (see 2 Tim 3:1-5).

We are in a battle for the mind (Eph 6:12). Various worldviews are competing for our thoughts, and the challenge is before us to think God's thoughts after Him and to go into the world with the message that Jesus Christ is still Lord. This is a message that must be presented reasonably, with proper evidence, so that God is glorified through Jesus.

Discussion Questions

1. Why should Christians be ready to suffer?

2. To what does the term "apologetics" refer? What does it not mean?

3. Give three aspects of apologetics. Why is each important?

4. How is apologetics a part of evangelism?

5. Why is apologetics important for the Christian?

6. How can the modern culture be described as "pluralistic"?

7. What are some modern challenges we face that demonstrate that we are in a battle for the mind? How do these issues show the need for apologetics?

Approach Matters

There must be no mismatch or contradiction between the message that is proclaimed and the tone of the messenger's proclamation. We must be winsome, generous, and gracious. If the gospel is to cause difficulty, it must be on account of its intrinsic nature and content, not the manner in which it is proclaimed. It is one thing for the gospel to give offense; it is quite another for its defenders to cause offense by unwise choice of language or an aggressive and dismissive attitude toward outsiders.

Alister McGrath, Mere Apologetics, 16

For the early Christian apologists in the time of the Roman Empire, the challenge was to introduce a message so novel that it was strange to its first hearers, and then to set out what the message meant for the classical age and its sophisticated and assured ways of thinking. For much of the advanced modern world today, in contrast, the challenge is to restate something so familiar that people know it so well that they do not know it, yet at the same time are convinced that they are tired of it.

Os Guinness, Fool's Talk: Recovering the Art of Christian Persuasion, 28

Confronting the Offense of the Cross

3

Why is biblical Christianity so important and yet controversial? Is it that Christians believe in God? No, for millions all over the world believe in God or some kind of supernatural power even though they are not Christians. Christianity is both significant and controversial because of what the Bible says about Jesus Christ—His identity as the Son of God, His death, and His resurrection. People must face the claims of the gospel, and once they do they will be forced to make a decision. Will they accept Jesus as their Lord and submit to the implications of His Lordship or will they reject Him altogether in favor of their own will? Before we point someone to specific evidences, we need to teach the facts of the gospel so that people can respond. Depending upon their response, we may then need to help them overcome obstacles by providing further evidence for why they should believe or how they can approach a variety of questions and doubts. The goal of apologetics should be clearly before us. We desire to get people to the cross of Christ so that they can be saved from their sins. The goal is always salvation.

Yet the cross of Jesus is offensive. Today we tend to dress up the cross, make it look nice, wear it, put it on bumper stickers, and generally soften its horror. The cross was humiliating and horrible. So what do we mean by "offense of the cross"? When people face Jesus at the cross they will be forced to choose between doing what is right in their own eyes (if they refuse the evidence) or accepting salvation from sin offered by Christ through His death and resurrection (if they accept the evidence). The problem is that we are not able to save ourselves. Our own standards are weak and flawed. We need the help that only Jesus can offer. When people reject Christ they are trying to do something (save themselves) that cannot be done. In order to accept the salvation offered by Jesus we must submit ourselves to His will, and this is offensive to many people.

Responding to the cross of Jesus Christ is the most important decision anyone will make. The task of the apologist is to help people overcome obstacles that keep them from Jesus so that they too can benefit from the wisdom and power of God through Jesus Christ. Since salvation is in no other name but Jesus (Acts 4:12), we must do all we can to help others meet Jesus. But this can only be done through His cross.

The apostle Paul clearly states the fundamental ("first importance") facts of the gospel in 1 Corinthians 15:1-4:

> Now I make known to you, brethren, the gospel which I preached to you, which also you received, in which also you stand, by which also you are saved, if you hold fast the word which I preached to you, unless you believed in vain. For I delivered to you as of first importance what I also received, that Christ died for our sins according to the Scriptures, and that He was buried, and that He was raised on the third day according to the Scriptures.

People must decide what to do with these facts. Will they believe or disbelieve? What will that mean for their lives? The controversy is not merely that someone died and was buried. The vital, offensive facts are that 1) Jesus died "for our sins," and 2) that He rose again. These are the claims that make Christianity unique and significant. They are also what many people do not like about the gospel, for we must accept that we are sinners in need of that salvation. So to some, the message of the cross is foolishness. To others, it is a stumbling block. To the saved, the cross is the power and wisdom of God (1 Cor 1:18ff). To unbelievers, it is a silly myth to be shunned and mocked.

Historical Importance

How important is it that we believe that Jesus actually died for our sins and that He really was raised from the dead? It would be difficult to overstate the importance of these facts. Paul's argument in 1 Corinthians 15 is, basically, that these make all the difference in the world.

> But if there is no resurrection of the dead, not even Christ has been raised; and if Christ has not been raised, then our preaching is vain, your faith also is vain. Moreover we are even found to be false witnesses of God, because we testified against God that He raised Christ, whom He did not raise, if in fact the dead are not raised. For if the dead are not raised, not even Christ has been raised; and if Christ has not been raised, your faith is worthless; you are still in your sins. Then those also who have fallen asleep in Christ have perished. If we have hoped in Christ in this life only, we are of all men most to be pitied. (1 Cor 15:13-19)

If we don't believe that Christ arose, then everything we do in the name of Christ is "in vain." Remember that it is by this gospel that we are saved (vv. 1-4). If the gospel is not true, then there is no salvation. We would still be in our sins. Also see how this is tied to the end of the chapter: "Therefore, my beloved brethren, be steadfast, immovable, always abounding in the work of the Lord, knowing that your toil is not in vain in the Lord" (v. 58). If we do not have confidence that Jesus died for our sins and rose again, then we will not have confidence that what we do for the Lord is worthwhile. We must believe in order to be confident that our work for Christ is important. Perhaps one reason why some people don't commit themselves completely to the Lord is that they are not as convinced as they ought to be that Jesus actually died for their sins and rose again.

Some argue that the "Jesus of history" is different from the "Christ of Faith." They say that the Jesus of history was only a man who did not die for our sins and who was not raised from the dead. They argue that the history in the Bible is not accurate. Instead, you can accept your own "Christ of faith," believing what you want about Jesus. Yet views like this show why we need to defend our faith. Jesus Christ, as presented in the Bible, is the real Jesus. He really died for our sins and was raised again. What we believe about Jesus historically is what the Bible tells us about Him. If we give this up, any claim to be Christians is empty.

Believing History and the Miraculous

On what grounds do we believe that the historical picture of Jesus in the Bible is true? On the same grounds that we believe anything in history is true. Do you believe that there was an ancient person named Aristotle? Do you believe there was an Alexander the Great? Julius Caesar? How about George Washington and Abraham Lincoln? We have seen none of these people in person, but the historical records show that they were real, and their accomplishments should be accepted beyond a reasonable doubt. Yet if we can believe what we are taught about these people historically, then we can also believe the biblical accounts of Jesus.

We are not saying that we should believe that everything ever written about anyone should be accepted historically. If a book or story is intended by the author to be read as a fairy tale, then we should accept it as such. No one argues that the Three Little Pigs is historical narrative. If a story is presented as legendary, then we can accept it as that. However, when a book claims to be historical, placed within a historical time-frame with real people and places, then that claim must be respected for what it is. And the Bible does indeed do this (see Luke 1:1-4 and 1 John 1:1-3).

Why would someone *not* believe that the material in the Bible is historical? Basically, the reason boils down to how a person thinks about reality (see the chapter on presuppositions). If people think that only the natural world is real, that there is no supernatural existence or God, then there is one basic aspect of the Bible that will offend them: miracles! Any account about a miracle (especially the resurrection) is automatically considered to be a fairy tale or legend, regardless of anything else indicated in the text. In analyzing one of David Hume's arguments against miracles (improbability based on "universal experience"), C. S. Lewis remarked, "We know the experience against them to be uniform only if we know that all the reports of them are false. And we can know all the reports to be false only if we know already that miracles have never occurred. In fact, we are arguing in a circle."[1]

Are miracles believable? If the existence of God is possible, then there is a possibility that He has supernaturally intervened in this world at some point in history. In fact, Bible believers know that God's intervention in this world is not only probable, but expected, since God is actively involved in his creation and wants to have fellowship with mankind. So unless one is of the mind to close all doors of possibility, miracles must be acknowledged as possible, if not probable.

By its very nature, science is limited. Neither God nor miracles can be put under controlled conditions in order to test and observe them. Miracles are unique events, not repeatable and testable. They are observable only once to the eyewitnesses who were blessed enough to see them. They fall outside of natural science, and therefore cannot be measured by a methodology that is inherently limited to natural events.

One cannot rule out historical documentation simply on the grounds that it records remarkable events: "if the documents are sufficiently reliable, the remarkable events must be accepted even if

---

[1] C. S. Lewis, *Miracles* (New York: Macmillan Publishing Co., 1952), 102.

they cannot be explained by analogy with other events or by an *a priori* scheme of natural causation."[2] If one rejects a record as untrue just because it contains an account of a miracle, then it reflects an anti-supernatural bias and not true investigation. Naturalists and liberal theists may have their preferences when it comes to the idea of God and how he should or should not work, but how can these preferences define "what really happened in history or what God has truly done?"[3]

Another echo of Hume's argument on universal experience was Troeltsch's historical argument based upon analogy. The idea is that the historian should not accept as historical fact any record of a past event for which there is no analogy in the present.[4] For example, the historian will not accept an account of a battle in which one side slaughters thousands of the enemy without suffering a single casualty because there is no modern analogy or experience that would show this to be reasonable. Since the historian has not experienced biblical miracles, then these should not be accepted as historical. However, this approach begs the question. How would an ancient historian living in the tropics come to believe an eyewitness account of someone who had traveled to lands covered with ice? He would have had no analogy for that experience; therefore he should not have accepted it. The historical evidence must be investigated on its own merit, not rejected because it records events that are out of the ordinary by modern standards.

Historical documents should never be treated lightly. We cannot decide before ever studying that something could not have

---

[2] John Warwick Montgomery, *History and Christianity* (Minneapolis, MN: Bethany House Publishers, 1965), 21.

[3] A. J. Hoover, *The Case for Christian Theism* (Grand Rapids, MI: Baker Book House, 1980. Rpt. of *Dear Agnos.* 1976), 145.

[4] Craig Blomberg, *The Historical Reliability of the Gospels* (Downers Grove, IL: InterVarsity Press, 1987), 78.

happened. We must let the documents speak for themselves. And when the biblical documents speak for themselves, they speak to the historical reality of Jesus' death, burial, and resurrection—the fundamental facts that will offend unbelievers and save believers. Yet these are the fundamental facts that must be taught and defended.

Discussion Questions

1. What do people need to be saved from, and why?

2. Why is salvation so important when we have so many ways we can choose to live?

3. Why do you think that people cannot save themselves from sin?

4. Read 1 Corinthians 1:18-23. How do different people view cross? Why do you think they view the cross this way?

5. Why would faith be vain if Jesus did not rise from the dead?

6. On what grounds should we believe anything historically?

7. Why do skeptics not accept miracles? Why should we accept or deny miracle claims?

Presuppositions

The question is not whether or not we have ideas, opinions, or preexisting points of view; the question is whether or not we will allow these perspectives to prevent us from examining the evidence objectively. It's possible to have a prior opinion yet leave this presupposition at the door in order to examine the evidence fairly. We ask jurors to do this all the time.

J. Warner Wallace, Cold-Case Christianity, 28.

The Problem of Presuppositions

4

Of monumental import to a discussion of the historical Jesus (especially miracles and the resurrection) and even the existence of God are the basic presuppositions and biases that people bring to the table. One would be hard pressed to overstate the case, as this problem practically takes front and center of most discussions about the Bible and the questions about Jesus Christ. Biases and presuppositions make or break a view. They will determine what a person will or will not accept about ultimate reality. "Basic assumptions or presuppositions are important because of the way they often determine the method and goal of theoretical thought.... One's axioms determine one's theorems."[1]

A *presupposition* is an idea or assumption that a person has before considering additional concepts. To *pre-suppose* something is to take an idea for granted in advance as an antecedent condition for further understanding. For example, when we touch something with our hands, we presuppose that our touch sensations will provide us with accurate information. We usually don't even think about it. If we see a ripple in an otherwise smooth body of water, we assume that there was a cause for that ripple, even though we may not have seen the cause.

We all have presuppositions and biases (a *bias* is a preconception that causes us to "slant" in a particular direction, for or against certain ideas). There is nothing wrong with that in and of itself, since we all must presuppose certain aspects of reality in order to function. We cannot know anything unless we first make some unstated assumptions about our perceptions. The problem with

---

[1] Ronald H. Nash, *Faith and Reason: Searching for a Rational Faith* (Grand Rapids, Mich.: Academie Books, 1988), 27-28.

presuppositions is that sometimes they get in the way of discovering truth or they might keep us from a proper understanding of what is right. Since presuppositions essentially predetermine what we will or will not accept as true, the question is whether or not they put us on the right or wrong side of truth. How do we know?

Does the fact of having presuppositions mean that we cannot objectively know the truth? Not at all. Truth is discoverable, and the point is to recognize something about ourselves that needs honest evaluation so that we won't get in our own way of discovering truth. The key to dealing with presuppositions is not to deny that we have them. People who deny their own presuppositions are not being honest with themselves or reality. The key is to be honest with our presuppositions, lay them "on the table" and, to the best our ability, critique them with an open mind while we continue to pursue truth. This does not mean that we are trying to be "neutral" about God, for that is not possible. It only means we are trying to be honest so that we can be committed to finding truth. Eddy and Boyd, in challenging the skeptical conclusions of modern scholarship, observed, "That which empowers scholars in principle to transcend their personal and sociological biases and make claims about reality is a resolute and uncompromising commitment to apprehend truth."[2] Further:

> The question is not whether we have biases: we all do. The question rather is, do we, as a matter of method and principle, strive to place our quest for truth ahead of our personal biases? Is our concern for truth in principle greater than, say, our concern for security and/or maintaining our current perspective at all costs? Do we allow our biases to

---

[2] Paul Rhodes Eddy, and Gregory A. Boyd, *The Jesus Legend: A Case for the Historical Reliability of the Synoptic Jesus Tradition* (Grand Rapids, MI: Baker Academic, 2007), 21.

predetermine our conclusions even in the face of clear and substantial counterevidence, or are we willing to allow evidence and alternative arguments to challenge our biases and possibly modify our conclusions?[3]

This is a real challenge. We may not even be aware that a bias is getting in the way of discovering truth. We should, at the least, start by admitting that we have presuppositions and biases. We should try to know what they are and how they affect our understanding of truth.

Presuppositions and Apologetics

What do presuppositions have to do with the study of apologetics? In a word, *everything*. First, presuppositions are at the heart of what we believe to be true. They are at the core of our worldview, and apologetics is all about defending and advancing a biblical worldview. The very reason why people maintain particular worldviews is because they have made assumptions that are foundational to the way they think about everything else. This is inevitable, but the question is, are we honest about the assumptions in the first place?

Second, presuppositions determine what we will or will not accept as *evidence* on behalf of a proposition. What are we willing to allow as evidence for or against a claim? How we answer this question is critical, for if we disallow evidence that is, in fact, solid and reasonable, then we have put ourselves in the way of discovering truth.

For example, naturalism is the philosophy that nature alone accounts for the way things are; there is no God who has anything to do with nature or reality. If this philosophy is the foundation of a person's worldview, then that person's conclusions about miracles

---

[3] Ibid., 24.

are already predetermined. Naturalists already "know" that there is no God who does anything in this world, so miracles could not have happened. Consequently, any miracle accounts, like we find in the Gospels, are obviously untrue and mythological; they cannot be accepted as historical, regardless of the claims of eyewitnesses or the reliability of the documents. Naturalistic presuppositions will not permit considering the evidence for miracles as being anything other than nonsense. As Antony Flew said in a debate with Gary Habermas on the resurrection of Jesus, miracles "are things that you just take to be impossible."[4] Habermas later pointed out, "Most critics deny the Resurrection because of an anti-supernatural bias against miracles, not because of inferior evidence."[5] The tension here is obvious.

In another debate between Gerd Lüdemann and William Lane Craig, Lüdemann skeptically said of the resurrection, "I think that is nonsense."[6] Yet, the reason it is "nonsense" to the modern mind is not because the history is bad or the evidence is lacking; rather, the fundamental assumptions about reality are getting in the way. Eddy and Boyd point out that the biblical claims "are not implausible, unless, of course, one rules out the possibility of the supernatural from the beginning."[7]

Because presuppositions may get in the way of someone accepting evidences on behalf of Christ, our first step in dealing with people may indeed be to go right to the heart of those presuppositions.

---

[4] Gary R. Habermas, and Antony G.N. Flew, *Resurrected? An Atheist and Theist Dialogue* (Lanham, Md.: Rowman amp; Littlefield Publishers, 2005), 71.

[5] Ibid., 106.

[6] Paul Copan, and Ronald K. Tacelli, eds., *Jesus' Resurrection: Fact or Figment? A Debate Between William Lane Craig & Gerd Lüdemann* (Downers Grove, Ill.: InterVarsity Press, 2000), 45.

[7] Eddy and Boyd, *The Jesus Legend: A Case for the Historical Reliability of the Synoptic Jesus Tradition*, 453.

Until people are honest about their own assumptions, we will be unable to penetrate the barriers that divide believers from unbelievers.

Ironically, it is often those who claim to be open-minded who can be quite close-minded toward Jesus and the Bible. Consequently, there are some scholars who are beginning to call attention to this. "To be sure, an open mind is a good thing. But a mind is open only as long as it is closing in on truth."[8] Our culture has been conditioned to doubt the Bible, but we need to reaffirm the fact that skepticism does not equate to scholarship. Because of "cramped starting points," many have concluded that the Jesus of the Bible cannot be the real Jesus of history. Yet, when we dig in and take a hard look at the skeptical arguments, we may find what "often are little more than presuppositions and not documented and argued conclusions."[9]

Ben Witherington also called attention to the problem: "Some modern scholars, including historians, simply assume that miracles *cannot* happen and therefore *do not* happen. This is a faith assumption actually, since no human being has exhaustive knowledge of present reality, never mind the past."[10] We should never decide ahead of time and before hearing the evidence what the truth of the matter must be. As the wise man said, "He who gives an answer before he hears, it is folly and shame to him" (Prov 18:13).

---

[8] J. Ed. Komoszewski, *Reinventing Jesus: How Contemporary Skeptics Miss The Real Jesus and Mislead Popular Culture* (Grand Rapids, MI: Kregel Publications, 2006), 16.

[9] Craig A. Evans, *Fabricating Jesus: How Modern Scholars Distort The Gospels* (Downers Grove, Ill.: IVP Books, 2006), 34.

[10] Ben Witherington III, *What Have They Done With Jesus? Beyond Strange Theories and Bad History — Why We Can Trust the Bible* (New York: HarperOne, 2006), 5.

Keeping an Open Mind toward History and Reality

The philosopher William James astutely noted, "a rule of thinking which would absolutely prevent me from acknowledging certain kinds of truth if those kinds of truth were really there, would be an irrational rule."[11] Setting up a wall in our thinking that prohibits something from being true, if that something really is true, is hardly rational. Nor is it biblical. Yet, here we are two thousand years removed from the events that we claim started Christianity. How do we accept something like the resurrection of Jesus?

The answer is that we must keep an open view of history. Accepting that Jesus was raised from the dead is grounded in the acceptance of the Gospel accounts as relating historical reality. But to accept the historical reality of the Gospel accounts requires that our worldview permits miracles to have actually occurred. If our worldview forbids that reality, then there is no evidence that we will accept that would convince us that the Gospels are reliable. A closed view of history and reality (i.e., that miracles could not happen) prohibits the skeptic from reaching any other conclusion. No wonder the assumption is made today that the story of Jesus is legendary or even mythological. Skeptical presuppositions can allow nothing else.

While we are not saying that every event in history must be explained by the supernatural, we are saying that we must keep an open mind about supernatural events. Again, as Eddy and Boyd point out, as a matter of principle, we must be "open to the possibility that evidence may at times require us to entertain the possibility that an event cannot be plausibly explained exclusively in naturalistic terms."[12] Truly keeping an open mind toward history

---

[11] William James, "The Will to Believe," in *Essays in Pragmatism*, ed. Alburey Castell (New York: Hafner Publishing Co., 1948), 107.

[12] Eddy and Boyd, *The Jesus Legend: A Case for the Historical Reliability of The Synoptic Jesus Tradition*, 53.

requires humility, in which scholars should "remain committed to following the evidence, wherever it leads, rather than narrowly stipulating what can and cannot count as evidence on the basis of certain presuppositions."[13] The point is to be open to that genuine possibility, and if we do, then there are compelling reasons for accepting that the Gospel accounts are indeed telling us what really happened. As Roberts put it, "if you look squarely at the facts as they are widely understood, and if you do not color them with pejorative bias or atheistic presuppositions, the you'll find that it's reasonable to trust the Gospels."[14]

We will look at evidence, but it is important to confront the issue of presuppositions early because it will continue to arise. We'll likely find that this one issue is one of the single most important matters in trying to persuade people concerning the truth of God, Christ, and Scripture.

How will this help us in our continued study of apologetics?

First, recognize our own presuppositions and be honest about them so that they do not get in the way of discovering truth. If we expect others to do this, we must be willing to do it ourselves.

Second, recognize that others will have presuppositions that will likely affect how they perceive the evidence that you might present. It may be that we must deal with those biases before getting to the actual evidence.

Third, understand that our modern culture has been conditioned to doubt and react skeptically toward supernatural and biblical claims. Knowing this can help us be better prepared for evangelistic purposes.

---

[13] Ibid.

[14] Mark D. Roberts, *Can We Trust The Gospels? Investigating the Reliability of Matthew, Mark, Luke, and John* (Wheaton, Ill.: Crossway Books, 2007), 20.

Fourth, remember that skepticism is not to be equated with scholarship. Don't allow yourself to be intimidated by skeptics who confuse those issues. Scholarship means that we keep pursuing the truth while continuing to evaluate our own assumptions. Without both of these processes, we are setting ourselves up for missing the whole point. Keep on pursuing truth. There is no substitute for digging in and working hard.

Discussion Questions

1. Why are presuppositions necessary?

2. Are there differences between biases and presuppositions? If so, what are they?

3. How are presuppositions related to apologetics?

4. Why is it important to acknowledge our presuppositions?

5. What does keeping an open mind about history mean?

6. If it is not rational to close the possibility of discovering something, then what are the implications for the philosophy of naturalism?

The Problem of Doubt 5

God desires active faith in Christians (Jas 2:14-26). As James again shows, this type of faith involves the mind, the emotions, and the will. If any of these ingredients are missing, faith will not be what it is supposed to be. For many, personal faith has failed, and they don't know what to do about it or where to turn. Some don't even realize when or how they "lost" their faith.

Why is faith in God and Scripture often rejected? There are many reasons, and likely it is not just one reason by itself. Contributing to the problem sometimes is simply a lack of information. One person has a question and does not know the answer or how to find it, so he gives up. Another does not realize that a problem could have been solved with more information, but she quits seeking answers. Ignorance, without searching for answers, can lead to doubt. For others, it may be an issue of pride. To become a Christian means that we have recognized we are sinners in need of God's salvation. Making a change toward God is a humbling experience. "God is opposed to the proud, but gives grace to the humble" (1 Pet 5:5). Pride is the nemesis of personal change, and change is necessary when coming to Christ. Still others have moral problems that get in the way of making the necessary commitment to God. Their lifestyles are opposed to the ways of God, and they prefer just to stay where they are. They feel it is easier to reject faith in God than to go through the pains of admitting error and changing. Sometimes the easiest way to stay where they are is to throw doubts about God and the Bible into the equation. After all, if God is not real, if Jesus did not rise from the dead, and if the Bible is not true, then there is no need to change anything. However, having doubts is no excuse for justifying poor behavior. Instead, they should be a catalyst for seeking truth.

Not everyone is trying to make excuses, though. Sometimes people do have questions, doubts, and concerns, not because they want to do what is wrong, but simply because they see what they perceive to be an inconsistency or they just have questions and they genuinely want answers. One writer observed:

> Many of us do struggle with questions of the truth of Christianity. We are not fighting God, the church, or our upbringing; we just want to know the truth. Is Christianity believable? Can one with a clear head accept that Christ is God and that the Bible is the inspired Word of God? There are issues here that demand an answer, and they are suppressed at a potentially great cost.[1]

How, then, do we begin to deal with doubt?

Address the Questions

Personal doubts need to be addressed, not just swept aside. If merely cast aside, those doubts will keep coming back and may create even more problems later. We may feel ashamed if we have doubts, but it is far better to admit and confront our questions and doubts, understanding that true faith does not need to fear questions. Those doubts, left unattended, can destroy faith. Yet the answers will not always be easy. Answers will not always come in nice, neat packages where every piece of the puzzle is wrapped up perfectly. Faith should not require that, however. Still, we must keep studying, thinking the issues out and following them through. If we try to by-pass the pains, we are robbing ourselves of tremendous growth. This is all a part of owning our faith and choosing to follow Christ, not because that's just the "way we were brought up," but because we are truly convinced and convicted about Jesus as our Lord and the Scriptures as God's word.

---

[1] Winfried Corduan, *No Doubt About It: The Case for Christianity* (Nashville, TN: Broadman and Holman Publishers, 1997), 14.

Paul wrote to the Corinthians about the resurrection of Jesus, stating that if the event did not happen, then everything else is in vain (1 Cor 15:1-19). At the end of the chapter, he told them to be "steadfast, immovable, always abounding in the work of the Lord, knowing that your toil is not in vain in the Lord" (v. 58). The reason this is important for the issue of doubt is that it directly relates to the confidence we have or do not have in serving Jesus. If doubt continues to grow, then we will not have the confidence, and our service will suffer. On the other hand, if we are confident (not in ourselves, but in God), then we can serve with the knowledge that everything we do for the Lord is worthwhile. We will never waste our time working for God.

The real question that nags us and leads to doubt is simply, "but is it true?" After all, in the final analysis, we are being asked to believe that Jesus rose from the dead. That is not exactly an ordinary experience. This is not something we encounter by direct experience, so our faith is being called into action over something that is highly unusual. How can we proceed with confidence?

The evidence is there, and this will be presented later. But there are some other issues related to doubt that need to be considered. William Lane Craig, in his book *Hard Questions, Real Answers*, offers some important suggestions for dealing with doubt, and we are going to think about a few of these.[2]

1. Understand that doubt not just an intellectual dilemma, but is actually more of a spiritual and emotional issue. Remember that we are involved in a battle for the mind (Eph 6:12), and you have an enemy that will stop at nothing to divert your attention from truth. If we think that questions and doubts are merely academic debates, we have missed the point. Doubt is a spiritual problem.

---

[2] William Lane Craig, *Hard Questions, Real Answers* (Wheaton, Ill.: Crossway Books, 2003).

Some scholars seem to think that doubting is somehow to be considered the best default academic and intellectual position. Yet seldom do they apply that same doubt to their own worldview and academic skepticism. There is nothing particularly redeeming about skepticism. Further, as Craig points out, some apparently confuse *thinking* about faith with *doubting* faith. We are encouraged to think about our faith, to try to better understand it and refine it as necessary. But this is not the same thing as doubting. So I want to echo Craig's words here because the principle is so important: "Look, I don't want to challenge your *faith*; I want to challenge your *thinking*. But I want to *build up* your faith."[3]

When doubts arise, don't just bury them under some academic rug as if your superior intellect has finally solved all the complicated issues at stake. Rather, take your questions and, yes, even your doubts, to God. When the psalmist just about lost his faith over the fact that unbelievers seem to be prospering so much, he went to the sanctuary of God and finally perceived their end (Ps 73). Go to God with your troubles. Say, with the sick boy's father to Jesus, "I do believe; help my unbelief" (Mark 9:24).

Since doubt is a spiritual issue, learn to use the spiritual tools God has given us for strengthening our faith. Faith comes through hearing His word (Rom 10:17). Never neglect Scripture, and never neglect prayer. Understand who your real enemy is (see Eph 6:10-18). You may find that those troubling issues have a way of being worked out. Be patient and hang in there.

Our emotions are involved as well, and this can become complicated. Os Guinness made the following observation concerning emotional doubt:

---

[3] Ibid., 34.

The problem is not that reason attacks faith but that emotions overwhelm reason as well as faith, and it is impossible for reason to dissuade them . . . [this kind of] doubt comes just at the point where the believer's emotions (vivid imagination, changing moods, erratic feelings, intense reactions) rise up and overpower the understanding of faith. Out-voted, out-gunned, faith is pressed back and hemmed in by the unruly mob of raging emotions that once a while earlier were quiet, orderly citizens of the personality. Reason is cut down, obedience is thrown out, and for a while the rule of emotions is as sovereign as it is violent. The coup d'état is complete.[4]

The problem with doubts is that once we begin to entertain them, they make us weak and vulnerable, open to other temptations and problems that may take us down paths we don't want to go. The spirit may be willing, but the flesh is weak, and that weakness is furthered by our weariness in doing good. We get broken down, buried beneath frustrations, and thereby create a cozy place in our hearts for doubts to nest and eventually hatch.

Once we understand the nature of the doubts we are having, the emotional issues involved, then we can begin to address them properly.

2. We need humbly to admit that our intellect and knowledge is frail and limited. Paul wrote that knowledge "makes arrogant, but love edifies. If anyone supposes that he knows anything, he has not yet known as he ought to know" (1 Cor 8:1-2). Paul had great intellectual achievements, but that did not matter when compared to knowing Jesus (Phil 3:4-8). The point is that we cannot afford to get too proud about our own intellectual abilities and knowledge. There is always room to grow.

---

[4] Os Guinness, *God in the Dark: The Assurance of Faith Beyond a Shadow of Doubt* (Wheaton, IL: Crossway Books, 1996), 25-26.

What does this have to do with the problem of doubt? Sometimes those doubts arise because either we think that we have discovered all the answers about an issue, or we think that a lack of finding an answer somehow disproves a particular proposition. For example, the problem of suffering can be subjected to this. One may argue that there is no good reason at all why God would allow innocent people to suffer, and many begin to doubt God because of the problem. This would be a failure to recognize that our knowledge is limited, and God may well have reasons that He does not even have to tell us about. On the other hand, one may think that because all the answers are not available, then we can never know or understand God and we should just give up because if God cared, He would tell us. This is arguing from ignorance (a logical fallacy). Either extreme misses the point. Our knowledge of how God operates is limited, but this should push us in the direction of trusting Him because, even though we do not have all the answers, God does. This is exactly the point made to Job (ch. 38). Lack of knowledge should be humbling, drawing us closer to God, not give us a reason to push away from God.

Further, try to remember the proper relationship between faith and reason.[5] The evidence can point us in the right direction, and we use our God-given reasoning abilities to try to understand, interpret, and draw conclusions. But reason (and that by fallible humans), in and of itself, can only take us so far (this is true in every area of study, including history and science). Our knowledge and intellect are limited, and so are our reasoning abilities. This is not to say that reason is unimportant, or that faith is not reasonable. It is to say, however, that we need to be modest and understand that sometimes we may draw improper conclusions or take a faulty path in our thinking. We must continually reassess where our thinking takes us and make corrections along the way.

---

[5] Craig makes this a completely separate point, but goes in a little different direction.

At the same time, we ought to do that within the boundaries of recognizing the greatness of God. God's thinking must take precedence over our thinking (see Ephesians 3:20, where we are told that God can do far above what we can even think). In this case, reason does not lord it over faith, but reason serves faith as we try to understand our faith better and help others by providing reasonable arguments.

Craig points out that we will always have questions, so the secret to dealing with doubt is "learning to live victoriously with one's unanswered questions."[6] We can do this if we understand the foundation for our faith and know that God is in control. We may even decide that there are some questions that are not as important as we thought, and so we can live with a lack of knowledge. But let us never think that because we do not have an immediate answer for something that this somehow means there is no answer.

3. *Continue to pursue your questions.* Keep studying and learning. Doubts that lead to the destruction of faith often come because people quit searching. If we let our doubts take over, we may just give up because we think answers are hopeless. But you might be surprised at when, where, and how those answers arise. Every Christian will have a "question bag" (as Craig puts it) with difficulties. Occasionally, you will find that you have the time to pull one of those questions out and go to work on it. There is something very intellectually and spiritually satisfying about pursuing a difficult question to the point that it is finally resolved in your mind. It may take quite a bit of time (even years), but the journey is well worth it. In the meantime, we do not need to put our faith on hold. We know that all answers ultimately are in God's hands.

Set aside time to study and learn. Once you solve one question, you will gain confidence in the Lord that will help you search out

---

[6] Craig, 39.

answers to others questions. There is no quick fix or easy road to solving difficulties. It takes time, hard work, and tears, right along with prayer and meditation in the Scriptures.

Alister McGrath points out, "doubt and faith are both states of mind or attitudes. Doubt can be a constant attitude of questioning toward God, where faith can be a constant attitude of trust and openness."[7] While we want to develop the attitude of faith more fully, we recognize that doubts can arise. Use any doubts to pursue faith at a deeper level, and we can grow through them.

Personal growth requires us to dig in and search for answers. We are not simply taking our beliefs for granted, but we are examining everything in seeking what is right and true. Keep on knocking; the door will be opened (Matt 7:7). Going through the process of dealing with questions and doubts does not mean we are tearing everything down we have ever learned. As Corduan pointed out, such examination may be "a matter of making sure all the nails are holding and applying a little more glue here and there. Unless a person is willing to go through such a process, his or her faith may always be suffering from a lack of conviction."[8] If we are nagged by doubts, it will be impossible to dedicate ourselves fully to Christ, for we will not truly know that our labor is not in vain (1 Cor 15:58). Dealing with the doubts will help us get over the hurdles so that we can truly sanctify Christ as Lord in our hearts, ready to make a defense of our hope in a hostile world (1 Pet 3:15). May God bless us and help us to that end.

---

[7] Alister E. McGrath, *Doubting: Growing through the Uncertainties of Faith* (Downers Grove, IL: InterVarsity Press, 2007), 53.

[8] Corduan, *No Doubt About It: The Case for Christianity*, 17.

Discussion Questions

1. Why do you think people sometimes reject faith in God?

2. How would you respond to someone who told you that he or she was "losing" faith or had doubts about God and the Bible?

3. Why is doubt a spiritual problem, not just an intellectual problem?

4. How can properly dealing with doubts help strengthen our faith?

5. Why is it important to understand the relationship between faith and reason?

6. How can recognizing our limitations on knowledge help us with doubts?

7. How can you learn to "live victoriously" with unanswered questions?

Where Does Intelligence Come From?

Are we or are we not capable of recognizing intelligence? If we are, why is it a stretch to infer from the presence of intelligence that there is an even greater Mind that is the source of it all? If we are not capable of recognizing intelligence, then on what grounds can opponents argue that they have the intelligent position? The skeptics' position can be no more intelligent than those whom they criticize, for there would be no standard of measurement and no hope of determining an ultimate intelligence. If our own minds are the mere product of non-intelligent chance, then how can we possibly know or reason that our arguments have an intelligent foundation? Yet if we wish to argue intelligence for ourselves, at some point we must begin to ask where it all came from.

Doy Moyer, Foreword,
Natural Theology by William Paley, 10

Resurrection 6

To make the case for the resurrection, we start with historical facts then reason from them to the most probable explanation for how the facts fit together as a whole. Craig Evans pointed out to a group of scholars dedicated to searching the historical questions, "Our approach is the same approach we would take if we were interested in the historical Alexander the Great or the historical Julius Caesar."[1] The point is not to be gullible or argue for Jesus merely on the desire to turn Jesus into something he was not. The essential case for the resurrection is an argument from the historical evidence, not an argument from wishful thinking. Ladd wrote:

> However, the resurrection is consistent with the known historical facts; it is indeed the one adequate explanation for these facts, and it is the uniform witness of the New Testament writers that God did in fact raise Jesus from the dead. Therefore faith is not a leap in the dark in defiance of facts and evidences, but is consistent with known facts and rests upon witnesses.[2]

The kind of historical evidence to which apologists can appeal is that which virtually all critical scholars can accept.[3] The apologist need not appeal to subjective, obscure, or questionable arguments. Rather, the case for the resurrection is found within the facts that are knowable and accepted by most who have studied them. The question then becomes what those facts actually point to and imply. Here is a brief overview: These facts include the death of Jesus by crucifixion, His burial, and a tomb that was empty on the third day

---

[1] Day of Discovery Productions, "Jesus: Man, Messiah, or More? An 8 part Video Series," http://dod.org/Products/DOD2121.aspx (accessed March 26, 2009).

[2] George Eldon Ladd, *The New Testament and Criticism*, 189.

after Jesus' death. The disciples, grieved after Jesus died, believed that they saw Jesus alive again, and because of this they went through radical transformations in which they were willing to die for their beliefs. The resurrection message became the main theme of the preaching in the first century. This message spread from Jerusalem where Jesus was crucified, and the church was born and increased quickly with Sunday as the primary day in which they came together for worship. James, a skeptical brother of Jesus, was converted based on the same belief of seeing the resurrected Jesus. Paul, also a skeptic, was converted to Christ, believing that he actually saw the risen Christ. Now these basic facts constitute what "virtually all scholars who deal with this issue" recognize as the "minimum of known historical facts surrounding this event."[4] Most scholars will not take much issue with these facts, though they may try to offer alternate explanations for them (such as the empty tomb explanations). The question is what to do with these facts and how to understand their significance. How should the facts be interpreted?

The concept of the historically minimal approach is important (though not a complete approach). This does not mean that history is minimized, but rather that one seeks the minimal facts necessary to make the argument without getting sidetracked into other peripheral issues. "This approach considers the data that are so strongly attested historically that they are granted by nearly every scholar who studies the subject, even the rather skeptical ones."[5] By simplifying the issue this way, one need not delve into a discussion of the inspiration and inerrancy of Scripture before presenting the resurrection evidence. Instead, apologists need only supply the minimum facts, argue for the resurrection based upon the evidence,

[3] Gary R. Habermas, "Introduction," in *The Historical Jesus: Ancient Evidence for the Life of Christ* (Joplin, MO: College Press, 1996), 158.

[4] Ibid.

[5] Gary R. Habermas, and Michael R. Licona, *The Case for the Resurrection of Jesus* (Grand Rapids: Kregel Publications, 2004), 44.

then deal with the implications that necessarily arise thereafter. The facts that are used in the historically minimal approach ought to meet the following two criteria, according to Habermas: "They are well evidenced and nearly every scholar accepts them."[6] By basing the discussion on these facts, the case for the resurrection becomes strong and the conclusion becomes difficult to refute. These are facts that must be addressed by everyone.

Minimum Facts

What are these minimal facts? First, Jesus died by crucifixion, a fact that is, according to the skeptic Crossan, "as sure as anything historical can ever be."[7] The Roman historian Tacitus, who shows a bias against the Christians, wrote:

> Christus was executed in the Principate of Tiberius by the governor Pontius Pilate; the deadly *superstitito* was checked for a time, but broke out again, not only in Judea, the origin of the evil, but even in the capital, where all hideous and shameful practices collect from every quarter and are extremely popular.[8]

Saying that Christ was "executed" almost certainly refers to crucifixion. The text also shows that Christianity "broke out again," which probably references the Christians' belief in Jesus' resurrection, as that would explain why the religion "broke out."[9] The support for the death of Jesus by crucifixion is extensive, and most scholars will not bother to question it.

---

  [6] Ibid.

  [7] John Dominic Crossan, *Jesus: A Revolutionary Biography* (San Francisco: HarperSanFrancisco, 1989), 145.

  [8] Mary Beard, and and Simon Price John North, *Religions of Rome: A Sourcebook* (Cambridge, UK: Cambridge University Press, 1998), 2:277.

  [9] Habermas, *The Historical Jesus: Ancient Evidence for The Life of Christ*, 187-90.

The second fact is that disciples of Jesus believed that they saw Him alive again after He had died. The key to this statement, for minimal purposes, is that the disciples *believed* that they saw Him alive again. That statement in itself does not say that they did, in fact, see Jesus, only that they believed it. Yet this speaks volumes. Given that the church started in the first century based upon the preaching of the resurrection of Jesus, this is a fact that can hardly be disputed. After all, the existence of the church based upon the belief that Jesus rose again must be explained. It should be noted, as Niebuhr argues, "We can gain nothing by disallowing the contribution they who were the witnesses and Apostles and prophets of the new age must have made."[10]

The intensity of the belief that Jesus rose from the dead is demonstrated in that the disciples who claimed to have seen Jesus alive again were willing to die for that claim. While this does not prove that the claims are true, it does show how much they believed the claims to be true. It proves the intensity of their faith. Origen, in the third century work *Contra Celsum*, makes this very point in favor of the resurrection:

> But a clear and unmistakable proof of the fact I hold to be the undertaking of His disciples, who devoted themselves to the teaching of a doctrine which was attended with danger to human life—a doctrine which they would not have taught with such courage had they invented the resurrection of Jesus from the dead; and who also, at the same time, not only prepared others to despise death, but were themselves the first to manifest their disregard for its terrors.[11]

---

[10] Richard R. Niebuhr, *Resurrection and Historical Reason* (New York: Charles Scribner's Sons, 1957), 179.

[11] Origen, "Contra Celsum," in *Ante-Nicene Fathers*, eds, Alexander Roberts, and James Donaldson (Peabody, MA: Hendrickson Publishers, 1994), 4:454.

Why is the willingness of the disciples to die for their claim so important for the evidence of the resurrection? The answer is that "liars make poor martyrs."[12] If they were lying about the resurrection of Jesus, there is no sound explanation for the historical fact that the majority of the apostles, along with Paul and James, became martyrs. The objection might be given here that many people have died for lies throughout history, which is undeniably true. The sincerity of those who give up their lives for a religious cause is not in question. Many believe in their cause and act upon their faith with tremendous devotion and zeal, willing to go to their deaths because they believe so strongly. Such devotion is to be commended. However, this objection misses the point. The issue is not just that believers died, but that it was those claiming to be eyewitnesses who were willing to die. The argument is focused on the first generation disciples, not those who came to believe later. People who die for their faith today are not in the same position as the apostles and initial witnesses of Jesus Christ. Modern martyrs act on a faith that they have been taught and received from others. The apostles, on the other hand, were making claims about what they had actually seen with their own eyes. This means that they knew, without question, whether or not they were telling the truth. Modern martyrs may be claiming to believe truth, but they are not the firsthand sources that the apostles claim to be, and they are not making the same types of claims.

The third fact of the historically minimal approach is that Paul, previously a persecutor of the Christians, went through a radical change, became an apostle of Christ, and claimed that the reason for it all was that he saw the risen Christ. Paul's testimony in 1 Corinthians 15 once again comes into play on this fact and stands on its own. This is explored in another chapter.

The fourth fact is that the tomb was found empty on the third day after Jesus had died by crucifixion. Evidence shows that the tomb

---

[12] Habermas and Licona, *The Case for the Resurrection of Jesus*, 59.

was *new* (Matt 27:57-60; so Jesus' body could not be mistaken for another body), *observed* (Mark 15:47; the women watched closely where Jesus was laid and would not have gone to the wrong tomb), and *secured* (Matt 27:62-66; sealed and guarded so that it could not be tampered with or the body stolen). All of this adds to the weight of evidence in favor of actual resurrection.

Some will dispute the empty tomb, and it is usually here where alternate explanations begin to find their way into discussions. Crossan, for example, argues that Jesus' body was "left on the cross or in a shallow grave barely covered with dirt and stones, the dogs were waiting."[13] The dogs took care of the body of Jesus, so that "by Easter Sunday morning, those who cared did not know where it was, and those who knew did not care."[14] Others offer the typical theories that have long been answered and shown to be faulty. Such ideas include the stolen body theory (the first offered by the Jewish leaders in Matthew 28), the wrong tomb theory, the hallucination theory, and the swoon theory. These theories have no historical support at all.

The question is what to make of the fact that alternate explanations are so often given. First, when an alternate explanation is offered, there is an implicit admission by the one giving the explanation that something actually did occur that needs explaining. If the whole story is a myth, then why bother to give alternate theories about the status of a real tomb? Why would skeptics feel the need to provide some kind of explanation? Second is that the alternate explanations regarding the empty tomb are really red herrings. They sidetrack from the real issue. The disciples did not believe that Jesus was raised from the dead just because they saw an empty tomb or because someone else told them about it. When the women initially saw an empty tomb, they thought someone had moved the body. The disciples' understanding of the Scriptures was

---

[13] John Dominic Crossan, *Jesus: A Revolutionary Biography*, 154.

[14] Ibid., 158.

certainly enlightened by the empty tomb (John 20:8-9), but their ultimate faith that Jesus was raised came about because they believed they saw, firsthand, Jesus alive again. Once that is understood, the empty tomb, as an empty tomb *per se*, no longer matters except to point out that if the body were still there, then they could not have actually seen Jesus alive again. The empty tomb is a necessary condition for the resurrection, but it is not sufficient in itself to prove the resurrection. Even so, if the enemies of Jesus could have presented the body of Jesus, they would have done so and all further talk of the rise of Christianity would have been over. If a dead body of Jesus were to have been produced, that would have been the end of the Christians even before the first conversions. However, while everyone can agree that Jesus died on a Roman cross, apart from the resurrection no one has been able to provide a sufficient explanation for 1) the whereabouts of his body after it went missing, and 2) the claims of the disciples to have seen Jesus alive again. If critics are to supply a proper, adequate explanation for the missing body coupled with the appearances, they need to provide first century historical evidence, not speculation based on a worldview that *a priori* does not permit the miraculous.

What Does it Mean?

The implications of the resurrection are far-reaching. Can one think of a more important event in recorded history? There is nothing more vital for the child of God than to believe that Jesus rose from the dead (1 Cor 15:12-19). Faith is in vain if He did not rise. Here was an awesome display of the power of God (2 Cor. 13:4), giving God's people the faith to know that they have been born again to a living hope (1 Pet. 1:3-5). Death has been conquered (Heb 2:14-17), and everything about our faith is worthwhile (1 Cor 15:58).

For evidential purposes, the resurrection is the key to accepting the Lordship of Jesus. He was "declared the Son of God with power by the resurrection from the dead" (Rom 1:4). This evidence should convince us to confess Jesus as Lord (Rom 10:9-10), submitting our lives completely to Him and His will. We should be able to say, with Thomas, "My Lord and my God" (John 20:28). We ought to confess, with Peter, "Lord, to whom shall we go? You have the words of eternal life. We have believed and have come to know that you are the Holy One of God" (John 6:68-69). The authority of Jesus is absolute, ultimately demonstrated by the resurrection.

Accepting the Lordship of Jesus has further implications for how we view Scripture. Jesus is the key for informing our attitudes about what we should think regarding the Scriptures. Whatever Jesus said or taught about Scripture is what we should believe and teach about Scripture. Accepting the Lordship of Jesus means accepting His attitudes, teachings, works, claims, and everything He stands for. How can it be any other way?

Discussion Questions

1. What is the purpose for using a "historically minimal" approach? What does it mean? Why is it useful for dealing with skeptics?

2. What are the basic facts? Can you present them? What significance does each fact add to the overall case?

3. What is the relevance of the "empty tomb"? Why is that alone not sufficient to prove the resurrection?

4. Why is the resurrection so vital to the Christian's faith? What are the consequences if it did not happen?

5. Discuss the Lordship of Jesus. What does it mean to call Him "Lord"? Why is the Lordship of Jesus crucial to apologetics? Why is it crucial to your life?

The Testimony of Paul 7

Paul's first letter to the church at Corinth demonstrates the importance of the death and resurrection of Christ. From the first chapter, and all through the epistle, Paul shows that Christ's death and resurrection are paramount to the way that Christians are to think and act, both toward God and toward each other. Especially significant for the resurrection is chapter 15, wherein Paul shows the historical importance of the resurrection as the foundation for the Christian's hope in overcoming death. Here we will focus on the historical question of Christ's resurrection.

Why is Paul's argument in 1 Corinthians 15 so important to the overall resurrection case? Since skeptical explanations for the empty tomb have proven fruitless, the argument critics typically now make is that the whole story is just legendary. However, Paul's resurrection argument in 1 Corinthians makes "legendary" explanations untenable.

Wolfhart Pannenberg writes, "The historical question of the appearances of the resurrected Lord is concentrated completely in the Pauline report."[1] Even when skeptical scholars deny historical kernels in the Gospels, they still must grapple with Paul's overall argument. They might dismiss the Gospels as late (which is debatable), but they cannot dismiss Paul as a separate, independent, and *early* source for the resurrection of Jesus. At the least, one ought to accept "Paul's intention of giving a convincing historical proof by the standards of that time."[2] Once again, historical intent plays a vital role in the argument. Did Paul intend to convey information about what really happened? As Pannenberg admitted,

---

[1] Wolfhart Pannenberg, *Jesus--God and Man*, trans. Lewis L. Wilkins and Duane A. Priebe (Philadelphia: Westminster Press, 1975), 89.

[2] Ibid.

one would be hard pressed to deny Paul's historical intent. Now if Paul intended to convey what really happened, and he did so within twenty-five years of the events about which he writes, and he had witnesses who could confirm what he writes, then the argument for resurrection is strong. It is unlikely that anyone would doubt any other historical event that had such strong, early testimony on its behalf. The difference is that the events about which Paul writes are supernatural, and critics do not like the implications.

Arguing a later date for the Gospels does not in any way diminish Paul's argument in 1 Corinthians 15 since it was written "very close to the events themselves."[3] There is no viable debate over the fact that Paul wrote 1 Corinthians within 20-25 years of the death of Jesus. For the present purposes, skeptical sources will suffice to make the point. Bart Ehrman notes that 1 Corinthians is considered to be one of Paul's "undisputed" letters that can be plausibly "situated in the early Christian movement of the 40s and 50s of the Common Era, when Paul was active as an apostle and missionary."[4] Marcus Borg dates the epistle to "around the year 54."[5] Robert Funk also dates the epistle to "around 54 C.E."[6] and Paul's actual vision within five years of the death of Christ, around AD 34 or 35.[7] Lynch argues that the "generally accepted letters," of which 1 Corinthians is a part, "are the earliest surviving writings of the Jesus Movement, composed between 50 and 60."[8] Crossan writes that the "resurrectional apparition" was "summarized by Paul as early as the

---

[3] Ibid., 90.

[4] Bart D. Ehrman, *The New Testament: A Historical Introduction to The Early Christian Writings*, 293.

[5] Marcus J. Borg, *Meeting Jesus Again for The First Time*, 105.

[6] Robert W. Funk, *Honest to Jesus: Jesus for a New Millennium* (San Francisco: HarperSanFrancisco, 1996), 259.

[7] Funk, *Honest to Jesus: Jesus for a New Millennium*, 264.

[8] Joseph H. Lynch, *Early Christianity: A Brief History* (New York: Oxford University Press, 2010), 44.

winter of 53 to 54 C.E."[9] Ehrman, Borg, Funk, and Crossan are among some of the most outspoken critics of the supernatural events of Scripture. The point is that even skeptics count 1 Corinthians among Paul's genuine epistles. No matter where one dates the written Gospels, clearly the resurrection account as given by Paul is both early and well attested. Because Paul wrote in such close proximity to the events, there were many people still alive who would have been in a position to contradict and invalidate the resurrection message. Paul's appeal to over five hundred at once, "most of whom remain until now," makes sense in this context. It would make no sense in a later context, or in a context that is not based in historical reality, for critics could easily have refuted Paul. Ian Wilson, who believes that people cannot know what really happened in the case of Jesus, writes, "The one incontrovertible aspect of this matter is the belief that Jesus had risen from the grave, whatever its origin, caught on very soon after the crucifixion and spread like wildfire. And it was embraced by an extraordinary diversity of people."[10] That hardly sounds like mythology. Paul's writings demonstrate the proximity to the events and the diversity of people who believed and claimed to have seen Jesus. This provides evidence that within twenty years of Jesus' death "the early Christians were passing on information about Jesus" in a stylized manner, "which would have facilitated the accurate transmission of that tradition. Paul was delivering to the Corinthians the exact message that had been given to him earlier."[11]

Another important implication from the proximity of Paul's writings to the events is that there was not enough time for legend theories about Jesus to become so fully developed. Skeptics have argued that the story of Jesus is a myth, containing borrowed

---

[9] John Dominic Crossan, *The Historical Jesus: The Life of a Mediterranean Jewish Peasant*, 397.

[10] Ian Wilson, *Jesus: The Evidence*, 142.

[11] Mark D. Roberts, *Can We Trust The Gospels? Investigating the Reliability of Matthew, Mark, Luke, and John*, 68.

elements from paganism, particularly the idea of resurrection. However, people who said they saw Jesus were still alive at the time, and they would have served as living checks to any mythological theories attempting to arise. Mythology takes time, and Paul's writings do not give nearly enough time for a resurrection myth about Jesus to have developed, especially when living witnesses could have easily contradicted the idea. This is particularly important considering that early Christians would have resisted such sweeping syncretism. The concept of bodily resurrection apart from end-time events was not easy to accept, especially in the Jewish culture. Jews would have tied the idea of resurrection to final judgment issues.[12] Further, the pagan world would not have thought of bodily resurrection as recorded in the Gospels. Stoics, for example, would have accepted the immortality of the soul, but that is not the same as bodily resurrection. There is no straight parallel with pagan religions on this point. The resurrection of Jesus Christ stands as a unique event in history.

Several have shown that, while there are similarities to be found between Christianity and pagan religions, the differences are far greater. Further, if any borrowing took place from one religion to another, then paganism borrowed from Christianity. The mystery cults "took note of the Christian movement and started to emulate it. Only after A.D. 100 did the mysteries begin to look very much like Christianity, precisely because their existence was threatened by this new religion."[13] The elements of paganism that sound like Christianity actually post-date the writings of the New Testament. Thus the evidence shows that the "theories that the resurrection was an idea incorporated into Christianity from pagan sources simply have no factual substance."[14] Eddy and Boyd argue, "If we had a cultural context that was conducive to legend making, and if

---

[12] J. Ed Komoszewski, M. James Sawyer, and Daniel B. Wallace, *Reinventing Jesus*, 255.

[13] Ibid, 237.

[14] Ibid., 255.

we have several centuries, or at least several generations, to allow for a legend of this magnitude to develop, the legendary-Jesus theory undoubtedly would be more compelling. But we have neither."[15] They point out that the notion of monotheistic Jews ascribing a divine nature to the Messiah and worshiping him, in spite of the fact that they would have been hostile to such ideas, shows that something other than legend making is at work.

Paul is clearly grounding his belief in history that is verifiable by multiple witnesses. This was a belief that was very early and very close to the historical events in question. Historians would love to have this kind of attestation to all the historical events they are investigating, and no better attestation exists for historical testimony than for the resurrection of Jesus. When it comes to Paul's arguments for the resurrected Christ, there is nothing wrong with the history; the problem lies more in the resistance to the implications that flow from that history. As Antony Flew said in debating the resurrection with Gary Habermas, one tries to discover what actually happened with a proper historical method, but "miracles are things that you just take to be impossible."[16] The problem is that a bias that rejects the history outright because of the contents of that history "is not a bias conducive to an open-minded historical investigation."[17]

What Else did Paul Know about Jesus?

Generally, seven epistles are accepted by skeptics as genuinely written by Paul. These letters include Romans, 1 and 2 Corinthians,

---

[15] Paul Rhodes Eddy, and Gregory A. Boyd, *The Jesus Legend: A Case for the Historical Reliability of the Synoptic Jesus Tradition*, 208.

[16] Gary R. Habermas, and Antony G.N. Flew, *Resurrected? An Atheist and Theist Dialogue* (Lanham, Md.: Rowman & Littlefield Publishers, 2005), 71.

[17] Ronald H. Nash, *Christian Faith and Historical Understanding* (Grand Rapids, MI: Zondervan, 1984), 92.

Galatians, Philippians, 1 Thessalonians, and Philemon.[18] Ehrman refers to these as "undisputed Pauline letters."[19] They would have been written sometime between A.D. 50-60, all within about thirty years of the death of Jesus. In order to stay with the evidence that cannot be very well disputed, and to keep from having to defend more than is necessary, the following will come from these "undisputed" epistles. What does Paul indicate that he knew about Jesus Christ in these epistles and why is Paul's knowledge important for understanding the historical Jesus?

Paul knew that Jesus was an Israelite, of the tribe of David (Rom 1:3; 9:5; Gal 3:16). He knew that Jesus was "born under the Law" (Gal 4:4). Jesus had a brother named James (Gal 1:19), to whom He appeared alive (1 Cor 15:7). Jesus also had other brothers (1 Cor 9:5). Paul knew that Jesus was poor (2 Cor 8:9), ministered among Jews (Rom 15:8), had twelve chosen men to serve with Him (1 Cor 15:5), and even knew that Peter was married (1 Cor 9:5). He knew that Jesus had instituted a "Lord's Supper" and knew the words that Jesus used in giving instructions for it on his betrayal night (1 Cor 11:23-25). Paul knew that Jesus was betrayed (1 Cor 11:23), killed by crucifixion (1 Cor 1:17-18) through the influence of his own countrymen (1 Thess 2:14-15), that he was buried and seen alive again (1 Cor 15). Critics think they can know "almost nothing concerning the life and personality of Jesus,"[20] but Paul concludes from his knowledge that Jesus is Lord.

There is more. What did Paul know about the character of Jesus? He knew that Jesus was meek and gentle (2 Cor 10:1). He understood that Jesus was humble, self-sacrificing, and obedient to the Father even unto death on the cross (Phil 2:6-8; Rom 5:19). He knew that Jesus' life and death was characterized by grace and love

---

[18] Funk, *Honest to Jesus: Jesus for a New Millennium*, 38.

[19] Ehrman, *The New Testament: A Historical Introduction to the Early Christian Writings*, 324.

[20] Rudolph Bultmann, *Jesus and the Word*, 8.

(2 Cor 8:9; Rom 8:35). Paul also knew that Jesus was righteous, even saying that Jesus knew no sin (Rom 5:18; 2 Cor 5:21). Paul saw the life of Christ as one to be emulated (1 Cor 11:1). He was practicing what he knew was at the heart of the gospel: the life, death, and resurrection of Christ. Paul knew the historical Jesus well and he called upon Christians to follow Christ's example.

Paul also knew the teachings of Jesus. For example, in addition to knowing what Jesus taught about the "Lord's Supper" (1 Cor 11), Paul knew Jesus' teachings on marriage and divorce (1 Cor 7), the rights of preachers to meet their material needs (1 Cor 9), and Jesus' purpose in going to the cross (Gal 1:4).

What is the point? Contrary to skeptical dogma, Paul knew quite a bit about the historical Jesus. Paul was in a much better position to know what he was talking about than those two thousand years removed from the events, whose worldviews begin with assumptions about reality that cannot conceive of the Jesus Paul knew. We'll go with Paul's knowledge as a reliable source of information about who Jesus was, what Jesus did, and what Jesus taught.

Discussion Questions

1. Why do you think that, according to 1 Corinthians 15:1-4, the death, burial, and resurrection of Jesus is of "first importance"?

2. Why do you think it is so important to accept the historical reality of the resurrection?

3. Think of who Paul was and when he wrote. Why is Paul's testimony so significant?

4. Why does it matter that Paul would have written within 25 years of Jesus' resurrection? How does that argue against myth-making?

5. How do you think Paul knew so much about the historical Jesus?

What Have Others Said? 8

How do we know that Jesus lived and was a real person in history? The gospel accounts of Matthew, Mark, Luke, and John are four ancient, independent sources that provide us with real information about Jesus. What Paul wrote, within twenty to twenty-five years of the events in question (1 Corinthians), is another ancient, independent source that skeptics have a difficult time dismissing. Though these sources are all compiled in the Bible, they were not originally written together or written in collusion with each other. They stand as their own sources and should be considered as such for historical purposes.

However, some people will argue that since these sources are biased in favor of Jesus, we need other sources to confirm the information, as if only hostile sources provide good information (so much for endorsements from good sources). This is a false assumption, for any writer is going to have a bias, but this does not automatically make the writer untrustworthy. If this were the case, the bias of modern skeptics would render their skepticism invalid on the same terms and their works should be dismissed. Consistency would demand as much.

But let's play their game for a few moments. Are there other sources, even non-Christian, ancient sources that help confirm the life of Jesus and others found in the Bible? Yes. However, we should remember a few things when looking at this material from ancient, non-Christian sources.

First, we should not expect ancient, non-Christian sources to sound like Christians. They are not writing to say that they support Jesus, so we should not expect them to support the divine nature of Jesus in any explicit way. They are not going to write in favor of the miracles. They are simply recording a fact or two about Christ or

Christians that reflects their own particular concerns at the time of their writing. They are not giving detailed accounts, but they do record information consistent with what the Gospels show to be true. Sometimes they do this perhaps unintentionally even though they are opposed to Christians.

Second, do not expect the ancient sources to record every event that the gospel accounts record Jesus doing. Not many ancient records are as detailed about someone as the Gospels are about Jesus, and there are not many surviving works for any ancient person or event. Some of the records indicating something about Jesus or His followers are just passing comments without any intent to provide much historical detail. Still, they show that Jesus was a real person in history who had influence. So if someone tells you that the Bible is the only source that mentions Jesus in the ancient world, you will know that this is not correct. Let's survey a few of these sources.

Ancient Historians and Officials

Tacitus
Cornelius Tacitus was a Roman historian in the first century (ca. AD 55-120). He was known as one of the greatest historians of that time. Among his works is one called the *Annals*, which cover the historical period from AD 14 (the death of Augustus) to AD 68 (the death of Nero). Here is one reference to Christ and Christians recorded in this non-Christian work (found in *Annals* 15.44). Nero was trying to pass off the guilt for the burning of Rome to the Christians, though many suspected he did it himself:

> Consequently, to get rid of the report, Nero fastened the guilt and inflicted the most exquisite tortures of a class hated for their abominations, called Christians by the populace. Christus, from whom the name had its origin, suffered the extreme penalty during the reign of Tiberius at the hands of one of our procurators, Pontius Pilatus...

From this non-Christian passage, we can see several facts: 1) The origin of the name "Christian" comes from the founder, named "Christus" (Latin for Christ). 2) Christus "suffered the extreme penalty," a reference which almost certainly is speaking of crucifixion. 3) Christus was put to death under the supervision of Pontius Pilatus (Latin), a fact recorded by all four gospel accounts (Matt 27; Mark 15; Luke 23; John 18-19). 4) The death of Christus occurred during the reign of Tiberius. Tacitus further records that upon the death of Christus, the "mischievous superstition" was "checked for a moment," but "again broke out not only in Judea … but even in Rome." This is consistent with Biblical history. When Jesus rose from the dead, Christianity proceeded to spread throughout the Roman Empire. Here, then, is a non-Christian source verifying fundamental elements of what the Bible says occurred in history.

Suetonius

Suetonius, another Roman historian, served as the chief secretary to the Emperor Hadrian (r. AD 117-138). Suetonius would have had access to important records. He wrote this about the Emperor Claudius: "Because the Jews at Rome caused continuous disturbances at the instigation of Chrestus, he expelled them from the city."

Claudius was trying to blame Christians for riots that had occurred in a Jewish community in Rome during AD 49, so he expelled the Jews from Rome. "Chrestus," in this reference, is most likely another variation of the name Christ (or even a misspelling of it, but this is not the point of the reference). Now compare this with Acts 18:1-2 where Luke records the same event. Biblical history is consistent with Roman history on this point.

Suetonius, in his work about Nero, also wrote about punishing Christians after the great fire at Rome. He said that the Christians were "a sect professing a new and mischievous religious belief."

What was so mischievous about what Christians believed? The most probable explanation for this is that the Christians believed in the resurrection of Christ. Whatever Suetonius was referring to, this confirms that Christians believed something very different from what typical Romans believed and practiced religiously. This helps confirm the fact that what Christians believed was not just an offshoot of either Judaism or paganism. Christianity was indeed unique.

Josephus

Josephus is a well-known ancient Jewish historian who lived from about AD 37-97. After Jerusalem was destroyed in AD 70, he moved to Rome and became a court historian for the emperor Vespasian. Though what Josephus wrote about Jesus is often disputed, there is little question that he at least refers to Jesus as a historical figure. In the context of a reference to James, Josephus calls James "the brother of Jesus, who was called Christ" (Antiquities 18). That simple reference supports the fact of James, the fact of Christ, and the fact that they were brothers.

The more debated passage from Josephus speaks of Jesus in positive terms as a wise man who appeared to his disciples alive again the third day. While a Jewish historian may not have written in support of Jesus, there is still strong evidence that Josephus did in fact reference Jesus and his followers. An Arabic version of the disputed passage seems more likely. In this passage, Josephus tells us that "Pilate condemned him to be crucified and to die. But those who had become his disciples did not abandon his discipleship. They reported that he had appeared to them three days after his crucifixion and that he was alive..."

This passage simply lists the facts. Jesus was crucified under Pilate's authority, and the disciples believed and reported that Jesus had appeared to them. There is not much to dispute in this. In another section of Antiquities (18.5.2), Josephus refers to John the Baptist as being put to death by Herod.

Now some of the Jews thought that the destruction of Herod's army came from God, and that very justly, as a punishment of what he did against John, that was called the Baptist: for Herod slew him, who was a good man...

...Now when [many] others came in crowds about him, for they were very greatly moved [or pleased] by hearing his words, Herod, who feared lest the great influence John had over the people might put it into his power and inclination to raise a rebellion, (for they seemed ready to do anything he should advise,) thought it best, by putting him to death, to prevent any mischief he might cause, and not bring himself into difficulties, by sparing a man who might make him repent of it when it would be too late. Accordingly he was sent a prisoner, out of Herod's suspicious temper, to Macherus, the castle I before mentioned, and was there put to death. (Ant. 18:5)

See Matthew 14:1-12 where the Bible speaks of John's death. The question is what to make of Matthew's report that John was put to death at the instigation of Herodias, whereas Josephus indicates another reason. However, there is no contradiction between the accounts, if one can accept the idea that often multiple reasons explain historical events. It is certainly possible that both Matthew and Josephus are correct, each stressing different reasons that both played a part in John's death (one personal and one political). Even so, Josephus' account verifies that John was a real person who was put to death by Herod Antipas. The Gospels were not making up some fictional character in order to help foist the Christ of faith onto unsuspecting disciples.

Thallus
Thallus is a historian who wrote some time around AD 52, just a few years after Jesus died on the cross. He wrote a history of the Eastern Mediterranean world that began with the Trojan War. The

work itself was lost, but there are other writers who quoted from it. One of these writers was Julius Africanus, writing in about AD 221. There is an interesting statement that Africanus made regarding something that Thallus wrote in the first century.

Africanus writes about the darkness when Jesus was on the cross (Matthew 27:45) and refers to Thallus, who apparently also wrote that a period of darkness occurred at that time. Africanus wrote, "This darkness Thallus, in the third book of his *History*, calls, as appears to me without reason, an eclipse of the sun." Keep in mind that this reference to an "eclipse" comes from less than 200 years after Jesus died. So the report of the darkness while Jesus was on the cross was known. Yet Thallus, an unbeliever, in an apparent attempt to deny any supernatural element of what happened tried to argue that the darkness was merely an eclipse of the sun. Here we find a very important point. When unbelievers try to argue for a natural explanation of something supernatural that we read in the Bible, they are verifying that something actually happened. If nothing at all happened, they would not feel the need to explain it away.

Pliny the Younger and Trajan

Pliny the Younger was a Roman author and administrator. He was a governor in Asia Minor and is known for his letters. One of his works, which dates to about AD 112, talks about Christians in the territory of Bithynia in Asia Minor. He was concerned about the influence that Christians were having and was not sure about how to deal with them. He wrote to the emperor Trajan asking what to do. In this letter, he wrote that Christians "were in the habit of meeting on a certain fixed day" and that they "sang in alternate verses a hymn to Christ, as to a god..." This shows that early Christians worshipped Jesus Christ as Deity and met regularly on a certain day (which, historically, was the first day of the week).

The emperor Trajan responded by telling Pliny that he should not seek out the Christians in order to punish them, but that if they do happen to get caught, they should have the opportunity to repent by renouncing Christianity and worshipping the Roman gods. If the Christians refused, then they should be severely punished.

There are several other ancient, non-Christian sources mentioning Christ and Christians, including the emperor Hadrian, the Jewish Talmud (2nd century), and Lucian (2nd century Greek). Many more references could be included, but these should suffice to show that there are plenty of sources outside of the Bible that speak about Christ and His followers. Remember, these are non-Christian sources, unbelievers who were not trying to support Jesus.

Of course, we could also show that there are many more sources written in the first two to three hundred years after Christ by early Christians. Just because they believed in Jesus does not discount them as historical sources. They believed because they considered that the evidence for Jesus was too strong to ignore. Believers today would agree.

While the non-Christian sources are not going to prove the resurrection, they do show the historicity of Jesus and the movement that grew *based upon belief in the resurrection*. At the very least, we have the evidence that Jesus Christ was a real person in history who died by crucifixion. His disciples believed that they saw Him alive again, and they began to preach this message wherever they went. They were willing to die for this message, and it is clear that the impact they had the ancient world was powerful.

Note: several sources have the quotes used, plus more. Among these readily available sources are:

Eddy, Paul Rhodes, and Gregory A. Boyd. *The Jesus Legend: A Case for the Historical Reliability of the Synoptic Jesus Tradition.* Grand Rapids, MI: Baker Academic, 2007.

Evans, Craig A. *Fabricating Jesus: How Modern Scholars Distort the Gospels.* Downers Grove, Ill.: IVP Books, 2006.

Geisler, Norman. *Baker Encyclopedia of Christian Apologetics.* Grand Rapids, MI: Baker Books, 1999.

Habermans, Gary. *The Historical Jesus.* Joplin, MO: College Press, 1996.

Strobel, Lee. *The Case for the Real Jesus: A Journalist Investigates Current Attacks on the Identity of Christ.* Grand Rapids, MI: Zondervan, 2007.

Witherington, Ben III. *What Have They Done With Jesus? Beyond Strange Theories and Bad History —Why We Can Trust The Bible.* New York: HarperOne, 2006.

Discussion Questions

1. Why do you think some would insist on finding non-Christian sources in order to verify facts from the Gospels?

2. How should non-Christian sources be accepted? What cautions do you think are important?

3. What should we not expect from non-Christian sources and why?

4. What types of facts are verified by the non-Christian sources? Why are these important (or not)?

5. Why should we *not* dismiss the Gospels and Paul just because they favor Jesus?

The Divine Messiah

9

"For in Him all the fullness of Deity dwells in bodily form" (Col 2:9). The biblical witness to the divine nature of Jesus is summed up in that passage. Jesus possesses all divine attributes. Here Paul "emphasizes that no element of that fullness is excepted. Whatever is characteristic of God as God resides in Christ. This includes both God's nature and his attributes."[1]

The identity of Jesus has long been a debated issue. Some called Him a deceiver (Matt 27:63). Some said that He led the multitudes astray; others said He was a good man (John 7:12). Some claimed that He was one of the prophets, such as Elijah or Jeremiah (Matt 16:14). His disciples confessed their faith that He was the Christ, the Son of God (Matt 16:16). After the first century there were continued debates about the nature and identity of Jesus. "The Christological controversies of the late second and early third century were thus a part of the internal dialectic of the Christian faith."[2] To avoid the extremes of adoptionism (Jesus was a good man whom God adopted as his Son) and modalism (Jesus was the same person as the Father who manifested himself in different modes), "the orthodox solution was to affirm at the same time the oneness of God, the deity of Christ, and the distinction of the Son from the Father."[3] Due to the efforts to try to explain all of this, the "Trinitarian" controversies of the fourth century were born. Though there have always been dissenters, the orthodox position defined and understood over the centuries was that Jesus was indeed God, and that the Father, Son, and the Holy Spirit are distinct

---

[1] Murray J. Harris, *3 Crucial Questions About Jesus* (Grand Rapids, MI: Baker Books, 1994), 66.

[2] Everett Ferguson, *Early Christians Speak*, rev. ed. (Abilene: ACU Press, 1987), 18.

[3] Ibid.

personalities, yet together one God. In modern times, the debate has not lessened. Liberal theology of the last couple hundred years has questioned the orthodox view and has tried to rediscover the historical Jesus. The result has been a denial of the Deity of Jesus in this modern era of skepticism.

> Today, one can find evidence virtually everywhere — on every continent, in both Protestant and Roman Catholic circles — that the theologically "in thing" is to contend for a Jesus who was only a man by nature and for a Bible that is virtually silent regarding the classical incarnational Christology of a two natured Christ — true God and true man in the one person of Jesus Christ. It is very much in vogue to believe that the better case can be made for understanding Jesus as only a man — a very unusual man, of course, with a special mission from God — and to explain the biblical ascriptions of divine qualities to Him in other than ontological terms.[4]

This quote accurately describes the modern mind-set even of some who are professed believers in God. Many are teaching that Jesus was not really God. Skeptics are saying that he never even claimed to be God, but that later disciples attributed Deity to him. This is why other discussions have focus on the reliability of the Gospel accounts and on Paul's account. If they are accurate presentations of Jesus, then they speak for themselves. However, the question here is, what does the Bible actually teach about the nature of Jesus Christ? Was He God? Was He just a man who had some extraordinary ability? Who was He?

---

[4] Robert L. Reymond, *Jesus Divine Messiah* (Phillipsburg, NJ: Presbyterian and Reformed Publishing Co., 1990), 2-3.

The Old Testament

First, consider the many prophecies and allusions (hundreds) concerning Messiah that the New Testaments shows were fulfilled in Jesus. We'll just survey a few. Some of these prophecies include references to the Messiah as being Deity. For example:

Isaiah 9:6 refers to the Messiah as "Mighty God" (*El Gibbor*). In Jeremiah 32:18, the name of "Mighty God" is identified as "Yahweh of hosts." Some have argued that "Mighty God" is not the same as "Almighty God," and therefore Jesus was not really Yahweh. Jeremiah connects the terms "Mighty God" and "Yahweh of hosts." To call Jesus "Mighty God" obviously attributes a divine nature to Jesus. "Yahweh" (or Jehovah) is the most precious name for God. "Jesus," short for Jehoshua, means "Yahweh the Savior." His earthly parents were told this would be His name (Matt 1:21). This was no accident. The Bible does teach that Jesus was Yahweh come in the flesh (John 1:1, 14). Consider further the following biblical connections:

1. Isaiah 8:13-14 refers to Yahweh as the one who would become a stone of stumbling and a rock of offense. The New Testament applies this to Jesus in 1 Peter 2:8.

2. Isaiah 40:3 speaks of the one who would come before "Yahweh" in the wilderness. This is applied to John the Immerser as he prepared the way for Jesus the Christ (Matt 3:3; Luke 1:76; John 3:28). John came before Yahweh in the flesh.

3. In Isaiah 42:8, Yahweh speaks of glory that belongs only to Himself, and that it would not be given to another. Jesus prayed about the glory that He shared with the Father before the world was (John 17:5). Isaiah 6 relates a vision in which Isaiah saw Yahweh sitting on his throne. John 12:36-41 records that statements spoken by Isaiah were uttered "because he saw His glory, and he spoke of Him." In context, this is a reference to Jesus. Isaiah saw "His" glory

and spoke of "Him"—Jesus. This connects Jesus to Yahweh's glory.

4. Isaiah 44:6 makes a clear statement concerning Yahweh: "I am the first and I am the last, and there is no God besides Me." It would stand to reason that anyone who claimed this would either have to be God, or he would have to be a liar. There can be only one first and last. The New Testament attributes this very phrase, "the first and the last," to Jesus (Rev 1:17-18; 2:8; 22:13-16). He is the first and the last, the alpha and the omega, the beginning and the end. These references teach that Jesus is Yahweh, for that cannot rightly be applied to anyone else.

5. Psalm 102 begins a prayer to Yahweh. A section of this very prayer is applied to Jesus in Hebrews 1:10-12, once again connecting Jesus to Yahweh. It would be difficult to reconcile how a prayer (or even a part of one) made to Yahweh could be thus applied to one who is not God. The application of this passage testifies to Jesus' divine nature.

These, and other, references taken together provide evidence for the deity of Christ being taught from the Old Testament. It was not an accident that such connections were made between the Testaments. Jesus was not coming to this earth to be just any other man; He was coming to be the savior of the world. Ultimately, only God Himself could fill this role.

What Do the Gospel Accounts Teach?

Based upon other discussions, it is appropriate to consider the testimony of the Gospel records. Do they teach that Jesus is Deity? There are at least three areas to consider: the claims of Jesus, the works of Jesus, and His acceptance of worship.

1. *The claims of Jesus.* While Jesus did not make many explicit claims to be God, He did make claims that uniquely identified Himself with God. Taken together, they support a case for Jesus'

understanding that He is God.

a. *He claimed to be one with the Father.* He did not claim just to believe in or love God; He claimed to be one with God (John 10:30). He did not refer to Himself as a son of God, but as *the* Son of God. See John 5:17-18 where they understood that Jesus was claiming the Father in a unique sense, and they believed that this was blasphemous, for He was "making Himself equal with God." Jesus claimed a unique relationship with God that no one else could properly claim.

b. *He claimed to have power to forgive sin.* Mark 2 records where Jesus, confronted with a paralyzed man, simply said, "Son, your sins are forgiven." The Jews thought this was wrong, for none "can forgive sins but God alone." In order to prove that He had the authority to forgive, Jesus healed the man. The claim to forgive sins is a divine claim.

c. *He claimed sinlessness* (John 8:29, 46; 18:23). Other biblical passages support this claim (Heb. 4:15), which puts Jesus in a position different from all others who have sinned (Rom 3:23). While this in itself may not prove Jesus is God, surely if Jesus had sinned He could not have convinced anyone He was God. His sinlessness is consistent with His divine claims.

d. *He claimed to have authority to judge the world* (John 5:25-27). He said that His words would judge in the last day (John 12:48). This high claim implies that either He understood Himself to be God or else He was the most conceited and arrogant man who ever lived.

e. *He claimed to speak the very words of God.* He said, "My words shall not pass away" (Matt 24:35). He put his own words on par with the words of God and Scripture.

f. *He claimed to be the only way to salvation* (John 14:6). One cannot be neutral about statements like this. Salvation is narrow and exclusive, found only in Jesus (Acts 4:12). (See the chapter on *Salvation: is there only one way to God?*).

g. *He claimed to be the Author and Giver of life.* "The Son of Man gives life to whom He will" (John 5:21). He called himself the "bread of life" (John 6:48), and the "resurrection and the life" (John 11:25). Who but God can have such intrinsic power and make such outstanding claims?

h. *Jesus claimed the highest loyalty from mankind.* He said that His followers must deny themselves to follow Him (Luke 9:23). He told His followers that they must love Him above all else, including family members (Luke 14:26; Matt 10:34-39). If Jesus did not think He was God, what else could He have been possibly thinking?

i. *He claimed to fulfill all of the Old Testament prophecies concerning the Messiah* (Luke 24:44). Considering how many prophecies there are about Messiah, this is an amazing claim. But Jesus fulfilled not just a few prophecies, but the entire purpose of the Old Testament. Since, as already shown, the Old Testament connects the Messiah to Yahweh, then Jesus' claim to Messiahship was also a claim to Godhood.

j. *Jesus claimed to be "I AM."* When speaking to the Jews about Abraham, Jesus said, "before Abraham was, I am" (John 8:58). This would take the Jews back to the time when Yahweh spoke to Moses in the burning bush, claiming to be "I AM THAT I AM" (Exod 3:14). In this statement, Jesus was claiming eternal existence and self-sufficiency. If He was not God, then this really was blasphemy.

To dismiss all of these as being superimposed upon Jesus by later disciples is not consistent with the evidence, and portrays later disciples as being more clever and deceitful than would be difficult to imagine. These claims are subtle, yet strong. Taken together, they argue that Jesus claimed to be God.

2. *The works of Jesus.* It was not enough for Jesus to make spectacular claims. He needed to back up what He said. This was the purpose for the works of Jesus: "the works which the Father has given Me to accomplish, the very works that I do, bear witness of Me, that the Father has sent Me" (John 5:36). John 20:30-31 states that the works Jesus did were intended to spark faith in those who know of them.

Jesus performed different kinds of miracles, but they can be classed under three categories: miracles over nature (e.g., calming the storm), miracles of physical healing (e.g., healing the paralyzed man), and miracles of resurrection (e.g., Lazarus). The point here is that Jesus worked various types of miracles in order to back up His claims. Whatever Jesus claimed, according to Scripture, was demonstrated by His works in many ways and in different circumstances.

3. *The acceptance of worship.* Another important biblical proof of the deity of Jesus is His acceptance of worship. The action of worship "is an acknowledgment of that being's deity."[5] The Bible teaches that the only one who is to be worshiped is God. Jesus recognized this Himself (Matt 4:10). While it is possible for someone to accept worship who is not God, Jesus' acceptance of worship was an implicit claim to be divine. Several examples of this are given in the gospel accounts (e.g., Matt 8:2; 9:18; 14:33; 28:9, 17). Of special note are three New Testament passages in this connection:

a. **John 5:23**. Jesus stated that all should honor the Son (Jesus)

---

[5] Robert M. Bowman Jr., and J. Ed Komoszewski, *Putting Jesus in His Place: The Case for The Deity of Christ* (Grand Rapids, MI: Kregel Publications, 2007),

just as they honor the Father. If He did not think that He was God, then He was guilty of blasphemy. This statement alone demonstrates the biblical teaching of the Deity of Jesus. For one to properly claim that he deserves the same honor as the Father, he would have to be divine.

b. **John 20:28.** After the resurrection, Jesus appeared to His disciples. Thomas was not present at the first appearance, and he doubted whether Jesus had really been seen. When Jesus appeared again, Thomas saw and made the following statement to Jesus: "My Lord and my God." There is no indication that Jesus tried to correct this. Jesus accepted this worship, as well as the reference to his Godhood. In fact, He responded to Thomas, "Because you have seen Me, have you believed?" (v. 29)

c. **Hebrews 1:6.** Referring to Jesus, the text says, "Let all the angels of God worship Him." The Bible shows that the angels knew that the only one they could properly worship was God (Rev 19:10). If they are told to worship Jesus, then this is a clear implication of the teaching that Jesus is God.

As earlier argued, the resurrection is the strongest proof of the divine nature of Jesus (Rom 1:3-4). So we should never lose sight of this evidence. Further testimony can be seen in the epistles (e.g., Paul's testimony, which is independent of the Gospels). The divine nature of Jesus is seen throughout Scripture, and we should respond to the evidence as did Thomas: "My Lord and My God."

Discussion Questions

1. Why do you think the debate over the identity of Jesus has been so controversial over the years?

2. Why do skeptics argue that the idea that Jesus is God was something invented by later Christians?

3. Review the claims of Jesus and think about what these claims imply about Jesus' identity. Also, what do they imply about how we should think of Jesus?

4. How do the works of Jesus back up His claims?

5. How should we respond to the evidence of Jesus, and why?

Jesus is Lord

We have now run out of alternative explanations for Jesus' extraordinary claims. The explanation that He was the world's biggest liar or a lunatic has no takers. The theory that these divine claims were attributed to Jesus in later legends is undermined by the thorough Jewishness of the Gospels and by the fact that the earliest material in the New Testament attests to the same view of Jesus as divine. The notion that Jesus did claim to be divine but in a mystical sense also does not fit the Jewish context of Jesus' teachings and the specific claims that He made. This leaves only one explanation standing: Jesus did claim to be divine, and He meant it literally. Ultimately, one of these explanations will have to be chosen; and the only one that fits the evidence is that Jesus truly is Lord.

Ken Boa and Robert Bowman, Jr.,
20 Compelling Evidences That God Exists

Salvation: Is there only one way to God? 10

"Enter through the narrow gate; for the gate is wide and the way is broad that leads to destruction, and there are many who enter through it. For the gate is small and the way is narrow that leads to life, and there are few who find it." (Matt 7:13-14)

"He who is not with Me is against Me; and he who does not gather with Me scatters." (Matt 12:30)

"I am the way, and the truth, and the life; no one comes to the Father but through Me." (John 14:6)

"And there is salvation in no one else; for there is no other name under heaven that has been given among men by which we must be saved." (Acts 4:12)

These are astounding claims. Who would have the audacity to say such things? Before Jesus, no one was claiming to be the *exclusive* manifestation of the one God. This was shocking to the core. As Ben Witherington noted, it's no surprise that Jesus got Himself crucified. The surprise is that he lasted three years in public ministry before it happened.[1]

The question before us is this? Are the claims true? Is there really only one way to salvation? Is Christianity exclusive? How do we reconcile Christianity with a pluralistic world?

Salvation in a Pluralistic World

In the *Case for Faith: the Film*, Lee Strobel tells the story of Charles Templeton, a man who at one time was a fundamentalist preacher

---

[1] Lee Strobel, *The Case for Faith: The Film* (Santa Monica, CA: La Miranda Films, 2008), DVD.

who worked alongside Billy Graham. Then he turned to atheism. His objection? "Are we to believe only Christians are right? After all, Christians have the audacity to say there is only one God—theirs—and that the gods of every other people on earth are spurious." After quoting Acts 4:12, he says, "Such an insufferable presumption!"[2] So who do Christians think they are to be so arrogant as to say that they are the only ones who got religion right?

In a pluralistic world, the idea of having only one right way is intolerable. Postmodernism's impact on religion means that there is no one single religion that is valid for everyone. Therefore, one of the worst things anyone can do today is to be intolerant of other religions. For postmodernists, what matters is not whether or not something is true, but whether or not it works for the individual. If it works, it must be right for that person or group. This is what a "post-truth" world looks like.

Of course, the real question is this: is it true? Is there really only one way to God? How would we know if there is, and how would we know that we found it? Rather than react emotionally to the idea that many are wrong, we need fundamentally to ask whether it is actually true.

There are multiple views about the concept of salvation. Salvation for eastern religions may involve a release from the Karmic cycle. Salvation for Naturalism means we must save ourselves and our environment. We alone are responsible for fixing the world. There is no salvation from sin needed. As Kurtz put it, "But we can discover no divine purpose or providence for the human species. While there is much we do not know, humans are responsible for what we are or will become. No deity will save us; we must save ourselves."[3]

---

[2] Ibid.

[3] Paul Kurtz, *In Defense of Secular Humanism* (Buffalo, NY: Prometheus Books, 1983), 16-17.

All the so-called salvations are missing the point and do not address the real problem in which we find ourselves.

In a pluralistic world, all ethical religions lead to God. In this view, all religions essentially teach the same God, so there are many ways to salvation. This type of system tends to tie everything to moral behavior. Since all the great religions teach a high moral behavior, like Christianity, then they all equally find their way to the Ultimate Reality (as some refer to God).[4] This view dethrones Christ as God, makes him out to be a prophet on par with any world or religious prophet, and places the experience of observing similar religious behavior and morality in a superior position to revelation. There is nothing particularly unique about Christianity, though it is still considered to be a viable practice as long as it doesn't claim to be the only way that is right. There is little emphasis on the problem of sin and the need for salvation from sin. Religion is simply humankind all trying to reach up to the same Ultimate Reality. The problem is that all of this really misses the point.

Even though there is some agreement on many issues like moral behavior (even then not always), there is great disagreement on major issues such as: Who is God? What is the nature of God? What is the nature of man? What of the problem of sin? What of salvation? Is Jesus the promised Messiah? Is He God manifested in the flesh? These are not minor issues, and Christianity differs from the major religions on these points. They cannot all be right.

Yet, the fact of religion universally demonstrates that we have a great need that cannot be fulfilled by this natural world. There is something not right, and we sense that, so we hunger for something greater. Jesus identified these problems and gave the solution to it.

---

[4] See, for example, John Hick, and et al, *Four Views on Salvation in a Pluralistic World*, Counterpoints (Grand Rapids, Mich.: Zondervan Pub. House, 1996).

Other views, more conservative in nature, focus on Christ as the one through whom salvation is found, but might still accept that those outside of Christ can be okay. Some insist we must remain agnostic about those who have not heard the gospel. Where can we turn?

The Biblical View

First, we must recognize the need for salvation because of the problem of sin. Since sin is universal, the need for salvation is also universal. The solution to the problem we all face is not simply to make us better people. That won't work by itself. The solution is God's grace (Eph 2:1-4).

The biblical doctrine of grace is unique. Only God has the authority to forgive sins (see Mark 2). So if we will know anything about salvation and forgiveness, it must come from the One who has the authority to tell us about it. This requires revelation of the mind of God (1 Cor 2:9ff).

Further, many passages point to the exclusive nature of salvation in Christ: John 3:16, 18; 14:6; 1 John 3:22-23 (see how one cannot deny Christ and say all religions are the same); 1 Pet 1:3-5; Rom 10:9-15; Acts 4:12. The whole New Testament shouts this theme.

Other biblical considerations show that in both the OT and NT other religions are seen as non-redemptive, even as part of the domain of darkness (Acts 19:26; 26:17-18; Col 1:13; Exod 20:3-6; Isa 37:18-19). Wrath is said to come upon those Gentiles who remain separate from Christ (1 Thess 2:16). On the other hand, conversion to Christ results in turning to serve the living and true God (1 Thess 1:9). Other religions are not considered merely inferior, but as dead wrong, because there is only one God, one Lord, one faith... (Eph 4:1-6).

Scripture teaches what has been termed "exclusivism" (often not meant to be a compliment). That is, salvation comes only through Christ, and those who are outside of Him will be eternally lost. Salvation depends upon explicit personal faith in Christ as Lord, though it is still considered as a gift of God's grace (Eph 2:8).

Why is Salvation Only in Christ?

If Christians are going to say that Christ is the only way to salvation, then they need to be able to give reasons why this is so. These are, in fact, the very points that show biblical Christianity to be different from every other world religion. Why is Christ superior? Why is Jesus Christ the only way? We could spend time getting to know all the various world religions—Islam, Judaism, Hinduism, etc.—but the following reasons are sufficient to demonstrate why Jesus Christ is the only way to God:

1. Because Christ is the only one who has come to this world – God manifested in the flesh—and died for the sins of the world. We should understand, as one put it, that God isn't looking down at different religious clubs (the Hindu Club, Muslim Club, Buddhist Club, Christian Club) and saying "I like the Christian club the best." Rather, He is looking upon all humanity and seeing people who are lost in sin, separated from Him, and He has responded by stepping into the world He made and taking that problem of the human condition of sin upon Himself in the most personal way.[5] Jesus became the sacrifice for sin that we might be forgiven (2 Cor 5:21; 1 Pet 1:18-21).

Some want to compare religions on the grounds of what works to make people better, but this misses the point. The question for religion is not which one makes us better people. There may be many religions that help improve a person's character, but that is not why we need salvation. The question is which one (or, rather,

---

[5] Strobel, *The Case for Faith: The Film.*

who) responds properly to the human condition of sin, and the only answer to that is Jesus Christ.

The ultimate superiority of Christianity over all other world religions is not the ethical system, as many religions contain a high ethics. It is not in the assumption of a high morality in itself. It is not in the rituals and practices that make Christianity unique. The superiority of it lies in the fact that Jesus, God manifest in the flesh, died for our sins and was raised from the dead, thus providing salvation from sin and the living hope through the living God. No other religion can begin to offer this. God responded to the human condition through Christ, taking sin upon Himself. One who rejects this rejects the only true means of dealing with the condition of sin.

2. Because Christ is the only one who can properly mediate between God and man. If the fellowship that was broken between God and man, due to sin, is to be bridged, then we need someone to stand in the gap and mediate. Only Jesus Christ can do this.

How so? One reason is because Christ is both God and man. As such, He knows and has the right to bridge the gap caused by sin. He is God's communication with mankind, and He is mankind's advocate before God (see John 1:1, 14; 1 Tim 2:5).

All other views about salvation must ultimately reject this truth about Christ. The divine nature of Jesus is the key to understanding the exclusive nature of the claim to salvation. No one else anywhere or anytime can represent us to God as Jesus can, and no one can represent God to us as Jesus can. Jesus is, at the same time, both our sacrifice and our great High Priest. Because of Jesus and His work, we have an advocate with the Father (1 John 2:1-2). No religious leader of any other religion can begin to touch this.

3. Christ is the only one who ever lives to make intercession (Heb 7:25). He intercedes for His people who have sinned. What other religion offers a living savior—even now—who intercedes to God on behalf of his people?

4. Christ is the only one who backed up His remarkable claims. Many people have made terrific claims without providing much support. The difference is that Jesus backed His claims up (see Mark 2). This was the purpose of His miracles and resurrection (John 20:30-31; Matt 11:2-6).

5. Because Christ is the only one who was raised from the dead, never to die again, and in fulfillment of his own claims and prophecies (Matt 16:21). The resurrection of Jesus is the ultimate proof. If this didn't happen, the rest is in vain anyway.

6. Because Christ is the ultimate Judge, we will all stand before Him (2 Cor 5:10). Again, God's Proof of a final judgment is the resurrection of Jesus (Acts 17:30-31). No one else in the entire religious world can claim to be judge then demonstrate it through resurrection. Because of this, Jesus is the only one who has a right to command everyone to repent and expect their obedience. His authority is absolute. No other religious leader or system has such a right.

Of course, just *calling* yourself a follower of Jesus isn't enough by itself (Matt 7:21-23). Faith in Christ and living by His will are necessary components of our salvation. However, this by no means indicates that we earn our salvation. Salvation is a gift of God's grace. Yet grace teaches us to live soberly, righteously, and godly (Titus 2:11-14). If we live just any way we desire apart from what God teaches, then we cannot say we are truly receiving God's grace.

Submission to the Lordship of Jesus requires us to listen to His authority and live by it. Our job is not to "pick" a religion that we think is going to save us.[6] Our job is to respond to the offer given by God by which He, in His grace and mercy, has responded to the human condition of sin and sent His own Son to die as a sacrifice for sin, then raised Him up to give us the hope of heaven. This religion of Christ is not one based upon mere emotion or experience, but upon the historical reality of God acting in this world on our behalf. God acting in this world through Jesus is what justifies the exclusive claims of Christianity.

Discussion Questions

1. How do the biblical claims about Christ and salvation indicate "exclusivism"?

2. Why do you think that saying there is only one way to heaven is so offensive in our world today?

3. Why is just focusing on the ethics of Christian behavior not going to be very convincing when arguing for salvation only in Christ?

4. What do you think we should be emphasizing to people lost in sin, and why?

5. What reasons are there for saying that Jesus Christ is the only way? Can you think of others not listed?

---

[6] Ibid.

Common Approaches to the Existence of God

11

Can you prove that God exists? Often, when people ask you this question, what they are looking for is some kind of scientific demonstration. Since God is intangible and unseen, then many question His existence. Naturalists, assuming that there is nothing outside of the materialistic universe, boldly claim that the evidence for faith in God is just lacking. Why hasn't God made Himself more plain and evident?

First, the issue, once again, often boils down to those pesky presuppositions. What are people willing to accept as evidence? That may well depend upon their presuppositions about reality. If they refuse to admit that something outside of the material world can be real, then they will not accept evidence for God, no matter how powerful.

Second, the primary historical argument for God's existence is the resurrection of Jesus, which is verified through eyewitness testimony and historical documentation. If God has indeed been seen in the person of Jesus and through His resurrection, then God surely exists.

Yet there are other legitimate avenues of argumentation available to the believer. Here we will overview a few of the chief arguments that have been popular through the years. As we do this, keep in mind the following:

1. All of these types of arguments share the same basic weakness: they can take us in the direction of God, perhaps even convince some people that there is a God, but they do not prove the God of the Bible or Jesus as the Son of God. In order to do that, one must still go the resurrection.

2. These arguments can serve as good "foot in the door" openers. That is, they can get someone started in the right direction and perhaps cause some to take the issue of God's existence seriously. One may then proceed to the historical evidences for Jesus and the biblical God. Still, though these arguments must be supplemented with more information, they can open doors with some unbelievers.

3. Like all arguments of this nature, these cannot provide the kind of scientific proof that some are seeking. God cannot be put into some test-tube for observation, and if that is what some are looking for in order to be convinced, they will likely stay unconvinced. For those willing to keep an open mind, however, the arguments will have merit.

The Cosmological Argument

"The heavens are telling of the glory of God; and their expanse is declaring the work of His hands" (Ps 19:1).

The cosmological argument is basic cause and effect reasoning. If there is an effect, then something must have caused it. That rationale is then applied to the existence of the universe (cosmos). Why is there something rather than nothing? What caused this universe to exist? Is the universe eternal? Did it just pop into existence out of nothing all on its own? Or was it created by something or someone greater? What other possibilities are there?

The simple argument is that "everything that exists has a cause of its existence," implying that if something exists, there must be another cause. But the objection can be made here that this would imply that God also must have a cause for His existence. The argument, so stated, is flawed.

However, the *kalam* (lit. "talk") argument has to do with material objects that have a beginning. The argument is not that everything has a cause, but that every contingent entity or object must have a cause. That is, if something can be shown to have a beginning, then what caused it to begin? God cannot, by definition, fall into this category (if He had a beginning, He would no longer be God, the great "I AM").

Is there evidence that the universe had a beginning? Two points of evidence help to argue in this direction. First, the universe is expanding, which implies a point in time when it must have began or from which it "exploded." Some counter by arguing for an "oscillating universe" in which it expands and contracts eternally. Yet there is no scientific proof for that theory. The expansion suggests a beginning point.

Second, according to the second law of thermodynamics, processes that occur within a closed system tend toward a state of equilibrium (or decay). With no energy being fed into the system, everything would eventually "burn up" and wear out. So how does this help the believer's cause? Well the question is simple: if, given enough time, the universe would burn out (reach "heat death"), then why hasn't it already happened if it did not have a beginning? Assuming that the universe is infinite, it should have already burned out. Yet, here we are. Here, unbelievers must propose a model that is neither scientifically provable nor observed anywhere. The universe cannot be eternal.

So, if the evidence suggests that the universe had a beginning, is it not reasonable to believe that something greater than the material universe – one who is not contingent (dependent on something else) but is necessary (does not depend on anything else)—created it? One might try to go into an infinite regress of causes, but eventually one must hit the first cause. This first cause we call God.[1]

---

[1] For a detailed analysis of the cosmological argument, see William Lane Craig, *Reasonable Faith: Christian Truth and Apologetics*, 3d ed. (Wheaton, Ill.: Crossway Books, 2008), 111-156.

The Teleological Argument

Teleology has to do with design and purpose. Various regularities in the universe imply that there is some purpose or design in the way things work. If there is evidence of design, then reason suggests there is a designer, one who actually purposed it all in the first place.

In 1802, William Paley popularized this argument with his "watch-watchmaker" analogy in his *Natural Theology*. If someone happened upon a watch, he would rightly assume, based upon its design, that an intelligent watchmaker made it. In fact, it is unreasonable to conclude otherwise. He argued that his conclusion was "invincible" and the atheist cannot maintain his position without absurdity.[2] Yet, plants, animals, and humans are far greater than a watch. Why would we conclude that we were not designed by a Creator?

This argument has undergone various revisions. Today we are likely to hear about the "evidence of fine-tuning."[3] That is, everything is just right for life to exist on earth. Collins gives a few examples, including the following:

- If the initial "beginning" of the universe had differed only slightly in strength (by 1 in 10^{60}), it would have either collapsed on itself or expanded too quickly—that's like firing a bullet at a target twenty billion light years away and hitting it.
- If the nuclear force that holds protons and neutrons together in an atom had been stronger or weaker by as little as 5 percent,

---

[2] William Paley, *Natural Theology*, 12th ed. (Chillicothe, OH: DeWard Publishing Co., 2010), 19-20.

[3] Robin Collins, "A Scientific Argument for Existence of God: The Fine-Tuning Design Argument," in *Reason for The Hope Within*, ed. Michael Murray (Grand Rapids, MI: William B. Eerdmans, 1999), 47-75.

life would not be possible.

- If gravity had been stronger or weaker by 1 in 10^{40}, life-sustaining stars like the sun could not exist.
- If the electromagnetic force were just a little weaker or a little stronger, life would not be possible.

Many examples can be multiplied. The sheer chance that life could have just existed without any help at all, purely by chance, is virtually impossible. Unbelievers respond by arguing that given enough time and enough alternatives (like an alleged multiverse), an existence like this is going to happen. Of course, when they argue this, they are arguing a faith, not a proven scientific fact. The evidence of design reasonably supports an ultimate Designer.

Intelligent Design Theory

From the mid to late 1980's, a newer design argument has been made based upon scientific principles and new findings. This is often termed the "Intelligent Design Theory." Proponents of this believe it is more scientific because "Intelligent design is detectable; we do in fact detect it; we have reliable methods for detecting it; and its detection involves no recourse to the supernatural." As such, "design is common, rational, and objectifiable"[4] It takes teleology further than before.

While proponents do not try to argue specifically for the biblical God, they do believe that the intelligence they are talking about is transcendent (beyond here). Thus there are important implications for faith in God as the ultimate intelligence.

This position was brought to the forefront of the science and religion debate when Michael Behe wrote *Darwin's Black Box*

---

[4] William A. Dembski, and James M. Kushiner, *Signs of Intelligence* (Grand Rapids, MI: Brazos Press, 2001), 19.

(1996).[5] Darwinistic assumptions were that the cell was simple, and evolution involved moving from the simple to the complex. Behe, a biochemist, argued that the cell is anything but simple. In fact, it is so complex that it is much more reasonable to accept that intelligence had a hand in it rather than blind chance. He addressed what he called "irreducible complexity," the idea that some structures and processes are complex enough that they cannot have anything removed and still be viable. In other words, gradual evolution does not account for the complexity found at the cellular level.

So while Intelligent Design Theory is not so much about defining God, it certainly does fit consistently with the teaching that there is a Creator who planned and purposed everything. So strong have such arguments been that Antony Flew, one of the premier atheistic philosophers of the twentieth century, finally changed his mind. Though he did not change to believe in the biblical God, Flew still moved in the right direction: "The only satisfactory explanation for the origin of such 'end-directed, self-replicating' life as we see on earth is an infinitely intelligent Mind."[6]

The Moral Argument

Why do people believe in right and wrong? Even those who argue that morals are relative to the society or the individual still have lines that they do not think should be crossed. All thinking people have some sense of "ought" and will react negatively when they think their "oughts" or "ought nots" have been violated. On what grounds can anyone say that anything is right or wrong?

C.S. Lewis is known for his use of the moral argument in *Mere Christianity*. Moral Law is not simply describing how people act,

---

[5] Michael J. Behe, *Darwin's Black Box* (New York, NY: Touchstone, 1996).

[6] Antony Flew, *There Is a God: How The World's Most Notorious Atheist Changed His Mind* (San Francisco: HarperOne, 2007), 132.

but how they *ought* to act based upon some kind of objective principle. Atheism, which is too simple according to Lewis,[7] acts inconsistently when it denies objective morality, for even atheists will try to tell others how they should act.

Lewis relates that he used to argue against God on the basis that the universe seemed so cruel and unjust. Then he realized his own inconsistencies, for how could he call something unjust if he didn't know what the standard of justice really was?[8]

Moral behavior of any kind is based upon some kind of standard. If that standard is merely found in the whims of people, only what they desire, then on what grounds can they require others to follow that standard? Relativism means that society or individuals determine their own standard. Even some atheistic philosophers, like Jean-Paul Sartre, have recognized that without God they merely have to determine moral values for themselves. Still, what if others disagree and decide on a different type of morality? How can anyone ever condemn that? Further, how can anyone praise it? Such a moral stance would be no closer or further to being better or worse. It would just be there, and no one can say it is good or bad. Yet, we know that this type of philosophy just won't work in the real world.

Imagine entering an archery contest, and when it came time to take your turn, the judges simply said, "Go," but you realize there is no target. There is nothing to shoot for. On what grounds can anyone say that you are closer or further from a perfect shot? Such talk would be ridiculous because it would have no meaning. Yet this is what happens when people try to define morality without an objective standard. Their talk becomes meaningless because there is no way to judge right or wrong. Who says how we ought to act?

---

[7] C.S. Lewis, *Mere Christianity* (NY: Macmillan, 1952), 46.

[8] Ibid., 45.

The implications for God should be obvious. If we cannot consistently take a merely human standard for morality, then how is morality to be explained? Is it not better understood within the context of a God who made us moral creatures? Goodness and badness are concepts that make the most sense in the context of One who defines the right and judges the wrong. And the only One who has a right to do so must be God, for no mere man or group of men can bear such authority.

There are more arguments for God's existence, but this survey hits the highlights of the more popular arguments. Taken together, the arguments form a cumulative case for God that cannot be lightly dismissed. They can serve as springboards for further discussion that leads to Jesus Christ.

Discussion Questions

1. What are strengths and weaknesses of arguments for God's existence that focus on scientific and moral issues?

2. How can these arguments open doors for further study and discussion?

3. Can you define the basic cosmological argument? How do you think the argument can be used in discussion with others?

4. What is teleology? Why is the teleological argument important?

5. Why do you think the newer Intelligent Design Theory has made an impact?

6. Why do you agree or disagree with the moral argument? How would you talk to someone else about morality?

Naturalism and Darwinism 12

"In the beginning God created the heavens and the earth" (Gen 1:1). This is the foundation for the Christian's worldview, and it stands in contrast to naturalism and the atheistic view of the general theory of evolution. What do you think of when you hear the word "evolution"? It's a loaded word, isn't it? Evolution can simply mean "change," but usually in its cultural context we think of Darwin's general theory of evolution. "Evolution" stands for the leading naturalistic idea for how all of the animals and people of this world came to be in their present condition. Here, our focus is mainly on naturalism as the background philosophy that underlies most Darwinian teaching.

The scientific establishment typically teaches naturalistic, Darwinian evolution as a fact. Richard Dawkins, an outspoken atheist, wrote, "Evolution is as much a fact as the heat of the sun. It is not a theory, and pity's sake, let's stop confusing the philosophically naïve by calling it so. Evolution is a fact."[1] Many think that naturalistic evolution is proven beyond any doubt, and to question it is to question science and to push a gullible, religiously superstitious agenda. But there is a difference between saying something is a fact and proving it to be so. There is a difference between the heat of the sun and a vast historical, mindless scenario that has not been seen anywhere.

Naturalism is based upon philosophical presuppositions. There are philosophical underpinnings to the discussions that focus on scientific matters and how this affects our view of the Bible. For example, the word "science" can be slippery. Science is a legitimate attempt to derive knowledge from observation, testing, and

---

[1] Richard Dawkins, "The Illusion of Design," *Natural History Magazine*, Nov. 2005.

experimentation based upon repeatable phenomena. Yet, science has limitations and is not the final determiner of all truth. In other words, while science is legitimate, "scientism," the "underlying presupposition" that "in order to be true knowledge, any discipline had to be science, implicitly pursued in the manner of the natural sciences," is not.[2]

Further, sometimes *science* is equated with naturalism, the philosophy that nature alone is capable of explaining everything. This is an idea that needs to be challenged because it cannot itself be scientifically demonstrated. If God cannot be proved by science, neither can naturalism be proved by science. As Ian Hutchinson, a nuclear physicist, put it, "what needs to be opposed is bad logic; it is not science but scientism: the unjustified belief that all useful knowledge is science."[3]

How does the Bible square with science? The Bible is not meant to be a modern scientific textbook. However, science does not inherently conflict with Scripture. The interpretations and philosophies of some scientists differ with interpretations of the biblical text. But this is not the same as science vs. the Bible. No human interpretation of either science or the Bible is infallible. When understood and interpreted correctly, science and Scripture are in harmony. Neither is the issue *science vs. faith*: it is the faith of some vs. the faith of others. Everyone has faith, including those who profess naturalism.

Macro and Micro

The distinction between *macroevolution* and *microevolution* has long been debated. *Macro*evolution is the idea that all present life forms (plants and animals) have developed over billions of years

---

[2] Ian Hutchinson, "Science: Christian and Natural," ASA Conference, 2002 <http://hutchinson.belmont.ma.us /hutchinson/asa2002/> Accessed 10-25-2016.
[3] Ibid.

from a single, common ancestor, as a result of unguided processes. It refers to "changes in the kinds of animals and plants on earth, changes that take place over long periods of time, with new forms replacing old ones."[4] The idea goes something like this: at some point in the past, billions of years ago, an explosion (the "Big Bang," though this, too, is challenged) gave rise to the universe, and eventually planet earth was born. Among the chemicals present in this newly-formed planet were those that make life possible. The conditions were just right, and a single living organism developed from the existing matter. Other organisms came from this first one, and these organisms began to take on various characteristics in response to their environment. Because of their ability to adapt and change, new forms arose, and changes continued. Through the process of natural selection over these billions of years, all living organisms evolved into their present state. New organisms and new kinds arose from older ones, coincident with major episodes of extinction.

Microevolution refers to smaller, limited changes within a kind of organism. Within a given kind, there are variations that arise from generation to generation. For example, many breeds of dogs exist with characteristics that are obvious, distinguishing one from another. Yet they are all dogs. The evidence for limited variations is readily seen, but the evidence that they arose from a completely different type of animal is missing. Vast speculation, not observation, is what fills in the gaps.

Here is what happens. Darwinists will often appeal to *micro*evolution as proof of *macro*evolution. They believe that *micro*evolution provides the mechanism and explanation of how *macro*evolution occurs. But in so arguing, they rarely use the macro and micro prefixes. One might argue, "Evolution has been shown to occur in laboratory tests. Thus, evolution is true." This is deceptive.

---

[4] Peter H. Raven, and George B. Johnson, *Biology*, 2d ed. (St. Louis: Times Mirror/Mosby College Publishing, 1989), 367.

What that means is, "microevolution has been shown to occur," which is true. From this they argue that, therefore, *macro*evolution is true. *Micro*evolution is true, but all it proves is that limited changes occur within given kinds. It does not itself prove that kinds have mindlessly changed into different kinds. When people say, "evolution is true," ask what they mean by "evolution." You may find that Darwinists don't like to make this distinction very much.

Biblically, the concept of limited changes is acceptable and even implied by the text. The Bible teaches that living things were created after their kinds (Gen 1). This includes mankind. "He made from one man every nation of mankind to live on all the face of the earth" (Acts 17:26). We may infer that God placed within Adam and Eve the genetic pool necessary to bring about the varieties of people. The same is true of plants and animals. Scriptures allows for the variety, but that is not a story of macroevolution (even though many theists argue for theistic evolution). What Genesis supports within the text itself is variation within kinds, not crossing of kinds.

A Theory without God

Darwinism, as founded on naturalism, is not friendly to the notion of God's existence or work in the world. By definition, typical evolutionary theory excludes the idea of intelligent guidance. For example, the American National Association of Biology Teachers issued an official statement regarding evolution:

> The diversity of life on earth is the outcome of evolution: an unsupervised, impersonal, unpredictable and natural process of temporal descent with genetic modification that is affected by natural selection, chance, historical contingencies and changing environments.[5]

---

[5] Quoted in Phillip E. Johnson, *Defeating Darwinism By Opening Minds* (Downers Grove, IL: InterVarsity Press, 1997), 15.

Note the terms "unsupervised," "impersonal, "natural" and "chance." When such Darwinists speak of evolution, they do not mean a process guided by God; they mean an unsupervised, impersonal process involving nature and chance. There is no room for God in the definition. The idea of *natural* selection excludes anything outside of nature (God). "Darwin was able to arrive at a successful theory when many others had failed because he rejected supernatural explanations for the phenomena that he was studying."[6] Julian Huxley, a champion of Darwinism, explained natural selection as that which "converts accident into apparent design, randomness into organized pattern."[7] It is unguided, random chance. Evolutionist Michael Ruse, in criticizing doubters of Darwin, wrote, "The very last thing that Darwin and his followers are trying to do is put mind into nature."[8] He further argued that "there is a lot of sympathy for the claims of the so-called new atheists," and that "if you are a Darwinian, then you ought to be at least an agnostic, if not an outright atheist."[9] Adding God to the mix does little to appease the champions of naturalism.

Sometimes naturalists argue that they are not trying to say anything about religion or God. They are only trying to explain nature. However, when they use the terms associated with Darwinian theory, such as "chance," "accident," and "unsupervised," they are implying that everything exists apart from and without God. They are indeed talking about the role of God, but in a negative sense. They are unwilling to consider intelligent contributions to design. As a famous evolutionist, George Gaylord Simpson, said, "Man is the result of a purposeless and natural process that did not have him in mind." This is why "biologists insist that evolution must be

---

[6] Raven and Johnson, *Biology*, 8.

[7] Julian Huxley, *Evolution in Action* (New York, NY: Mentor Books, 1953), 36.

[8] Michael Ruse, "What Darwin's Doubters Get Wrong," *The Chronicle Review*, March 12, 2010, B8.

[9] Ibid.

unsupervised and why God's purposes are not listed among the things that might have affected evolution."[10] Naturalism is the underlying worldview. If they admit that God had anything to do with it, their worldview must change. Richard Dawkins, who spoke of the "illusion of design," wrote that Darwin "discovered a way in which the unaided laws of physics—the laws according to which things 'just happen'—could, in the fullness of geologic time, come to mimic deliberate design. The illusion of design is so successful that to this day most Americans (including, significantly, many influential and rich Americans) stubbornly refuse to believe it *is* an illusion. To such people, if a heart (or an eye or a bacterial flagellum) looks designed, that's proof enough that it is designed."[11]

Here is the rub: naturalism is a philosophy that cannot be substantiated by science. Let the naturalist demonstrate by scientific means (observation and experimentation) that nature is all there is, and that everything can be explained by nature alone. No scientific test, through experimentation and observation, can do this. Their reliance on naturalism as a foundation is as much a faith as is a Christian trusting God. They trust what they cannot see or scientifically prove as much as any theist. It is a double standard that insists that naturalism is the default explanation for everything while demanding scientific proof from theists that there is a God.

An Information Problem

Macroevolution is about massive changes over time resulting in the formation of new and complex organs, body plans, and life forms. This involves new organs, new genes, and new types of organisms, all the way up to humans. Evolutionists will argue that what they are teaching is not about origins, but before evolution can even begin to work, there must be an accounting for the first life forms. As Meyer put it,

[10] Johnson, *Defeating Darwinism by Opening Minds*, 15.
[11] Richard Dawkins, "The Illusion of Design," Nov. 2005.

No undirected physical or chemical process has demonstrated the capacity to produce specified information starting 'from purely physical or chemical' precursors. For this reason, chemical evolutionary theories have failed to solve the mystery of the origin of first life— a claim that few mainstream evolutionary theorists now dispute.[12]

What we need to see evidence for is not variation in kinds or even reproductive isolation (speciation). What we must see is the evidence that natural selection and chance have *actually created new information from the beginning*. Can Darwinists prove that mindless mutations or purely natural processes are capable of providing vast quantities of new and beneficial genetic information? There is "no description of any mutations which are actually known to have the kind of information-creating power which would be required for creative evolution."[13] Examples of *micro*evolution, which is all they can provide, are not enough to prove what they require. Just showing that "change" occurs is not enough. Showing similarity is not enough. Ask for an example of *macro*evolution, with all its alleged creative abilities, and we get a speculative story based upon philosophical and methodological naturalism. Plus, we might get vilified as religious nuts who don't believe in science or reason.

Natural selection can only select from what is there. Creating new information is another matter. Mutations are random, and seldom beneficial, but even these do not add the necessary information into the existing gene pool. This information problem is a serious one, especially for those denying God. Everything we know about

---

[12] Stephen C. Meyer, *Darwin's Doubt: The Explosive Origin of Animal Life and the Case for Intelligent Design.* New York: HarperCollins, 2013. vi.

[13] Phillip E. Johnson, *The Wedge of Truth: Splitting The Foundations of Naturalism* (Downers Grove, Ill.: InterVarsity Press, 2000), 42.

information is that it comes from intelligence. Devoid of Mind, this cannot adequately be explained. Meyer writes,

> Although we don't know of a material cause that generates functioning digital code from physical or chemical precursors, we do know—based upon our uniform and repeated experience—of one type of cause that has demonstrated the power to produce this type of information. That cause is intelligence or mind. As information theorist Henry Quastler observed, "The creation of information is habitually associated with conscious activity."[14]

A Mind Problem

This brings us to the mind problem. If naturalism is true, then it must also account for the evolution of the mind. Not only must it account for the creation of vast complex organs and new genetic information, it must account for the rational, reasoning part of mankind. If true, then this means that the ability to think and reason is the result of unintelligent chemical and material processes. In other words, non-intelligence produced intelligence. Where is the science for this?

The theory essentially turns us into mere machines or robots, with proponents arguing that free will is an illusion.[15] There is nothing except the material of the brain. There is no real "self" that controls the machinery of the brain. This is an illusion. Instead, the brain is a material circuit, and natural selection gave us the illusion of being single entities who feel, love, hate, and make decisions. Does this have any moral implications?

---

[14] Meyer, *Darwin's Doubt*, vi.

[15] Cf. Sam Harris, *Free Will* (NY: Free Press, 2012), 5, 39-40.

Johnson observed: "There is no scientific evidence that the brain, or any individual cell within the brain, either was or could have been created by matter unassisted by preexisting intelligence. The scientists who believe that natural selection made the brain do not do so because of the evidence but in spite of the evidence."[16]

To naturalists, the mind is produced by a material process and therefore cannot be fundamentally different from matter. Consequently, the mind is not distinct from the brain. The mind involves information that is coordinating the neurons of the brain in such a way as to produce the capacity to think. Yet information itself is not matter. It may be imprinted on matter, but the information does not come from mere matter. Information comes from intelligence, and this aspect of the mind is not explained through strictly naturalistic causes.

When we see the pictures of the evolution of humans, we are seeing the story, not observation. When we see the charts depicting the evolutionary trees of the various types of animals, we are seeing the vast speculation, not observed phenomena. But the story has been told so many times and identified as "science," that to question it is to question the authority of science. To ask for observed evidence of macroevolution will only serve to put us at odds with their version of science. The story is one of vast speculation founded upon the assumption of philosophical naturalism. We are certainly within our rights to challenge those assumptions, and we should not be intimidated by those who use science in a way that steps beyond its inherent limitations.

---

[16] Johnson, *The Wedge of Truth*, 123.

Discussion Questions

1. Why is the difference between *micro* and *macro* evolution important? Why would many today not like to make this distinction?

2. How can microevolution be understood in a biblical context? Why does macroevolution not fit the biblical context?

3. How can we tell that Darwinism is a theory without God? What does this tell us about the presuppositions of Darwinists? Why won't theistic evolution work with true Darwinists?

4. How is naturalism itself a philosophy? Why is this important to recognize?

5. Why do you think that the battle between evolution and creation is important? Why do you agree or disagree that what a person believes about this issue can affect behavior?

6. Why is "information" and "mind" a problem for Darwinists?

7. Do you think that Darwinism would have implications for morality? If it is true, what do you think would that mean for moral accountability?

The Problem of Evil   **13**

One of the greatest challenges to the Christian's faith is the problem of evil. There are at least three reasons for this. First, the problem is one that strikes at the very heart of the good and holy God in whom we believe. Because of this, it serves as an apparent proof of atheism, something that unbelievers can point to and argue that the biblical God is not consistent with evil or suffering. Second, the problem is universal in that people everywhere and throughout all ages have suffered from evil. There is nowhere to go where we will not run into the problem in some form. Third, the problem is practical. This is not about some great philosophical debate as much as it is ordinary people who have to grapple with a loved one riddled with disease or having to cope with the loss of a child. The problem is real, not simply a hypothetical construct in a classroom or a thesis.

Gideon's Question

A biblical example shows that the problem has been around for a long time. Judges 6 describes how the children of Israel had again sinned, so the curses of the covenant were taking their toll on the people. The Midianites were raiding the country, devastating crops, and humiliating the people, who were hiding in caves to escape. The angel of the Lord appeared to Gideon, saying, "The LORD is with you." Gideon's response shows that he believed there was an inconsistency: "O my lord, if the LORD is with us, why then has all this happened to us?" (v. 13) That is the question echoed through time. If God is with us, then why does He let us suffer? If God cares, then why did He let someone we love die a painful death? Why does He not keep us from feeling the pain and sorrow we so often encounter? How can God really care about us under adverse circumstances?

Habakkuk had a similar question: "How long, O LORD, will I call for help, and You will not hear? I cry out to You, 'Violence!' Yet You do not save" (1:2). Habakkuk could not understand why God was not taking action sooner, why God was allowing the wickedness to continue that brought so much pain and suffering. He was told that he needed to wait on God, who will take care of matters in His own time. This was not easy.

Whatever we feel about the problem of evil and the pain that we feel, we are reflecting what so many have already felt. There is nothing new about this problem, but it still persists as one of the major obstacles to faith in God. How can we possibly continue to believe in a God who allows evil and suffering to persist so strongly in this world?

Evil vs. God's Attributes

In our present context, "evil" refers to whatever we may consider to be "bad," whether it be moral evil (sin) or natural evil (natural disasters that cause suffering). Suffering is included and is typically the consequence of moral or natural evil. The logical problem of evil centers around two of the major attributes of God: His omnipotence (power) and His goodness (or love). The primary assumption of the problem is that the existence of evil is not compatible with the existence of an all-powerful, all-good God. Why so? The reasoning goes like this: if God is powerful enough to prevent evil, but will not, then He cannot be considered good. If God is good enough to prevent evil, but cannot, then is not all powerful. But since evil is real, then there is no justification for believing in an all-powerful, all-good God.

The difficulty of this, on its face, is that we don't always have the knowledge at our disposal to tell why some forms of suffering exist. We believe in a God who is omnipotent (all-powerful), omniscient (all-knowing), omnibenevolent (all-good), and who created the world. Yet we must also recognize that the world contains evil (all of this is part of what is sometimes called the "Theistic Set" – propositions that we accept as fundamental to the God in whom and we believe and the world in which we live).[1] Are there any viable reasons why such a God would allow evil to coexist with Him?

Solutions

Many have attempted to solve this problem through the centuries. Some have argued that evil is just an illusion that we conquer through the control of our minds. This is more in line with eastern religions, but it is self-defeating. Wouldn't the fact that our minds can be deceived into thinking that evil is real itself be an evil? Others have argued that the universe is better with evil in it. Yet it is one thing to say that we can become better in character based upon the way we respond to the fact of evil, but quite another to say that God purposed evil in the world so that it can become better. Understanding and properly responding to the way things are in reality does not mean that this was the way it was supposed to be in its purpose. Something happened to change everything.

Still others argue that good and evil are necessary counterparts. That is, good cannot exist without evil, as it is a necessary balance to good. However, if the biblical God is real, then He necessarily existed without evil. This means that good can exist without evil, but evil, which finds its very definition in falling from the standard of good, cannot exist unless there is something that we can call good. In other words, to say that something is evil, we must have a measuring stick for calling it evil, and that standard must be good. Good is not measured by evil, but evil is measured by good. Of course, this also means that whoever brings up the problem of evil

---

[1] Ronald H. Nash, *Faith and Reason: Searching for a Rational Faith* (Grand Rapids, Mich.: Academie Books, 1988), 181. For a more thorough discussion of the problem, you might read chapters 13-15 of this book.

ought to be prepared to show what that standard is. If they don't have a standard, then how can they rightly say that something is evil? This is one reason why, though the issue is a problem for the theist, it is just as much, if not more so, a problem for the atheist. Atheists speak as though they think evil is real, but they cannot define the ultimate standard by which to call something evil. They have a major problem here.

Augustine suggested that evil is a privation (the absence) of good: "For evil has no positive nature; but the loss of good has received the name 'evil.'"[2] When goodness is removed, what is left is evil. This is similar to light and darkness. Darkness is the absence of light, and so evil is absence of goodness. Perhaps so, but we might add to this that evil, particularly moral evil, is a *perversion* of what is good. A good desire can be twisted so that a person seeks to fulfill it in an evil way. This results in overtly sinful action (Jas 1:13-17).

If we are discussing the biblical God, then we need to see how the Bible deals with this issue. Biblically, God and evil are not mutually exclusive, as is clear from the fact that so many passages address the problem of sin. The Bible certainly does not ignore the issue. For example, the book of Job meets the problem of suffering head on, but shows that there can be reasons for suffering that we do not know or perhaps even can understand. We must recognize our own limitations on knowledge and not assume that God should somehow answer to us. Further, the book of Ecclesiastes has a bit to say about the problem of oppression and issues related to living without God. Yet the wise man asks, "Who knows what is good for man?" (6:12) Who is in the position to know what is best for us? Who are we to make demands upon God? The point is that we must be extremely careful when we draw conclusions about God since we are not in a position to completely know His mind and His ways.

---

[2] Aurelius Augustine, *The Works of Saint Augustine.* (Kindle Edition, 2015), loc. 19023.

Such passages highlight that God, in addition to being both good and powerful, is also all knowing and all wise. Once these attributes of God are on the table, we must allow for God's wisdom and knowledge to be a part of the total solution. We cannot dismiss these attributes of God, then deny God on the basis of His not knowing what He was doing or why. Since God is able to do far more abundantly beyond what we can think (Eph 3:20), we must allow that He has reasons we may never understand.

Two Key Issues

We would not want to oversimplify the problem of suffering. Nor would we suggest that we know all of the reasons why suffering would occur, as God may well have purposes unknown to us. Again, our knowledge is limited. God is sovereign and will function as He sees fit, for He alone knows what is good for man. Still, there are some key issues that help us put a framework around the problem and gain a little better understanding. Two of these we will briefly address: free will and the justice of God.

Free Will. Scripture shows that free will played a large role in how evil entered the world. Adam and Eve were placed in the garden and given the ability to choose whether or not they would obey God. The consequences for disobedience were clearly stated (death), and when they sinned they had no one to blame but themselves (even though the serpent played a role). Because they abused their free will, sin entered the world and, with sin, a flood of bad consequences (Gen 3). The world that we see today is not the same as it was when it was created. Creation itself was brought under futility (Rom 8), and death, with its attendant suffering, came with it. Suffering thus entered the world because of abused free will. Plantinga wrote:

> The fact that free creatures sometimes go wrong, however, counts neither against God's omnipotence nor against His

goodness; for He could have forestalled the occurrence of moral evil only by removing the possibility of moral good.[3]

Free will is linked to the problem of suffering in several ways. First, we suffer for personal wrong choices that we make (see Psalm 51 for David's recognition of this). Second, others are affected by the choices that we make. Third, future generations will be affected by the choices we make. So the problem of evil extends beyond our own actions into the lives of others both now and later. This is one reason we must be careful with our choices (see, for example, how this worked in the life of Lot in Genesis 13-19).

The bigger question, though, is why God would make us with the ability of free choice when there was such a risk. An alternative, of course, would be to make us robots, but what would be the point of that? It seems that part of this answer must be seen through the concept of being made in God's image (Gen 1:26-27). There are probably facets of being in God's image that we do not even begin to understand, but there is one clear example of why being in God's image is so important: we are given the capacity to choose love. God is love, and if we do not have the capacity to freely choose love, then how can we be in His image? Thus if God were to make creatures in His image, this would necessitate giving the moral capacity to love. Love seeks a loving response, and Jesus said that loving God and loving neighbor are the greatest commandments (Matt 22:36-40). This would not be possible if we were not creatures of free will, for there is no such thing as forced love. Yet the ability to love also entails risk, for if we have the capacity to love, we also have the ability to choose not to love. Choosing not to love will also have consequences, however adverse.

The Justice of God. God's justice is connected to His holiness. Because He is holy and righteous, He cannot simply ignore the

---

[3] Alvin C. Plantinga, *God, Freedom, and Evil* (Grand Rapids, MI: Eerdmans, 1977), 30.

problem of sin. Part of our understanding here must be informed by the horrible nature of sin itself. C.S. Lewis commented, "When we merely say that we are bad, the 'wrath' of God seems a barbarous doctrine; as soon as we perceive our badness, it appears inevitable, a mere corollary from God's goodness."[4] In order for God's holiness and justice to mean anything, there must be consequences for sin. Why? Because of the nature of sin itself. Not only is sin a transgression of God's law (1 John 3:4), but it is a falling short of God's glory (Rom 3:23). We need to see sin as a violation of the very nature and character of God, not just a breaking of a few arbitrary rules. Adam and Eve's sin was not simply eating a piece of fruit; it was rebellion against God's nature. That cannot be overlooked without any judgment whatsoever, for it would make a mockery of God's holy nature.

Further, the justice of God means that evil does in fact have a day of reckoning. This is one of the fundamental teachings of the New Testament. There will be a day of judgment (Acts 17:30-31). All things will be set straight, and God with His people will be vindicated. No one will question God's power and goodness in that day.

When people ask why God has not taken care of evil, they are missing a couple of important factors. First, God has done something about it. Every judgment in Scripture, from being kicked out of the Garden of Eden to all the judgments on the various nations, shows that God did something about evil. Further, God's greatest act of judgment is also His greatest act of love, for both love and judgment meet in the cross of Jesus. No one can rightly throw suffering up in the face of God given the reality of the cross. God Himself entered suffering for the sake of taking care of this problem of evil. He has in the process made it possible for us

---

[4] C.S. Lewis, *The Problem of Pain* (NY: Macmillan Publishing Co., Inc, 1962), 58.

all one day to escape this world of suffering. He has done something about it. Second, God will do more about it. That, once again, is judgment.

Given that all have violated the character of God through our sins, the real question is not so much why God allows good people to suffer. The real question is, *why does God do anything kind for bad people?* We are the bad people because of sin, yet God continues to show mercy and compassion. Why does He continue to do this for us when clearly He doesn't have to? Because of His great love. It's that same love that we are to reflect in our free will actions. All of this is God's grace at work.

On the Day of Judgment, people will not be pleading for fairness, but for mercy. God's grace is extended even now through our own suffering. The question is, how will we handle it? If we react like we should, we can grow through suffering. We can cultivate character, learn patience, gain wisdom and hope (James 1:2-5), and even help others. We can look beyond this world of suffering, which serves to remind us how ugly sin really is, and see the reward that He offers (Heb 11:24-26). Through Christ's death for us, we can know that whatever happens to us, He loves us (Rom 8:31-39) and He will not allow us to be tempted beyond our ability to bear (1 Cor 10:13). God be thanked that we are given the grace to make it beyond this present suffering to the rich reward of heaven.

Discussion Questions

1. Why is the problem of evil and suffering more than just a philosophical issue?

2. How can we know that we are not alone in feeling the pain of life? What does biblical history show?

3. What attributes of God does the problem of evil primarily strike against? How does that make it a real problem?

4. What should we keep in mind about our knowledge and why?

5. What is evil? How can we find a true definition of it?

6. Why is the issue of free will so important? How does "love" fit into this?

7. Why is God's justice so significant in helping answer the problem? What does God's justice guarantee in the end?

A Most Unreasonable Thing

It is a most unreasonable thing to suppose that there should be no future punishment, to suppose that God, who had made man a rational creature, able to know his duty, and sensible that he is deserving punishment when he does it not; should let man alone, and let him live as he will, and never punish him for his sins, and never make any difference between the good and the bad; that he should make the world of mankind and then let it alone, and let men live all their days in wickedness, in adultery, murder, robbery, and persecution, and the like, and suffer them to live in prosperity, and never punish them; that he should suffer them to prosper in the world far beyond many good men, and never punish them hereafter. How unreasonable is it to suppose, that he who made the world, should leave things in such confusion, and never take any care of the government of his creatures, and that he should never judge his reasonable creatures!

Jonathan Edwards,
The Complete Works of Jonathan Edwards

The Problem of Hell 14

The problem of hell is, in some ways, another facet of the problem of evil. Hell is eternal separation from God and from all that is good and blessed. How can we believe in a loving, powerful God who would also cast people into an eternal destination of pain and torment? Hell is not to be taken lightly. Eternity is serious business no matter what side of the issue one takes, and what is at stake is everything. Reconciling the dire and horrible nature of hell with a God who desires all to be saved can be a challenge, but it needs to be understood within the entire biblical context. Both biblically and philosophically, hell is compatible with an all-loving and all-powerful God. So what are some of the principles that can help us put the issue into perspective?

First, the question of hell is not an isolated issue to be understood apart from all of the other evidence that supports God and the Bible. Whatever one may think of hell does not change the evidence for the resurrection of Jesus or the comprehensive case for Christianity. The issue of hell does not disprove the Bible or Christianity, even if people don't fully understand the nature of hell or why it must exist. As Groothuis observed:

> Hell is an apologetic problem for Christianity because it demands that we square the love of God with the eternal punishment of some of God's creatures. But this problem should not be wrestled with in isolation from the cumulative case for Christian theism made in these pages (and elsewhere). A philosophical problem, even a vexing problem, need not sink an entire worldview. This does not mean that Christians should shy away from believing in or teaching this doctrine; it does mean that we should

approach it with humility and not apart from the evidence for Christianity as a whole system.[1]

Second, objections to hell are based upon emotional responses against its severity, not upon factual information or evidence to the contrary. People react against hell because they don't like it as a concept. However, we must not confuse disliking something with proof against its existence. We may not like what hell represents (and we shouldn't like it). We may think it says something unsavory about God and eternity (though, in reality, it doesn't). We may not like the concept of hell for a variety of reasons, but these reasons are not based upon facts that disprove the evidence for its existence. In terms of the reality of hell, whether or not we like it is irrelevant if it is real. Therefore, what matters is whether or not hell is real. Our feelings need to be tempered by that truth, for reality cannot be altered by our emotions against it. If hell is real, an adverse emotional reaction would not therefore mean that we are exempt from its consequences. So the question is not, "How do I feel about hell?" The question is, "Is hell real?" Then, what evidence would lead us to the conclusion that hell is real?

Third, in connection to the previous point, the denial of hell is based upon redefining both who God is and what our conception of ultimate justice is in connection with God's character. Because we don't like hell as a concept, then we essentially try to reshape God into the mold we think He ought to fit. God "can't" do it this way because it offends our modern sensibilities, so either He must not exist or He must actually have something else in mind. In our minds, God, who is all about love, is not a God who could actually support a notion like hell, so God, justice, or both must be denied or remade. This reshaping of God into our image is then supported by our view of what ultimate justice should be. Whatever it is, we

---

just know that ultimate justice should not be eternally painful. Since we wouldn't conceive of such a terrible penalty, then obviously God couldn't. This all sounds too familiar. "You will not surely die," said the serpent to Eve (Gen 3:1-5). The essence of the devil's lie is that God doesn't mean what He says, especially when it comes to punishment. The trick in getting us to bite the forbidden fruit is to plant the idea that God isn't really going to be that strict after all and the punishment for rebellion won't be quite as bad as it sounds. Thus, hell will only be temporary at best and annihilation at worst. How do we know this? Our self-imposed personal standards just tell us. We know better than God, and if that's not the way it is, then we'll just deny God.

Fourth, the primary reason for accepting the reality of hell is based upon the Lordship of Jesus. The argument here is almost identical to the argument for accepting a high view of Scripture. If Jesus was raised from the dead, then Jesus is Lord (an argument combined with His claims and works). If Jesus is Lord, then what Jesus teaches is true. Jesus taught the reality of hell. Thus our warrant for accepting the reality of hell is based upon the Lordship and teachings of Jesus. Anyone denying hell will have to deal directly with the authority of Jesus.

What did Jesus say about hell? Jesus uses the imagery of Topheth in the Valley of Ben-Hinnom from the Old Testament. This valley was just outside of Jerusalem. Here many practiced the idolatrous form of child sacrifice referred to as passing their children through the fire (see 2 Chron 28:3; 33:6; Jer 7:31-32; 32:35). The place was a fire pit (as the meaning of Topheth seems to indicate) and represented that which was an abomination and a place where there could be no fellowship with God. One can only imagine the smoke, the worms, and the stench that would be found there. *Gehenna* is the New Testament term for this valley, and thus is a fitting description of eternal separation from God. Jesus said that hell (*Gehenna*) is where the "worm does not die and the fire is not quenched" (Mark

9:47-48, quoting Isaiah 66:24). He referenced hell as a "sentence" for wickedness (Matt 23:33). It is where the soul and body meet destruction (Matt 10:28). Hell is conceived of being "outer darkness"; "in that place there will be weeping and gnashing of teeth" (Matt 25:30). It is the "eternal fire which has been prepared for the devil and his angels" (Matt 25:41). Hell is "eternal punishment" (Matt 25:46). If Jesus is Lord, then how we feel about these statements is irrelevant. If we accept Jesus as Lord, then we accept what He taught and adjust our lives accordingly.

Fifth, biblical writers, prophets, apostles, and teachers continually spoke of two themes: 1) God's grace, and 2) God's justice in judgment. "Behold then the kindness and severity of God" (Rom. 11:22). Even a casual reading of Scripture shows that they had no problem reconciling God's mercy with harsh judgments; they are not mutually exclusive ideas. If we have a problem today, it is likely due more to misconceptions on our part about divine grace and justice. However, the biblical warrant for accepting both is clear. Paul wrote the following in a context of both grace and judgment:

> And we know that the judgment of God rightly falls upon those who practice such things. But do you suppose this, O man, when you pass judgment on those who practice such things and do the same yourself, that you will escape the judgment of God? Or do you think lightly of the riches of His kindness and tolerance and patience, not knowing that the kindness of God leads you to repentance? But because of your stubbornness and unrepentant heart you are storing up wrath for yourself in the day of wrath and revelation of the righteous judgment of God, who will render to each person according to his deeds: to those who by perseverance in doing good seek for glory and honor and immortality, eternal life; but to those who are selfishly ambitious and do not obey the truth, but obey unrighteousness, wrath and indignation. (Rom 2:2-8)

Notice that God's judgment "rightly" (in truth) falls on those who are wicked. His wrath is not arbitrary, unjust, or out of control. Further, those who ignore the severity of God are, ironically, thinking lightly of God's kindness. God's mercy is continually demonstrated as He gives time for repentance. He is unwilling that anyone perish, but that all come to repentance (1 Pet 3:9). Yet He gives us that option, not forcing anyone to obey, but warning all that failure to obey has its consequences. The time God gives is purely a matter of His grace, for no one deserves it. To argue that God is immoral for bringing judgment is to make a farce out of His grace. It cheapens what God does in extending His hand out to sinners who do not deserve His kindness by essentially saying that all people, no matter what they have done and no matter how evil they continue to be, in the end deserve God's favor. Yet when does any sinner *deserve* God's favor? All have sinned and fall short of His glory (Rom 3:23).

This brings us back to the issue of the nature of sin and what we actually deserve. The reason "grace" means anything is because it is undeserved. Grace is marvelous and often misunderstood. By its very nature, we do not deserve it. No one, in judgment, will be asking for fairness, for grace is not about fairness. Rather, we will ask for mercy, again undeserved. If we really want what we deserve, then we will not be happy with the final result. If we really want fairness, then we are asking for hell. But how can we say that we really deserve hell? How can eternal hell be a just punishment for a few sins here?

Remember that sin is not only a violation of God's law, but is also a rebellion against His glory. The law reflects the glory of God, who is infinitely holy, and who must act with justice if this holiness is to be vindicated. We are created to be henceforth eternal. If we reject God and rebel against His nature, then we will continue on eternally without Him. This we call hell. How can we say that we should be in God's presence when our actions have indicated to

God that we don't want Him in our lives here? If we have repudiated God's word, then we judge ourselves unworthy of eternal life (Acts 13:46). Hell is the consequence for rejection of God's glory and authority in favor of our own. If we insist on retaining our own autonomous authority apart from God now, then we must recognize what eternity is like without God's presence when He gives us completely over to our own will. Hell is not some kind of medieval dungeon with laughing demons and evil torture devices. Dante's Inferno does not define hell for us. The devil will be there (Matt 25:41), but he will not be in charge and he will not be laughing and whipping anyone. Further, while the descriptions of hell in physical terms evoke painful images in our minds, the ultimate tragedy is that God isn't there. Paul captures this point when he writes of those who do not know God: "These will pay the penalty of eternal destruction, away from the presence of the Lord and from the glory of His power" (2 Thess 1:9). Being away from God's presence and glory is the essence of eternal ruin in hell. The true issue of hell is not about fearing some physical fire, worms, darkness, and gnashing teeth. It is about a final separation from God. That realization will, indeed, be a pain far beyond what any physical description can represent.

People use the problem of hell in order to deny God, but, again, such a denial is based upon an emotional reaction, not the facts. If we can admit the power, wisdom, knowledge, and understanding of God, then we have to admit that God has information and knowledge that we don't have. He has wisdom and understanding that we don't have. He sees the universe as a whole, under an umbrella of the total picture of reality. We see but a speck of reality based upon our limited, finite knowledge. We must acknowledge that God has the wisdom, understanding, and knowledge to know exactly how ultimate justice does and should operate. He knows the full extent of both His own glory and the problem of sin. He also has the right to carry out final justice and judgment. Just because we don't understand it all doesn't mean it isn't real. When we stand in judgment over God based upon our finite understanding of both hell and who He is, then we are essentially saying that God does not know what He is doing. We know more than God. We have the ability to reason over and judge God's actions and intentions. Because we don't understand how God could send anyone to an eternal hell, we must use our own standards in order to argue that such a God is not worthy of our devotion. Do we stop to consider that our knowledge is incomplete? That our personal standards aren't exactly the best for judging the infinite? That our understanding lacks far more than we care to admit? If we can be skeptical of God, why can't we be so skeptical of our own finite reasoning?

Accepting both the reality of hell and God boils down to trust. When Abraham was faced with the knowledge of the destruction of Sodom and Gomorrah, he may not have fully understood all of God's reasons, but he still showed his faith. "Shall not the Judge of all the earth deal justly?" (Gen 18:25) Whatever the outcome and however God would accomplish justice, Abraham knew that God would do what is right. Can we not have the same sense of trust and faith in God with eternal justice? Our acceptance of hell is not a matter of completely understanding it. It is not even a matter of liking it. It is a matter of whether or not we can trust that God knows what He is doing. For our part, we need to concentrate on doing His will and leave the rest in the hands of the Almighty. The only alternative is to deny God in order to fashion our own understanding of reality. In denying God we end up creating our own god in our faulty image. This cannot be acceptable.

Discussion Questions

1. Why is the concept of hell considered to be a problem for many?

2. Why should we not consider the issue of hell apart from other evidence for God and the Bible?

3. Why do emotional considerations cause people to reject hell? Why is this a problem?

4. How do God and justice get redefined in the process of denying hell?

5. What is our primary reason for accepting the reality of hell? Why does this really matter?

6. What did Jesus say about hell?

7. What two themes did the prophets, apostles, and others often focus on? What does this tell us about how they would have viewed the issue of God's justice?

8. How does the nature of sin help us understand the problem of hell?

9. What is the real tragedy of hell and why?

Postmodernism 15

Oxford's the word of the year for 2016 was "post-truth." According to Time Magazine online,[1] post-truth "describes a situation in which feelings trump facts." It is called an "apt choice for countries like America and Britain, where people lived through divisive, populist upheavals that often seemed to prize passion above all else — including facts." The definition that they give for post-truth is as follows: "relating to or denoting circumstances in which objective facts are less influential in shaping public opinion than appeals to emotion and personal belief."

Further, "the word dates back to 1992, but Oxford saw its usage explode by %2,000 this year" (in 2016). They are applying this primarily to the political climate of our age, and then suggest, "it may become the defining word of our time." It is not difficult to see how the term broadly fits the way our culture has been moving for some time. This includes the way people think of religion and Scripture. The more familiar term over the last several years for this way of thinking is *postmodernism*.

Truth is paramount to the Christian. "I am the way, the truth, and the life. No one comes to the Father but through Me," Jesus said (John 14:6). Truth is what sets us free from sin (John 8:32). Yet the nature of truth means that it is objective. That is, truth is outside of us. It is not created by us, but rather discovered. Truth does not change to fit the whims of fallible people. Further, whatever stands as objective truth is truth for everyone everywhere. God is the ultimate source of truth, and all the works of God's hands are "truth and justice" (Ps 111:7). The truth of the Lord is everlasting (Psalm 117:2).

---

[1] Katy Steinmetz. *Oxford's Word of the Year for 2016 is 'Post-truth,'* http://time.com/4572592/oxford-word-of-the-year-2016-post-truth/ (accessed 2-28-2016).

The problem is that we now live in an age in which truth is no longer held in high esteem by many. Truth is being suppressed in unrighteousness (Rom 1:18). In fact, many question whether there is even anything we can really call truth. We have culturally shifted to a point where all that can be called truth is held suspect. We are in the era of "post-truth" or "postmodernism." It is considered not so much a "cultural theory but rather an (anti-)philosophical view flowing from a 'suspension' of the notion of truth."[2]

Postmodernism refers to an age "after modernism," but how does that make sense? Modernism typically refers to a mindset growing out of the enlightenment period that places a premium on science and rational thought. Through rational thought and the naturalistic scientific method, truth was seen as discoverable and knowable. Though Christians disagree with the philosophy of naturalism (more modernistic than postmodernistic), at least there was a common agreement on the idea that people can discover and know truth.

But postmodernists have "outgrown" that notion, and now there is a battle between traditional reason and the postmodern denial that truth is objective. To the postmodernist, truth cannot be proved in any objective way because we are essentially trapped in our language prisons, able only to express subjective feelings. Science, history, reason, and evidence cannot tell us anything except what those who report about it believe. Feeling and intuition tell us more than reason or evidence, so we need to go with what we feel. Since there is no absolute truth, then everything, including our morality, is relative and person-dependent. There are no objective standards by which to judge anyone or anything; all ethical views should be tolerated (and this is, ironically, seen as absolute).

---

[2] Hugh Tomlinson, "After Truth: Postmodernism and The Rhetoric of Science," in *Philosophy: A Text with Readings*, ed. Manuel Velasquez, 9th ed. (Belmont, CA: Thomson and Wadsworth, 2005), 501-02.

In the postmodern view, traditional morality is seen as oppressive. Because the Bible is expressed in such absolute terms, postmodernists reject its fundamental principles. They may have some interest in spirituality as long as they can define it on their own terms. It's okay to be religious as a postmodernist, but it is not good to teach that your religion is the only way. All religious views are equally valid—except the one that claims to be the one right way. Anyone paying attention to culture these days can readily see this attitude.

The Shift in Thinking

This shift in thinking has affected all levels of society: education (including history and literature), religion, politics, science, medicine, law ... name it. The shift has resulted in what some have simply called "the death of truth." Part of our problem is that we have a hard time recognizing it because it is not based upon distinct claims. McCallum put it this way: "Unlike Darwinism, postmodernism isn't a distinct set of doctrines or truth claims. It's a *mood*—a view of the world characterized by a deep distrust of reason, not to mention a disdain for the knowledge Christians believe the Bible provides. It's a *methodology*—a completely new way of analyzing ideas."[3] Further, "Relativism says that truth isn't fixed by outside reality, but is decided by a group or individual for themselves. Truth isn't discovered, but manufactured. Truth is ever-changing not only in insignificant matters of taste or fashion, but in crucial matters of spirituality, morality, and reality itself."[4] In other words, we aren't just talking your favorite flavor of ice cream.

The impact of this shift in thinking has hit strongly at the collegiate level. Allan Bloom noted in 1992 that "almost every student entering the university believes, or says he believes, that truth is

---

[3] Dennis McCallum, ed., *The Death of Truth* (Minneapolis, Minn.: Bethany House Publishers, 1996), 12.

[4] Ibid., 31.

relative."[5] These students come from all the various religious and economic backgrounds, and the mood has only deepened through the years. They see relativism as a moral postulate, the "condition of a free society." This is what they have been taught from early on. Bloom continues:

> The danger they have been taught to fear from absolutism is not error but intolerance. Relativism is necessary to openness; and this is the virtue, the only virtue, which all primary education for more than fifty years has dedicated itself to inculcating. Openness -- and the relativism that makes it the only plausible stance in the face of various claims to truth and various ways of life and kinds of human beings — is the great insight of our times.[6]

In postmodern thinking, there are at least two ideas that permeate: 1) all morals and ideas are relative, and 2) we should tolerate most ideas and practices (except, of course, for those views that say we shouldn't tolerate everything). In other words, we must agree with the postmodern mindset to be acceptable. Seeing how this affects the way people think about truth and morals is not difficult. Beckwith and Koukl, in 1998, observed, "Today we've lost the confidence that statements of fact can ever be anything more than just opinions; we no longer know that anything is certain beyond our subjective preferences. The word truth now means 'true for me' and nothing more. We have entered an era of dogmatic skepticism."[7] Further:

---

[5] Allan Bloom, *The Closing of the American Mind* (NY: Simon and Schuster, 1987), 25. Bloom was a professor at the University of Chicago. He passed away in 1992.

[6] Ibid., 25-26.

[7] Beckwith, Francis J. and Gregory Koukl, *Relativism* (Grand Rapids, MI: Baker Books, 1998), 20.

When truth dies, all of its subspecies, such as ethics, perish with it. If truth can't be known, then the concept of moral truth becomes incoherent. Ethics become relative, right and wrong matters of individual opinion. This may seem a moral liberty, but it ultimately rings hollow. 'The freedom of our day,' lamented a graduate in a Harvard commencement address, "is the freedom to devote ourselves to any values we please, on the mere condition that we do not believe them to true."[8]

In this way of thinking, tolerance is required because no one is in a position to say that anyone else is "wrong." Right and wrong are judgmental terms that are more rooted in absolutist ideas.

Signs of the Times

Since postmodernism is not really identified by a set of distinct doctrines, then how do we know when we have come up against it? First, it is everywhere. We really don't need to go far at all to see the affects of postmodern thinking. Second, there are strong indicators that we are around postmodern concepts. For example:

- *Political Correctness* generally refers to the idea that we should go out of our way not to offend certain groups. Our society has created a hyper-sensitive atmosphere in which we have to change the way we say everything so as not to offend anyone. While Christians are to be sensitive to others, not trying to offend, political correctness takes matters into the moral realm. For example, if we say that homosexual practice is morally wrong and sinful, we have violated the political correctness of our day and will be labeled as bigots for doing so (and yes, that is quite inconsistent, but that doesn't matter if it achieves the PC

---

[8] Ibid.

goal). Calling something a sin is not politically correct as it implies a spiritual standard to which all are amenable.

- Along with the above, we are expected to accept an aspect of multiculturalism and pluralism that allows for any and all diversity, even if it goes against biblical morality. We can see how hard advocates push the homosexual marriage agenda. We are expected simply to let them do what they wish, and we are not supposed to condemn or criticize the movement. Otherwise we are intolerant, and that kind of intolerance is considered intolerable.

- Educational standards have declined. There has been a shift from the teacher as one who imparts knowledge to the learners as those who create their own learning experience. Further, the emphasis has shifted more to improvement of self-esteem rather than on the traditional reading and writing of years past.

- How we view history and literature is also affected. History is not seen so much as what actually happened, but more just the expression of how a group perceived that something happened. History can be altered. The focus on literature is not so much on what an author intended to convey to an audience, but rather how we can subjectively determine our own meaning and how it makes us feel.

Perhaps we can see how this type of philosophy can affect even our Bible study and religious practices. Instead of trying to understand, for example, what Paul meant when he wrote something, our focus becomes simply what a text means to us regardless of what it originally meant. Or instead of asking what pleases God in worship, we are more concerned with how we feel about it, so we are more prone to worship as we like and take the emphasis off of God's authority. All of it becomes a subjective better-felt-than-told mentality.

The Postmodern Problem

First, postmodern thinking cannot logically be maintained. If postmodernists proclaim, "there is no such thing as truth," ask if that statement is true. If they insist, "don't push your morals on us," ask them if they are pushing their morals on you by telling you what you should and shouldn't do. If they tell us that language cannot be understood objectively, ask them what they mean by that. This type of thinking is logically self-defeating.

Second, to take relativism to its conclusion, how can they say that anything at all is right or wrong? Why would they oppose torturing a baby, for example? If they have no standard of judgment, who is to say that doing anything you feel like, even to the destruction of others, is wrong? But the moment they say something is wrong (or right for that matter), they have assumed a standard by which to make those judgments. It is inevitable. Now what exactly is that standard and who decides it?

Third, for reality to mean anything, truth is unavoidable. The law of non-contradiction is that something (like a word or an object) cannot be both what it is and what it isn't at the same and sense. Language of any kind assumes this to be true. If postmodernists are going to make arguments or write articles then they, too, must assume the truth of that principle. Else why talk or write at all? If we can just create our own meaning, then I can take what the postmodernist says and twist it to fit my own agenda. What's to stop me? Who can say it is wrong? What standard will they use to make a judgment about it? How can they say I've misrepresented them?

Fourth, the principle of tolerance is abused by postmodernists. They are generally inconsistent in their application of it. In truth, they want to tolerate only those things that fit their agenda, but will they tolerate those who teach that homosexual practice is sinful?

That abortion is morally reprehensible? That Jesus is the only way to heaven? The point is that they are selective in how they apply it and they aren't very tolerant when people disagree with their agendas.

Fifth, we should let the evidence speak for itself. The reason we teach that Jesus is the only way is not just because He made some outlandish claim. Rather, He provided the necessary evidence through the resurrection, demonstrating that He is Lord (Rom. 1:3-4). If He is Lord, then He certainly has the right to tell us how to get to heaven.

Truth is necessary (try denying it without affirming). Truth is attainable (or none of us can understand anything). Truth is objective, outside of ourselves and coming from a source that is greater than us. And truth is real. It is what separates us from all that is false and destructive. We can surely agree with the following: "The more we study and understand postmodern culture, the more we will see how desperately people still need absolute, objective truth. In a world where everyone's position is true, nobody's position matters. The result is a lonely vacuum waiting for answers that matter to fill it."[9]

---

[9] McCallum, 211.

Discussion Questions

1. Why do you think that people have a hard time accepting "truth"?

2. What is "relativism"? Why do you think so many believe morals are relative?

3. Besides the ones given, can you think of any other "signs" of postmodernism in our culture?

4. Between modernism and postmodernism, what do you think is more influential today and why?

5. How would you try to show a postmodernist the truth about Jesus?

Efficient Cause

In the world of sense we find there is an order of efficient causes. There is no case known (neither is it, indeed, possible) in which a thing is found to be the efficient cause of itself; for so it would be prior to itself, which is impossible. Now in efficient causes it is not possible to go on to infinity, because in all efficient causes following in order, the first is the cause of the intermediate cause, and the intermediate is the cause of the ultimate cause, whether the intermediate cause be several, or only one. Now to take away the cause is to take away the effect. Therefore, if there be no first cause among efficient causes, there will be no ultimate, nor any intermediate cause. But if in efficient causes it is possible to go on to infinity, there will be no first efficient cause, neither will there be an ultimate effect, nor any intermediate efficient causes; all of which is plainly false. Therefore it is necessary to admit a first efficient cause, to which everyone gives the name of God.

Thomas Aquinas, Summa Theologica, 10

The Problem of Atheism 16

Atheism is around us. There is a breed of atheism that is quite aggressive, sometimes termed "the new atheism." Some are putting signs on billboards and the sides of buses espousing their atheism. These atheists are anything but quiet and unassuming. They are actively seeking to destroy faith in God. They use science as their platform for arguing that there is no need for God.

Sometimes it is assumed that the only ones who must give a defense of their belief system are those who believe in God. As believers, we are supposed to have the burden of proof, and the default "needs no defense" position is atheism. We need to challenge this assumption, for unbelievers are not neutral bystanders. They have taken a position, a worldview that itself needs to be defended in rational discussion. We should never assume that unbelief is the natural victor. To the contrary, belief in God or gods is so universal through time and locations that if anyone is going to make a case about what is natural, belief in the supernatural has clearly been more accepted. This does not prove God, of course, but it does show the propensity of mankind to believe in something or someone greater than themselves.

Further, while unbelievers are going to challenge believers with philosophical issues like the problem of suffering or evil, they are not without a variety of problems that plague their views. Are they capable of providing a more significant worldview? A greater meaning to life? A stronger hope? A better life? What exactly will they offer for the betterment of humanity? And if they are correct, what difference does it really make in the end? They need to give answers.

What an Unbeliever Believes

To say that some are unbelievers is not to say that they do not believe anything. Everyone believes something; everyone exercises faith in a worldview. The denial of one idea will mean the affirmation of something else. To say, "There is no God" is itself an affirmation that this material world is sufficient to explain itself. This point is important because proving a negative is almost impossible. Surely atheists cannot prove that there is no God, so they may cry, "unfair," if called upon to do so. Further, just because the atheist cannot prove there is no God does not in itself prove that there is a God. Fair enough. The theist must still take a burden of proof.

What then does the unbeliever have to defend? If proving there is no God is unreasonable, then what are they positively affirming? Basically, the atheist should be called upon to defend brute materialism or naturalism—that naturalism is capable of explaining everything. Where is their scientific proof that nature alone can account for everything in the universe? They don't have to prove there is no God. They just have to show that naturalism adequately explains the universe—and not just the raw materials of it but also the intangible features like mind and conscience. They should be willing to defend that matter is all there is, and that matter must be either eternal itself or it created itself out of nothing with no intelligent forces behind it. But if they cannot prove that, then at the least they should admit that they have a faith in something that cannot be scientifically demonstrated. How are they so different from theists in that regard?

Further, the atheist should be willing to defend the notion that life came from non-life. After all, if there is no intelligent Creator who made everything, then where did life come from? If life and intelligence is not eternal (as would be the case with God), then there must have been a time when there was no intelligence and no life. What about the idea that consciousness came from non-consciousness? They believe their ability to think rationally arose from mindless matter. So how do they know they can think rationally at all? If rational thought is the chance, mindless by-product of irrational causes, then what guarantee does anyone have that they are intelligent in any sense? C.S. Lewis observed that

> no account of the universe can be true unless that account leaves it possible for our thinking to be a real insight. A theory which explained everything else in the whole universe but which made it impossible to believe that our thinking was valid, would be utterly out of court. For that theory would itself have been reached by thinking, and if thinking is not valid that theory would, of course, be itself demolished.[1]

In other words, brute materialism cannot really account for thinking, much less to provide the foundation for having real insight. It's self-defeating, and any worldview that defeats itself is not worth holding. Can the atheist's view of science reasonably account for all this? This is what they should be willing to defend.

They should also be willing to defend the notion that since we are the result of mindless, irrational forces (per their view), then we are essentially material machines with no ultimate responsibility and accountability. Atheists may try to argue against God based upon the problem of evil, but how does their worldview help the issue? They believe in a world with evil and suffering but with no sense of judgment, final justice, or setting things right in the end. Once dead, there is nothing. So ultimately, why would it matter whether we were murderers or humanitarians? Both end up in the same place with no ultimate judgment. Does this not sound a bit like the problem that the writer of Ecclesiastes was dealing with?

---

[1] C.S. Lewis, *Miracles* (NY: Macmillan Publishing Co., 1960), 14-15.

Philosophers have long asked, "Why is there something rather than nothing?" If it was possible that nothing existed, then why are we here? How does naturalism account for this? Which is more reasonable to believe? That 1) existence is uncaused, unplanned, without design and intelligent force driving it, or 2) we are the products of rational intelligence and it is our task to understand our purpose? Are we missing something here?

Then, what exactly is our basis for morality? Atheists can believe in morality, but can they really justify that belief if we are merely material processes at work with no ultimate accountability? It is one thing to say, for example, that rape, incest, and racism are wrong, but without an ultimate standard by which to judge these issues, how does one actually justify saying that they are wrong or evil? Who says? Why? What is the ground for moral outrage? They may wax bold about the problem of evil, but they have no foundation for really calling something "evil" in the first place. The objection rings hollow in a purely materialistic worldview.

What is the basis for the meaning of life? Who defines our purpose for existence? Without a Giver of meaning, who is to say why we are here and what we should be doing? Just think, in the atheistic world, all that has ever been done, all the progress ever made, all the accomplishments for the good of humanity—everything— will come to nothing. On what basis can the atheist argue otherwise and why would it matter?

The Despair of Unbelief

Unbelief has consequences, of course. What real hope will it offer? What meaning will it give to life? It is this very problem that leads to a sense of despair, as Ecclesiastes shows. Atheism has been described as "a journey without a destiny, a body without a soul, a religion without reason, life without meaning, a faith without hope, and a universe without God."[2] Once we take God out of the picture, we lose that sense of everything God stands for and provides. As one cynic declared, "God is dead, Marx is dead, and I'm not feeling too well myself."

How, then, can atheism provide for a fulfilling way of life? You can hear it in the atheist's own words. Existentialist and atheist Jean-Paul Sartre recognized the despair of atheism, speaking of "abandonment," which he says means that "God does not exist, and that it is necessary to draw the consequences of his absence right to the end." He further wrote,

> The existentialist ... finds it extremely embarrassing that God does not exist, for there disappears with Him all possibility of finding values in an intelligible heaven. There can no longer be any good a priori, since there is no infinite and perfect consciousness to think it. It is nowhere written that 'the good' exists, that one must be honest or must not lie, since we are now upon the plane where there are only men. Dostoevsky once wrote, 'If God did not exist, everything would be permitted'; and that, for existentialism, is the starting point. Everything is indeed permitted if God does not exist, and man is in consequence forlorn, for he cannot find anything to depend upon either within or without himself.

He recognized that "if God does not exist" then we are not "provided with any values or commands that could legitimize our behavior" so we are "left alone" and "condemned to be free."[3] He believed in responsibility, but once again we must ask, "To whom or what are we ultimately responsible?"

---

[2] Steve Kumar, *Christianity for Skeptics* (Peabody, MA: Hendrickson Publishers, 2000), 78.

[3] Jean-Paul Sartre, "Existentialism," in *Existentialism from Dostoevsky to Sartre*, ed. Walter Kaufmann (NY: Meridian, 1975), 352-53.

Bertrand Russell was another well-known atheistic philosopher who was honest about the despair brought about by his own position. Here is what he wrote:

> That man is the product of causes which had no prevision of the end they were achieving; that his origin, his growth, his hopes and fears, his loves and his beliefs, are but the outcome of accidental collocations of atoms; that no fire, no heroism, no intensity of thought and feeling, can preserve an individual life beyond the grave; that all labour of the ages, all the devotion, all the inspiration, all the noonday brightness of human genius, are destined to extinction in the vast death of the solar system, and that the whole temple of Man's achievement must inevitably be buried beneath the debris of a universe in ruins—all these things, if not quite beyond dispute, are yet so nearly certain, that no philosophy which rejects them can hope to stand. Only within the scaffolding of these truths, only on the firm foundation of unyielding despair, can the soul's habitation henceforth be safely built.[4]

And what hope will the unbeliever provide in death? Once again, in the words of a well-known agnostic orator, we note what Robert Ingersoll said at his own brother's graveside:

> While yet in love with life and raptured with the world, he passed to silence and pathetic dust. Yet, after all, it may be best, just in the happiest, sunniest hour of all the voyage, while eager winds are kissing every sail, to dash against the unseen rock, and in an instant hear the billows roar above the sunken ship. For whether in mid-sea or among the breakers of the farther shore, a wreck at last must mark the end of each and all. And every life, no matter if its every

---

[4] Bertrand Russell, *Why I Am Not a Christian, and Other Essays on Religion and Related Subjects* (New York: Simon and Schuster, 1957), 107.

hour is rich with love and every moment jeweled with a joy, will, at its close, become a tragedy sad and deep and dark as can be woven of the warp and woof of mystery and death. ... Life is a narrow vale between the cold and barren peaks of two eternities. We strive in vain to look beyond the heights. We cry aloud, and the only answer is the echo of our wailing cry...⁵

In the unbelievers' own words we can see that they have nothing positive to offer in the end. No sense of ultimate justice can be found in the worldview. No particular meaning can be heard for life —just an echo of a wailing cry. That is the best they can offer as any kind of "firm foundation" for a "soul's habitation." Hardly, though, can such "unyielding despair" provide safety for life or death.

Does all this prove that there is a God? No. That's not the point of this discussion. The point is that when we are considering alternate worldviews, we need to know what we are getting. If unbelievers are going to speak against God, then they need to be able to defend their own view and the dire consequences that stem from it. What exactly is the worldview's worth anyway?

As Jesus taught the need for His own to count the cost of being disciples (Luke 14), surely we also need to count the cost of being unbelievers. "Look at what you give up by becoming a Christian," one might say. "Yes," says the believer, "but look at what you give up by *not* becoming a Christian." The cost of unbelief is a steep price to pay for the few years on this earth. Weigh it against eternity.

---

⁵ Robert Ingersoll, "Tribute at His Brother's Grave," in *Wit, Wisdom, and Eloquence*, ed. R.L. Gray, 4th ed. (Atlanta, GA: The Harrison Co., 1930), 317-18.

Discussion Questions

1. Why would we say that "you cannot prove there is no God" does not in itself prove God?

2. Why should the unbeliever take a burden of proof in the debate over God?

3. Restate in your words what the atheistic positively affirms. Why should they be willing to defend it?

4. Why do agree or disagree that the issue regarding life coming from non-life and consciousness coming from non-consciousness is important?

5. Why would we say that if we are products of irrational forces then we would have a hard time trusting our own thinking abilities?

6. Summarize the essential position seen in the words of Sartre, Russell, and Ingersoll. Why is hearing the consequence of unbelief in their own words important?

Jesus and Apologetics 17

How did Jesus defend Himself? To what did Jesus appeal as proof for His identity and authority? How did Jesus use evidence? These questions are important because, as disciples of Jesus, we want to know how He dealt with matters so that we can imitate Him. So now we turn our attention to the question of how Jesus Himself used apologetics.

To do this, let's remind ourselves about what is involved in apologetics: 1. There is positive evidence offered on behalf of God; 2. There is defending against objections made by those who oppose, and 3. There is the offensive against the views of those who oppose. Did Jesus engage in these activities? Let's survey a few of these examples.

Jesus and Positive Evidence

John 5 provides a good case study of how Jesus used evidence. Jesus had healed a man on the Sabbath and was accused of breaking the Sabbath as a result. In the ensuing discussion, Jesus appeals to several witnesses in order to establish His identity as the Son of God. Based upon the Law, Jesus understood well the principle about witnesses and testimony. "If I alone testify about Myself, My testimony is not true" (v. 31) The Law taught that "on the evidence of two or three witnesses a matter shall be confirmed" (Deut 19:15). So what witnesses could Jesus point to on His own behalf?

First, Jesus appeals to John (the immerser) who "testified to the truth" (v. 33). John 1 records John's testimony. Second, Jesus appeals to His own works as greater than John's testimony (v. 36). That is, His miracles demonstrate that He spoke the truth. Third, Jesus points to the Father "who sent Me" and "testified of Me" (v. 37). On at least three occasions the Father spoke from heaven concerning

Jesus: first in His baptism (Matt 3:13-17), second in the transfiguration (Matt 17:1-8), and third when Jesus was troubled and asked, "Father, glorify Your name" (John 12:28). The Father replied, "I have both glorified it and will glorify it again." Jesus then pointed out that the voice "has not come for My sake, but for your sakes" (v. 30). All of these events were attended by other witnesses. John, of course, was there at Jesus' baptism and as a result was able to point to Jesus as the Lamb of God who takes away the sins of the world (John 1:29). Fourth, Jesus refers to the Scriptures as a witness to His identity. The Scriptures "testify of Me," said Jesus (v. 39). The entire Old Testament pointed to Jesus, and after the resurrection He told His disciples that "all things which are written about Me in the Law of Moses and the Prophets and the Psalms must be fulfilled" (Luke 24:44). A study of the Scriptures should lead one to faith in Jesus. Fifth, Jesus said that Moses specifically was a witness of Him (vv. 45-47). So Jesus specifies not only Scripture (which would include more than the Pentateuch), but Moses as the one who testified, "for he wrote about Me" (v. 46). For example, Deuteronomy 18 is a specific prophesy from Moses that finds its ultimate application in Jesus as the Prophet who was to come (see Acts 3:17-26).

Jesus was not afraid to point to evidence on His behalf. If two or three witnesses confirmed a matter, here Jesus presented five. These witnesses were varied, could be investigated, and provided overall strength and support to the claims Jesus made. He laid out the evidence on His own behalf, and they could not refute it.

Matthew 11:2-6 also shows how Jesus pointed to evidence. When John's disciples came to Him asking, "Are you the Expected One, or shall we look for someone else?" Jesus immediately pointed them to the evidence, based upon what they could "hear and see." They were not expected merely to take Jesus' word for it without any evidence. Rather, based upon the evidence, they could determine if Jesus really was the "Expected One" (i.e., the Messiah). Listen to what He said and look at what He did.

Mark 2:1-12 further records a good example of Jesus pointing to a miraculous work as proof that He was the Son of Man with authority to forgive sin. A paralyzed man carried by four men was let down through a roof in order to get to Jesus. Upon seeing this display of faith, Jesus said, "Son, your sins are forgiven." But this sounded blasphemous to the scribes who saw and heard this. Only God has the power to forgive sins. So what would Jesus do? Would He simply say, "Just believe Me. I have the authority"? Or would He prove it with evidence? He opted for proof. "So that you may know the Son of Man has authority on earth to forgive sins..." then He healed the man. Thus His miracles served an apologetic purpose. The evidence spoke for itself. Jesus was who He claimed to be, just as Nicodemus confessed, "Rabbi, we know that You have come from God as a teacher, for no one can do these signs that You do unless God is with him" (John 3:1-2). All of the signs were given so that we may believe (John 20:28-31).

Jesus and Defense

There is a sense, of course, in which the testimony Jesus offered in John 5 (the five witnesses) was in defense in His claim to be one with the Father. He was accused of blasphemy and He responded by appealing to the evidence on His behalf. So in one sense it is difficult to separate the positive evidence from the defense. Both dovetail into each other very well. But there were other occasions in which Jesus was essentially attacked and needed to respond. Here are some examples:

Matthew 21:23-27 reports that the chief priests and elders came to Jesus and began questioning Him about His authority to act as He did. It was a legitimate question, for Jesus had been in the temple teaching and had recently drove money-changers out. How could He do this? Jesus did not get upset that they questioned Him. His was no "how dare you" kind of reply. He simply asked them a question about John's baptism. Was it from heaven or men? They knew they were in trouble and could not answer it without getting trapped themselves. Jesus had turned the tables again with a simple question, showing that sometimes a well-placed question serves as a defense, too. How was it a defense? The point is that once they answered the question about John honestly, then they would also know the source of Jesus' authority. Sometimes answering one question will make other answers more obvious. They could see what Jesus did. They knew what He was claiming. They just needed to follow the evidence where it took them and honestly admit what they knew to be true all along.

Matthew 22 records what we often think of as the day of controversy in which several different groups came to Jesus and challenged Him in some way. Read it and see how calmly Jesus reacted, how well He responded, how one by one He silenced His critics. Jesus' defense of Himself was never an unreasonable display of anger. It was not a matter of digging down into the dirt and making wild accusations. His defense was a well-reasoned approach, asking basic questions, getting His critics to think through their attempts to trap Him. They were the hypocrites in the situation. They were the ones who failed to understand the Scriptures and the power of God. Jesus did not simply make these charges. He showed his accusers where they missed it. Defending Jesus is not about simply denying what a critic says; it is to be a reasoned and thoughtful reply with God and Scripture at the focal point.

There was even occasion for Jesus not to respond verbally. "Like a lamb that is led to the slaughter, and like a sheep that is silent before its shearers, so He did not open His mouth" (Isa 53). As Jesus stood before His accusers, He allowed them to abuse Him without protesting. This, too, was in fulfillment of prophecy and helped establish His identity. The Messiah would not be one who would fight back in some physical way. To fulfill Isaiah 53, Jesus had to endure the suffering and reproach. He is the suffering Servant and Savior, so when the time called for it, Jesus simply kept His mouth shut in fulfillment of the Scriptures. Even in His silence, He is defending His identity. Perhaps sometimes the better thing to do is to let God's enemies destroy themselves through their folly. Quietly watching them self-destruct may be the best option on occasion.

Jesus and Offense

After Jesus silenced His challengers, He went on the offense in Matthew 22:41-46 by challenging His critics with a question: "What do you think about the Christ, whose son is He?" Their answer was true: "The son of David." Jesus replied, "Then how does David in the Spirit call Him 'Lord,' saying, "The LORD said to my Lord, Sit at My right hand, until I put Your enemies beneath Your feet"'? Now the question is begging to be asked: "If David calls Him 'Lord,' how is He his son?" They could not answer. By going on the offense, Jesus was able to demonstrate that the position His challengers held toward the Messiah was not tenable or consistent. How could they rightly challenge Jesus the way they did when they couldn't answer questions about the nature of the Messiah from the Old Testament? They were supposed to be the experts, and their credibility suffered for their inconsistencies.

Matthew 23 continues with Jesus going on the offensive. He talks about the hypocritical stance taken by the Pharisees and shows that they were more interested in outward show than they were in sincerely serving God. Granted that Jesus had insight into their motives that we may not be able to have today, the point is still that sometimes the positions held by critics of Jesus need to be exposed for what they are. If the views held by unbelievers are not tenable, it is certainly fair to point that out and to show why.

The Greatest Apologetic

The greatest apologetic of Jesus is, once again, His resurrection. We have been focused on the resurrection as the primary apologetic of the New Testament. So it is with Jesus, too. When the scribes and

Pharisees asked for a sign, He replied that the only sign He would give them was "the sign of Jonah the prophet" who was three days and nights in the belly of the sea creature. Jesus said that this event pointed to His own resurrection.

After the great confession by Peter, Jesus began "to show His disciples that He must go to Jerusalem, and suffer many things from the elders and chief priests and scribes, and be killed, and be raised up on the third day" (Matt 16:21). Once the disciples understood who Jesus really was (the Christ, the Son of the Living God), the focus shifted to His purpose for being here, which necessitated that He suffer, die, and be raised again. By the resurrection, Jesus was "declared the Son of God with power" (Rom 1:4).

Following His Example

Of course, much more can be said about the apologetics of Jesus.[1] We can see from this brief study that Jesus was engaged in apologetics on a number of levels. He offered positive evidence. He defended Himself against challenges. He sometimes went on the offensive in order to show the folly of His opposition. In following the example of Jesus, the apostles and Christians of the first century did the same, as the book of Acts demonstrates.

We began our lessons by showing that apologetics covers proof, defense, and offense. Since Jesus engaged in these, then we can follow His example and, when needed, provide the positive evidence for Him, defend Him against attacks of the unbelieving, and demonstrate the folly of unbelief. Of course, not everyone accepted Jesus. We are not suggesting that when Christians engage in these activities that they will convert everyone. Even when Jesus

---

[1] See Norman L. Geisler, and Patrick Zukeran, *The Apologetics of Jesus* (Grand Rapids, MI: Baker Books, 2009). Not many books are written solely on the apologetic methods of Jesus, which makes this work especially useful on this topic.

performed miracles, there were witnesses who still refused to believe. All we can do is lay the evidence before them and let them decide what to do with it. Yet while we lay the evidence on the table, let us do all we can to represent Jesus properly.

Discussion Questions

1. Why was it important for Jesus to provide positive evidence for His identity?

2. Can you think of other examples of Jesus using evidence on His own behalf?

3. In what ways did Jesus defend Himself? What other examples are there?

4. Why did Jesus go on the offensive at times? What role does this play in apologetics?

5. Why is the resurrection the greatest apologetic? What can we learn from this?

Jesus is God

When Christians affirm that Jesus is God, they are simply being faithful to the explicit teaching of the Bible. After all, the New Testament does, indeed, call Jesus Christ "God," not once, but several times. It also affirms that Jesus is "Lord," repeatedly doing so in contexts that equate Jesus with YHWH, the God of the Old Testament. In addition, the New Testament assigns a variety of other divine names or titles to Jesus (such as Bridegroom, Savior, and the first and the last). It gives Jesus all these names in the broader setting of a pervasive attitude of exalting the name of Jesus above every other name. If we are to be faithful to the teaching of the Bible, we must acknowledge Jesus Christ as our great God and Savior.

Robert Bowman; J. Ed Komoszewski; Darrell L. Bock.
Putting Jesus in His Place:
The Case for the Deity of Christ

Apologetics in Acts 18

The book of Acts serves many purposes. It is a key to understanding other New Testament subjects: the church, salvation, and as a backdrop to the epistles. It is an inspired account of the apostles carrying out the great commission to take the gospel into the world. Yet the focus is more upon Peter and Paul than any of the others. As a second part to the Gospel of Luke, Acts shows the fulfillment of the kingdom: in Luke the kingdom was at hand; in Acts the kingdom is realized as Christ now sits on the throne of David (Acts 2). This kingdom is not of men, but of God, who, through the Holy Spirit, demonstrates His rule and authority in the spread of the gospel (cf. Acts 5:38-39). Further, Christ's reign as king extends not only to Jews, but also to Gentiles who are often seen as receptive to the message (beginning in chapter 10). Acts confronts both Jews and Gentiles on their own terms and nothing can stop the spread of the gospel. The victorious march of Christ and His disciples is well under way, and the book even ends abruptly in a way that implies the story is not over. Acts is only the beginning.

Acts has a narrow focus. It is seen as a history of the church, but it is not a comprehensive history. Yet the history shows how God is behind the movement. The growth of Christianity was not merely a human achievement. So there must be a reason that Luke, writing as a corollary to the gospel of Luke, recorded the specific information that he did (compare Luke 1:1-4 with Acts 1:1-3). Our focus here will be on the apologetic purposes served by the book of Acts. As with other areas in apologetics, we find the disciples engaging in providing positive evidence, defending against attacks, and sometimes going on the offensive.

In Relation to Jews, Romans, and Pagans

It appears that at first the Romans saw the Christians as another sect of the Jews, so they basically left Christians alone. Luke does demonstrate a connection between Christianity and the religion of ancient Israel. For example, Paul takes a vow and participates in Jewish ceremony (Acts 21). Timothy is circumcised so that he can effectively work among the Jews (Acts 16). James speaks to the relationship of Jews and Gentiles (Acts 15 and 21). In fact, the appeal to the Old Testament is tremendous in Acts, demonstrating to the Jews the false nature of the charges brought against both Stephen (Acts 6-7) and Paul (Acts 21-22). As an apologetic to the Jews, Luke shows that Christ (and by extension, Christ's people) is the fulfillment of all that God prophesied in the Old Testament (see Acts 3:22-26). Yet the Jewish leaders are the ones who are credited with being the first to persecute Christians and stand in opposition to the gospel (Acts 4-5). They are the fierce opponents of Christ while the gentiles are often seen as being more receptive to the gospel message. So Christianity is not the same as Judaism, but there is a connection to ancient Israel as its Messianic extension and fulfillment.

What is the relation of Christians to the Romans in the book of Acts? Again, as an apologetic, we might note how Roman officials come across as somewhat unconcerned or impartial about matters relating to Christians. Perhaps because they saw Christians as an offshoot of the Jews, they didn't really care about them. For example, when Gallio, proconsul of Achaia, had a case brought before him, he drove the accusers away and told them to see to it for themselves since it was not a matter that concerned his judgment (Acts 18:12-17). Sergius Paulos, proconsul of Cypress, was actually favorable toward the gospel, even though Elymas, a Jewish sorcerer, was trying to get in the way (Acts 13). When a riot broke out in Ephesus, the town clerk quieted the people and told them that there was no real cause for the uproar against Paul (Acts 19). Then, when Paul is kept in prison (for his own protection), Felix, the governor of the region, spoke with Paul about the gospel but doesn't appear to have taken the charges against Paul very seriously (Acts 24). Both Herod Agrippa and Festus agreed that if Paul had not appealed to Caesar, he should have been set free (Acts 26).

The point is that Jewish leadership is once again seen as being in opposition to the gospel while the Roman authorities don't really care. The Roman official who did mistreat the Christians—Herod Agrippa I, who had James killed (Acts 12)—did so to please the Jews. But clearly, Christianity is portrayed as harmless in terms of the political situation in the Roman Empire. The opposition of Jews in Acts shows that Christianity is distinct from Judaism (which showed hostility to Christians). But the portrayal of the Christians in Acts also shows that they are not a threat to the Romans politically. Christians were not a "menace to law and order throughout the Roman Empire."[1]

Acts also serves as an apologetic against paganism. If Christians are not just another sect of the Jews, then what are they? Are they another pagan religion? Luke shows that this cannot be the case, and the way that Christianity opposes idol worship and pagan practice takes front and center. Idolatry and the practices that are associated with paganism are clearly condemned as false and ungodly (Acts 14:15-18; Acts 15 and the instructions to Gentile Christians; Acts 17:22-31; Acts 19). Christians were certainly not pagans and they avoided any appearance of such.

Christians, then, are separate from Judaism, not a political threat to the Romans, and not associated in any way with paganism. They were not going to start any riots, insurrections, or political overthrows, but neither should they be confused with any existing religious groups. Thus part of Luke's apologetic purpose is to show the uniqueness of Christianity. Even today, that is one of our important tasks in demonstrating to the world the uniqueness of

---

[1] Donald Guthrie, and Alec Motyer, eds., *The New Bible Commentary: Revised* (Grand Rapids, MI: Eerdmans, 1970), 971.

Jesus Christ and what He offers. There is salvation in none other than Jesus Christ (Acts 4:12).

Peter, Paul, and the Nature of Christianity

Who were going to be the initial leaders among the Messiah's people? Not just anyone, of course, but those who were established as leaders and proven to be by no less than God Himself. In other words, there needed to be authoritative information put out about the apostles and leaders of God's people, for not just anyone was qualified to lead the efforts in spreading the gospel.

The apostles are seen as a united group of leaders in Acts. They worked together for the common cause of Jesus Christ, even working signs and miracles to demonstrate that they their authority came from God (Acts 3-6). Though the position of Peter was obvious, how would the early church respond to a persecutor like Paul? Acts shows both Peter and James (the Lord's brother) approving of Paul and his work for Christ after his conversion. Paul's conversion is narrated three times in Acts, which places great significance on the event and shows that Paul truly was chosen by Christ to be an apostle. Thiessen observed:

> The need for representing Paul's experience in his missionary labors and his arrest and imprisonment in the right light is supplied by the various visions that were vouchsafed to Paul, assuring us that God approved of his work and that his opponents were fighting against God and Christ.[2]

Acts shows that the apostles, including Paul, were acting by God's authority. This apologetic stands in contrast to the idea that Christianity was just some trumped up man-made religion just like

---

[2] Henry Thiessen, *Introduction to the New Testament* (Grand Rapids, MI: Eerdmans, 1943), 185.

the pagans. No, Christians had the divine approval of the Holy Spirit with them (see Acts 5:32). Christianity, then, is seen in Acts as coming from God. The nature of Christianity is that it is supernatural in origin. The role of the Holy Spirit is significant throughout Acts in order to make this case.

Not only are the apostles united in Acts, but so are Christians in general. This was a unified effort, not merely a bunch of people going their own way and doing their own thing. Even though there is a contrast to paganism and a separation from Judaism, Christ's body was composed of both Jews and Gentiles—the all flesh of prophecy (Acts 2). By demonstrating this point, Acts shows that the gospel is indeed for everyone (Acts 10:34-35). Geographically, Acts starts in Jerusalem but then the gospel spreads "to the remotest part of the earth" (Acts 1:8). All people are to hear about Christ.

Further, Christianity is solidly built on the resurrection of Jesus. The book of Acts works as an apologetic for this one basic fact: the resurrection is the reason why Christians exist at all. Without the resurrection, there would be no Christians and no spread of the gospel message. Note once again how Acts begins by saying that Jesus "presented Himself alive after His suffering, by many convincing proofs ..." (1:3). The resurrection is proclaimed without fear by both Peter and Paul (Acts 2, 3, 13, 17, etc.). Luke shows that the resurrection is the primary apologetic of the early church. In other words, the church did not make up the gospel; the gospel is what gave birth to the church.

The nature of the gospel also meant it would be opposed, and Acts shows that there was plenty of opposition to the disciples of Jesus. The persecution of the apostles (Acts 3-4), the martyrdom of Stephen (Acts 7), the widespread persecution starting in Acts 8, the killing of James and imprisonment of Peter (Acts 12), and the continuing opposition all show the truth of Paul's statement: "Through many tribulations we must enter the kingdom of

God" (Acts 14:22). Even so, whenever they were persecuted, they met that persecution with faith and conviction in the power of Jesus Christ. The gospel flourished when opposed. Every effort to block the spread of Christ's message was futile and only enhanced the growth of the kingdom. Christians have a reason to rejoice and a motivation to overcome the obstacles they face. The hope they have in Christ is worth defending, and this message is just as true today as it was then.

This, then, is the defense of the gospel. Christ warned that His people would be dragged before the courts, flogged, persecuted, and put to death. Yet Christians boldly stood up for the truth, proclaiming salvation in Christ alone (Acts 4:12). Why would they do this if they were lying about it? What did they have to gain by preaching the resurrection when they knew they would be opposed? Why would they claim to have seen Jesus alive after He died–unless they were telling the truth? They defended the gospel because they had seen the risen Christ. Acts is the ongoing testimony of this fact.

Acts Then and Now

The world of the first century is very much like today's world. It didn't have the technology of today, but the mindsets and attitudes are not that different. The first century world was pluralistic, accepting a number of religions and practices. Yet, the exclusive nature of Christianity later caused the pluralistic world to turn against Christians. Further, even though so many people were religious, in one sense, the first century world was still quite secular and unspiritual. Even the Pharisees were lovers of money and praise (Luke 16:14; Matt 23). Immorality was rampant and false philosophical ideas were everywhere in the Roman Empire. "By the time of Jesus and Paul, philosophers had long questioned the existence of the official gods. Political leaders, even the priests of these gods, were often motivated more by social and political goals than by personal religious belief."[3] They were not completely unconcerned about religion, but many religious practices were more ritualistic than anything else. As today, many viewed religion as something that served their ambitious ends, whether socially or politically, but the focus was still very worldly. People are often still "religious," yet very worldly.

The world of the book of Acts was a world in sin. This fact is highlighted in the last chapter of book when Paul quotes from Isaiah 6:9-10 (Acts 28:26-27). Isaiah 6 is about Isaiah's call. He saw the glory of God and reacted by recognizing his own sin and the sins of those around him. God commissioned Isaiah to preach to people who wouldn't even listen. These are people desperately in need of salvation. They needed salvation in Isaiah's time. They needed it in Paul's time. They need it today. The gospel will always be relevant to address the sinful human condition.

That same problem of sin that existed in ancient Israel, in the first century, and in the modern era is what makes our world ripe for the gospel of Jesus Christ. As then, people are looking for answers now. They desire something more than what this world gives, something to provide solutions to the greater problem of sin. We sometimes complain that people today are not interested anymore. The world just doesn't seem to care. This didn't stop Christians in the first century. Why should it stop us from trying now? As long as God lets us live here, there will be opportunities and responsibility. The world is in need of answers, and we have those answers in the Scriptures. The book of Acts gives us insight, then, not only to the first century spread of the gospel, but to our own world that is just as much in need of what Christ gives. If the gospel of Christ could be effective back then—preaching the resurrection, reaching out to all with the message of salvation—we should find encouragement

---

[3] James S. Jeffers, *The Greco-Roman World of the New Testament Era: Exploring The Background of Early Christianity* (Downers Grove, Ill.: InterVarsity Press, 1999), 92.

today for effective teaching. Let us not waste our opportunities to reach out with the same message of salvation, for there is salvation in no one else but Christ (Acts 4:12).

Discussion Questions

1. What are some of the purposes of Acts and how do these purposes fit with our needs today?

2. Why was it important for Christians to establish a connection to the Old Testament?

3. Why did the Christians need to show they were different from Judaism? From Paganism?

4. How is the exclusive nature of Christianity demonstrated in Acts?

5. Why was it important to show that Christians were not threats to the Roman government? How should that inform our efforts today?

6. What role did the Holy Spirit play in the spread of the gospel? How about the preaching of the resurrection?

7. How is our modern world like that of the first century? How can this help us in our efforts?

Living Apologetics 19

Apologetics is evangelistic in nature. Souls are at stake in the fight for truth. Consequently, we are not just trying to win arguments and debates; we are trying to win souls for Christ. Therefore, *how* we converse with others is vital. Paul wrote to Timothy: "The Lord's bond-servant must not be quarrelsome, but be kind to all, able to teach, patient when wronged, with gentleness correcting those who are in opposition, if perhaps God may grant them repentance leading to the knowledge of the truth, and they may come to their senses *and escape* from the snare of the devil, having been held captive him to do his will" (2 Tim 2:24-26). Paul's humble spirit comes through here as he imbibed the very attitude of God who is not willing that any should perish but that all should come to repentance (2 Pet 3:9). God's desire is that all be saved and come to the knowledge of truth (1 Tim 2:4). If our desire is something other than this, perhaps we should not be doing apologetics.

Why would we say this? An approach bent on winning debates for its own pleasure is more geared toward glorifying the man, not God. A debate can be beneficial if done properly, but when we argue in ways that distort truth so that we can win a point, we overstep our boundaries. This is partly what Paul meant when he wrote the weapons of our warfare are not carnal (2 Cor 10:3-5). That is, we must not stoop to worldly ways and ungodly methods in order to win fights. The weapons that God has given us are sufficient taking down the strongholds of the world and bringing every thought captive to Jesus Christ. We need to trust God in this.

If God's concern is the salvation of souls, then our concern ought to mirror this attitude. Jesus did not come to this earth merely to beat opponents in argumentation. He came to seek and save the lost. If we are going to honor Jesus for what He did, then our efforts should be directed toward those same efforts. Taking an approach that emphasizes self and personal reasoning abilities diminishes the honor that belongs to our Lord.

Defend Christ with Grace

The apostle wrote about this very point. "Conduct yourselves with wisdom toward outsiders, making the most of the opportunity. Let your speech always be with grace, as though seasoned with salt, so that you will know how you should respond to each person" (Col 4:6). Obviously, what we say is extremely important. We cannot convert anyone to truth unless we actually speak the truth. Yet, Paul reminds us that how we go about it is just as important as the content of our message. Truth presented with a bad attitude or lack of kindness does no one any good. Truth is to be spoken in love (Eph 4:15) and with a desire to "give grace to those who hear" (v. 29). Kindness is always in order when we are defending our Lord.

Further, we need to remember that part of the purpose in apologetics is to remove stumbling blocks and open doors. We don't want to slam doors by an unsavory attitude that serves only to turn people off to the message. If we get in the way of the message because we are not behaving as we ought, then once again we are not glorifying God but ourselves. Therefore, in defending Jesus Christ (and all that goes with this) let's make sure we represent Him honorably so that glory goes to Him in all things. Once we have sanctified Christ as Lord in our hearts, then we are in a position to give a defense of our hope, with gentleness and reverence (1 Pet 3:15).

Our job is to proclaim the excellencies of God (1 Pet 2:9-10) and to glorify Him in all that we do (1 Cor 10:31; cf. Col 3:17). Whatever good we may accomplish finds its value in glorifying God, not men. The Corinthians, who apparently put great stock in the wisdom of men, needed to learn this lesson. Paul indicated that even though the cross is foolishness to men, it is the power and wisdom of God through the cross that saves us from our sins. So when he preached to the Corinthians, he did not come to them "with superiority of speech or of wisdom." Rather, he was with them "in weakness and in fear and in much trembling." His message to them was not "in persuasive words of wisdom, but in demonstration of the Spirit and of power." Why? Paul's answer is straightforward: "so that your faith would not rest on the wisdom of men, but on the power of God" (1 Cor 2:1-5).

To defend Christ with grace means that we are kind in our approach, getting ourselves out of the way, and giving all the glory to God. The power of God's word will hold its own. We need not embellish it or hide it. Let God's power shine through your presentation of His message.

Promote Christ with Righteous Living

Peter wrote that we must keep our behavior excellent among Gentiles (unbelievers), "so that in the thing in which they slander you as evildoers, they may because of your good deeds, as they observe them, glorify God in the day of visitation" (1 Pet 2:12). This teaching coincides with what Jesus taught about His disciples being lights in the world: "Let your light shine before men in such a way that they may see your good works, and glorify your Father who is in heaven" (Matt 5:16). While we recognize that we are far from perfect, we should understand that proclaiming allegiance to God on the one hand and living in a way that betrays this claim on the other hand will create stumbling blocks for others. The consequences of causing others to stumble will not be pretty (cf. Matt 18:6).

In order to live effectively for Christ, people must see beyond us to the Lord Himself. They need to know that it really is the Lord Christ whom we serve (Col 3:24). Therefore, we are to present ourselves to God as living and holy sacrifices (Rom 12:1) with the added privilege: "do not be conformed to this world, but be transformed by the renewing of your mind so that you may prove what the will of God is, that which is good and acceptable and perfect" (v. 2). Our duty to the world is to live like Christ. Not only would we fail God, but we fail those in the world when we try to live like the world.

Peter reminds his readers of the need to be holy. "Prepare your minds for action," he wrote, with our hope fixed on the grace of Christ. We are to be "as obedient children" and "like the Holy One" who has called us. "You shall be holy, for I am holy" (1 Pet 1:13-16). In this light, the best way to offer apologetics to the world is by being holy and completely dedicated to God (Christ sanctified in the heart). This will promote Christ more than the mere words we might say. People need to know that we are different precisely because we are committed to Jesus as Lord.

Make the Most of Opportunities

Paul wrote to the Colossians that we are not only to speak with grace, but we are to be "making the most of the opportunity." We are to walk carefully, "making the most of your time, because the days are evil" (Eph 5:15-16). So once we have sanctified Christ in our hearts and are striving to live holy lives, we should be looking for opportunities to act for the good of others. God's people have been redeemed (bought back out of sin) and purified so that they can be God's special possession, "zealous for good deeds" (Titus 2:14).

"Let us not lose heart in doing good, for in due time we shall reap if we do not grow weary. So then, while we have opportunity, let us do good to all men, and especially to those who are of the household of faith" (Gal 6:9-10). There may be times when it seems that our efforts aren't going anywhere. Perhaps as we deal with people who have questions and doubts, we may feel that all of our discussions fall on deaf ears. The process can get old when it seems that no one is paying attention. Hang in there, Paul says. We will reap the reward for patience in the end.

Why is doing good for others important for apologetics? Because doing good will help open doors for further study. People can see that you are serious about what you claim to believe. You are a helper, looking for ways to be a blessing and benefit to others. You are the one who consistently and proverbially (and literally) helps the older lady across the street. You are the "Good Samaritan" of the parable in Luke 10, not the ones who pass by the other side when someone is truly in need. People will know that you care, and when they know this, they will care more about what you have to offer. Just look for opportunities to help. Be a blessing, and it may surprise you who might be willing to listen as you speak of Jesus.

Now Get Ready

When we are living like we should in Christ and finding ways to help others and do good for them, let's make sure we are ready because sooner or later the questions will likely come. Once again, Peter wrote that Christians must be "ready to give a defense" for the reason of the hope within them (1 Pet 3:15). They may want to know why you live the way that you do. Why are you so sacrificial? Why do you go out of your way to serve others? Why did you engage in that act of kindness? Whatever the particular questions, the point is that you are ready to defend your faith and hope. You should not be terribly surprised when people want to know about it.

Yet what if someone asks you a question that you really don't know how to answer? There are difficult questions after all. How can we be expected to know how to answer all of those? Remember that the primary concern is being able to answer for your hope, which is directly related to the salvation that you have in Christ. Beyond that, however, the issue of dealing with questions we don't know the answer to is a legitimate concern. What should we do?

First, don't panic. No one can be expected to answer every conceivable question that might be asked. There is no way to know exactly what topics or questions may arise in the course of a conversation. Others may indeed throw in some question that seems odd to us. Stay calm.

Second, take the questions seriously. It may be that the others are not really after the truth, but that is not ours to judge, especially so early in a conversation. We need to take the questions seriously and try to respond appropriately. If in the course of the discussion they make it clear that truth was not the goal, then at least you have done what you could.

Third, when a question arises that you don't know the answer to, use that as an opportunity to study. You can easily say something like, "I'm not sure about that answer. Let me study it and let's get back together..." If you do this, though, make sure that you don't put them off. Get back to them. But don't just give an answer that you haven't thought out either. People don't like a know-it-all. When you take the "let's get together again" attitude, you are actually creating another opportunity that may lead to future studies. If the person at this point says, "no, that's okay," then at least you have done what you could. Make every effort to keep studying. Do it with meekness and fear. Again, the attitude is vital. Defending Christ with self-pride is self-defeating.

Never underestimate the value of living a godly life in defending the faith. Let your own life serve as an apologetic to the world. May God bless you as you go out into the world and stand for Him. May God defeat you if you ever try to live against His divine purposes.

Discussion Questions

1. In what way is apologetics part of evangelism?

2. What are the most important tasks in doing apologetics and why?

3. What does it mean to speak with grace? Why is this important for apologetics?

4. How does righteous living promote the cause of Christ?

5. How can we make the most of our opportunities today? Can you come up with a few ideas for how to do good for others in today's world? How will doing these things open doors for discussion?

6. What are we to be ready to do and why?

7. How should we react if someone asks a question to which we don't know the answer?

Who Borrows from Whom?

That the closest parallels to the New Testament miracles all postdate the life of Jesus suggests that if anyone borrowed from anyone else, it was not Christianity from paganism but rather the Greco-Roman religions from Christianity. The more the Jesus-movement grew and spread, the more others would have tried to compete by modeling their holy figures to some degree on the stories of Jesus with which they became familiar.

Craig Blomberg, Can We Still Believe the Bible? 188

Can We Trust the Bible? 20
Part 1

How can we be so sure that what the Bible tells us about historical matters is true? How can we trust that the documents are conveying actual historical and eyewitness testimony about Jesus Christ? Focusing particularly upon Jesus and the Gospels here, the general skeptical assumption today is that the Gospels are accounts made up by later Christians who paint a portrait about Jesus as divine, but do not give a real picture of the true Jesus of history. We are told that we cannot learn much at all about the real Jesus by looking at the Gospels. They might have some historical nuggets in them, but they are not reliable sources for the historical Jesus. How do we even begin to respond?[1]

As a preliminary point, we should recognize that the skeptical arguments are based upon assumptions about what can or cannot be true in history (presuppositions again). These are not demonstrated facts. If our worldview did not permit miracles or resurrection, then we would be required to argue that the Gospel accounts are not accurate history. Our worldview would give us no other option but to come up with another explanation that cannot include the supernatural. Critics have biases that require them to reject anything that involves supernatural activity. We should not be surprised, then, to encounter their skeptical arguments.

Of course, challenging skeptical assumptions does not automatically prove that the Bible gives us an accurate portrayal of the real Jesus. So how can we argue for the reliability of the Gospel records?

---

[1] This begins several essays that ought to be read for a fuller discussion. Any one essay alone cannot cover it all, and even then there is so much more than can be said. The appendix essays, which are longer, cover additional facets of the issues surrounding the believability of Scripture.

The Oral Culture of the 1st Century

First, we need to be aware that before anything was written down, the stories were being told orally. This has caused some to assume that if they were oral, they could not have been accurate.[2] However, orality studies have shown that oral cultures were, in fact, able to maintain consistency in their story-telling.[3] Those who spoke the messages and told the stories publicly were concerned about not straying from the true story-line. They had freedom to use their own vocabularies and personalities, but not to change the core facts. There was an "elasticity of oral tradition."[4] What helped keep them in check were the audiences who were familiar with the stories. Oral cultures had built-in check and balance systems to maintain accurate story-telling. The Gospels reflect this kind of culture, which is one reason we see both similarities and differences in the way the writers conveyed the information. This was perfectly in line with their culture and styles, and does not in any way conflict with the biblical doctrine of inspiration. Further, many have realized that there are fundamental differences between ancient oral cultures and the modern post-Gutenberg print culture where accounts can simply be copied and mass-produced. Failure to see the differences can result in anachronistic fallacies by making modern demands of the written text that the ancient writers never would have considered. If we are going to be fair to the writers, we need to study them within their own cultural context, not ours.

---

[2] Bart D. Ehrman, *The New Testament: A Historical Introduction to the Early Christian Writings*, 4th ed. (New York: Oxford University Press, 2008), 61.

[3] Paul Rhodes Eddy, and Gregory A. Boyd, *The Jesus Legend: A Case for the Historical Reliability of the Synoptic Jesus Tradition* (Grand Rapids, MI: Baker Academic, 2007), 237-68.

[4] Michael R. Licona, *Why Are There Differences in the Gospels?: What We Can Learn from Ancient Biography* (Oxford University Press, Kindle Edition, 2016), loc. 251.

What Historians Want to Know

A basic principle to keep in mind when considering the reliability of the biblical records is that when subjected to the same tests that are used of other ancient documents, the Bible surpasses every expectation. When historians look at ancient documents, there are certain matters that they want to know about the texts. Following we want to give a brief sampling of what types of questions are asked about ancient documents, then see how the Bible fares.

Boyd and Eddy's *Lord or Legend?* provides a good starting point for introducing the types of questions historians want to know about ancient documents. They observe, "When evaluated by the same criteria critical historians typically use to evaluate ancient documents, the Gospels give us many reasons to conclude that the image of Jesus they present is historically reliable."[5] They ask a series of ten questions that reflect what historians want to know when they evaluate ancient documents. The questions can be asked in various ways, and you are encouraged to study these questions in depth as this is very introductory, but the basic issues can be expressed as follows:

1. *Do we possess copies that are reasonably close to the originals?*

Without question, the biblical documents fare better in this area than other ancient documents. We have copies that are much closer to the originals than any other ancient work by comparison. For example, there is a small fragment of the Gospel of John that dates to within 50 years of when the Gospel was initially written. Thousands of fragments and copies exist for the New Testament dating between 50-1500 years from when they were written. Complete copies begin to appear within 300 years (not long at all by ancient standards). Many copies are close enough to the

---

[5] Gregory A. Boyd, and Paul Rhodes Eddy, *Lord Or Legend? Wrestling with the Jesus Dilemma* (Grand Rapids, MI: BakerBooks, 2007), 77.

originals that if the texts were any other ancient source, no one would reasonably doubt their credibility. Nothing else begins to come close to what we have for Scripture. We will look at this more specifically later, but rest assured that this is not an area that critics can complain about. The Bible as a whole is the best attested ancient work ever. Period.

2. Did the authors intend to convey reliable history to the readers?

If the writers were intending to convey fiction, then we would not want to take the Gospels as historical reality. However, if authorial intention is clearly to tell about what really happened, then we must give them the benefit of any doubt. In other words, the normal way of approaching ancient history is to assume that the writers knew what they were talking about unless we have solid reason to discount what they say. Let's see how Luke answers this question:

> Inasmuch as many have undertaken to compile an account of the things accomplished among us, just as they were handed down to us by those who from the beginning were eyewitnesses and servants of the word, it seemed fitting for me as well, having investigated everything carefully from the beginning, to write *it* out for you in consecutive order, most excellent Theophilus; so that you may know the exact truth about the things you have been taught. (Luke 1:1-4)

One cannot seriously read Luke and think that he meant to convey anything other than real, historical information. Notice how he spoke of "things accomplished," "handed down" from eyewitnesses, and the ability to "know the exact truth" about these matters. Luke's intent is clear. However, some believe that the writers intentionally fabricated their material or that they intended to write fiction, primarily on the grounds that the writers include miracle accounts. The assumption simply does not comport with the facts or with what the writers actually claimed. The bottom line is this: if the Gospels did not have miracle stories, no one would be questioning whether or not they intended to convey real history. If our worldview permits the miraculous, we have no reason to question the historical intent of the Gospels.

3. Were the authors in a position to know what they were talking about?

The best situation is when an author was an eyewitness or if he had direct contact with eyewitnesses. Usually, the closer to the events, the better the information will be. Now look at Luke's opening statements again. He had direct contact with eyewitnesses and investigated everything. Matthew was a direct eyewitness, as was John. Mark is said to have written much of what Peter, an eyewitness to Jesus, taught.

Critics argue that eyewitnesses were not involved in the writing of the Gospels, but, remember, their presupposition requires the conclusion. Even if the Gospels were written as late as the AD 70's, the oral tradition went right back to Jesus Himself. There were eyewitnesses still around through most of the first century who could testify. Paul wrote within 20-25 years of Jesus' resurrection and pointed to people who saw Jesus alive again (1 Cor 15). The point is that these were people in a position to know—much more so than modern critics 2,000 years removed from the events in question. Peter wrote, "For we did not follow cleverly devised tales when we made known to you the power and coming of our Lord Jesus Christ, but we were eyewitnesses of His majesty" (2 Pet 1:16). Either this was a direct, blatant lie, or he knew what he was talking about.

Given the wealth of evidence pointing to the idea that they were in a position to write about Jesus, the burden of proof falls to those who want to deny it. If these were any other sources, historians would believe they are generally reliable. There is simply no reason to deny reliability to the biblical writers—unless, of course, our worldview requires a denial of the supernatural.

4. Did the author's bias distort their historical reporting?

But, we are told, the fact that the writers have a bias that they are trying to prove negates their ability to tell the truth about Jesus. Accordingly, the writers wanted to invent a Jesus who was divine, so they put the words in Jesus' mouth and made up miracle stories. Really? We grant that the writers had a motive for telling about Jesus. They were not "academic historians," but were simply followers of Jesus trying to get the message out to a variety of audiences. But does that mean they couldn't tell the truth about Jesus? What would be their motivation for doing this?

Such assumptions would render all history virtually worthless. Why? Because the fact is that most people want to write about subjects that they are personally invested in. Historians today choose topics that they are passionate about. If we used this criterion to deny reliability to the Gospels, we would, by the same standard, deny the skeptics their ability to adequately speak about their views. If being passionate, emotional, and personally involved in a situation makes us unable to tell the truth about it, then we are all in trouble, for there is no such thing as a totally unbiased position. By that criterion, all history is a farce. If anyone is passionate about anything, we'd have to say that the person is incapable of telling the truth about the subject.

Of course, it is possible to distort the history due to bias, and sometimes that does happen. However, that needs to be demonstrated, not simply assumed because skeptics don't like what is being said. Where is the actual counter-evidence? Considering the nature of the history being told—history that would get the writers into serious trouble—what motive would they really have for fabricating it? Why would they risk their lives for stories that they knew were not true?

5. *Are the reports consistent with what we know about eyewitness testimony?*

Another way of asking this question relates to whether or not there are incidental details or casual information included in the accounts that are typically found in eyewitness accounts. The inclusion of such material bolsters reliability. Boyd and Eddy observe:

> What is interesting about the Gospels, however, is that they do include incidental detail while giving us every reason to believe they were intended to pass on historically rooted tradition of actual events of the past. Not only this, but some of this detail has been independently confirmed as reflecting the situation of first-century Palestine—a point that can bolster our estimation of the reliability of these works.[6]

The types of examples given for this include Aramaisms (words and expressions that indicate Aramaic origin, as in Matt 27:46) and the inclusion of personal names. For example, note the name of Cleopas in Luke 24:18. Why is the name even here when it was not necessary to the account? Perhaps his name is here because he became a respected teacher in the early church. This, again, would bolster reliability. Richard Bauckham, in his work on *Jesus and the Eyewitnesses*, presents a compelling case that the use of names in the Bible supports its historical reliability.[7]

The point is that the Gospels contain the types of details that we would expect from eyewitness accounts and traditions that go back to the original sources. Once again, the Bible passes this test. More to follow...

---

[6] Ibid., 102.

[7] Richard Bauckham, *Jesus and the Eyewitnesses: The Gospels as Eyewitness Testimony* (Grand Rapids, Mich.: William B. Eerdmans Pub. Co., 2006).

Discussion Questions

1. How is it possible for people who live in oral cultures to keep their stories straight? Why do you agree or disagree that ancient story-telling might be like the more modern "telephone" game in which people whisper something in another's ear so that by the time it goes through several people it is completely changed? How is the game different?

2. How do you know that the biblical authors intended to convey historical information? Besides Luke 1, what other biblical examples can you identify that indicate historical intent?

3. Why were the authors in a good position to know what they were talking about? How do you think we should judge when someone is in a position to know?

4. How can bias distort reporting? How does distortion happen? How can someone with a bias accurately convey good information?

5. What are signs of eyewitness testimony? How do you think this affects the Gospels?

Can We Trust the Bible?
Part 2

21

Continuing from the previous reading, in which we are introducing the basic questions related to what historians would want to know about ancient documents:

6. Is there "self-damaging" material in the documents?

The point here may be surprising to some. We would think that "self-damaging" material in a document would hurt its credibility, but the opposite is actually true for historical integrity. If a document contains self-damaging material, then it demonstrates that the author's purpose was not to sugar-coat everything and gloss over problems. This, in turn, strengthens the historical credibility, for the author's motive was to tell what really happened. The author had nothing in particular to gain, and he was willing risk hurting his own cause in order to faithfully tell what happened.

Do the biblical documents contain self-damaging material? Yes. Boyd and Eddy provide a sizable list of such instances in the Gospels.[1] Here are a few examples:

- Jesus' own family and friends did not believe in Him. They thought He had lost His senses (Mark 3:21; John 7:5).
- People in Jesus' hometown rejected Him, which affected His miracle-working (Mark 6:2-5).
- His disciples were unable to exorcise demons (Mark 9:18).
- The disciples were sometimes painted in a bad light. They were obstinate and fought among each other (Mark 9:34).
- Jesus was betrayed by a close disciple and another denied Him (Mark 14).

---

[1] Gregory A. Boyd, and Paul Rhodes Eddy, *Lord or Legend? Wrestling With the Jesus Dilemma* (Grand Rapids, MI: BakerBooks, 2007), 108.

- Women were the first to testify about seeing Jesus alive again (Mark 16). Given that the testimony of women was generally not regarded as reliable, it would be unlikely that an author in this time period would make this up if he wanted to put his cause in a favorable light. We'll revisit this later.

Why would Christians who are fabricating stories about Jesus put details in the accounts that would normally be considered a little embarrassing? The Bible does not hide faults or gloss over embarrassing issues. This lends greater credibility to its historical authenticity and trustworthiness.

7. Are the documents reasonably self-consistent and consistent with other documents that tell about the same events?

Internally, if an account of something is filled with inconsistencies, then it won't be considered so reliable. Each Gospel account when considered on its own merits is self-consistent (note: in secular history, even some inconsistency can be expected without a document losing all of its credibility). What critics have more trouble with is how the Gospel accounts relate to each other. There are both similarities and differences, particularly between the synoptic Gospels (Matthew, Mark, and Luke), and these can be controversial. Critics often point to alleged discrepancies between the Gospels to try to minimize their credibility. Some think that the differences "represent irreconcilable conflicts."[2] Of course, much of that depends upon the perspective brought to the discussion and what one will allow as a credible explanation.

Keep in mind that these Gospel accounts were originally meant to be read out loud, not studied silently in an isolated situation like we often do today (since they didn't have multiple copies yet). The

---

[2] Bart D. Ehrman, *The New Testament: A Historical Introduction to the Early Christian Writings*, 4th ed. (New York: Oxford University Press, 2008), 63.

variations that we find are perfectly consistent with an oral cultural context. In fact, the similarities and differences are what we would expect in such a cultural setting.

That said, it is important to recognize the difference between a difficulty and a true contradiction. In logic, the law of non-contradiction says that something cannot be both what it is and what it isn't at the same time and in the same sense. We grant that there are difficulties, but a contradiction means that there are mutually exclusive statements that cannot be reconciled because there are no plausible explanations. Those who charge the Scriptures with error need to be able to show either that there is a clear contradiction or that statements do not comport with reality in some way. However, such charges against the Bible have not been sufficiently sustained. Much of what are considered to be discrepancies are answered by the literary and cultural context of the documents. New Testament scholar Ben Witherington noted, "Taking into account all contextual issues and all conventions that I know of that were operative in the day and time of the NT writers, I have yet to find a single example of a clear violation of the principle of noncontradiction in the NT."[3]

Certainly this topic has a great deal more to it. The "synoptic problem" has been the topic of many books, articles, and debates. For our present purposes, however, the answer to the question as to whether the documents show reasonable consistency is "yes." They demonstrate the kind of consistency that would engender basic trust in virtually any other type of historical document.

8. *Are the recorded events believable?*

Probably here more than with any other question, the role of presuppositions comes back into play. Whether or not we consider

---

[3] Ben Witherington III, *The Living Word of God: Rethinking The Theology of the Bible* (Waco, Tex.: Baylor University Press, 2007), 117.

something believable depends on what we allow as part of our worldview reality. To the naturalist, miracle stories will not be believable because the supernatural is not allowed in the first place. But let's ask a few questions here:

Is it believable that there is a God who created humankind? If so, then is it believable that this God would want to communicate with us, particularly if we have been made in His image? If God would want to communicate with us, then is it believable that He, as Creator, has the power to impact and influence events in this world? Is it believable that God is sovereign and can intervene in creation at His will? If these things are not believable, then what are believable alternatives? Our answers to these questions will determine whether or not we think miracles are believable. Yet, if we believe in God, then what is the problem? Paul asked Agrippa, "Why is it considered incredible among you if God does raise the dead?" (Acts 26:8) Once we accept the premises that God exists and that He is sovereign, why should there be a problem with the idea that He can actually do something in His creation?

Once people get over that philosophical problem with the existence of God, the question really boils down to this: is there evidence that events have occurred which find a more reasonable explanation by an acceptance of the supernatural than by purely natural processes alone? If so, why wouldn't the events be believable?

9. Is there other literary evidence that help to establish the reality of the events recorded in the examined documents?

People often ask if there are other documents aside from the Bible that corroborate the events we read about in the Bible. Indeed, it is desirable to have other literary evidence. But it is important to keep in mind a few thoughts.

First, we are dealing with ancient history, which means there will not be a great amount of literary evidence for any particular event.

This is true not just about Bible events. Any ancient event, which includes anything and anyone from Alexander the Great to Julius Caesar, is not going to have overwhelming literary support. Much of what is written about ancient history comes from sources that were much later than the people or events in question. Generally that is not a problem for ancient historians.

Second, keep in mind that the Gospels were written as independent accounts.[4] They were not written together and initially passed around together. They stand as separate, autonomous records (even if some form of interdependence can be established, they are still separate sources). We can add to this the record of Paul in 1 Corinthians which, as we shall see later, serves as an early, independent source all on its own.

Third, with all of that in mind, the fact remains that there are other sources that corroborate some of the events in the Bible.[5] These sources include Thallus, Pliny, Seutonius, Tacitus, Josephus, and others. These are non-Christian sources, and later we will survey some of them to see what they wrote. They do not deal with many specifics recorded in the Gospels, and they do not write much about Christ, but what they do corroborate is significant. Through their writings we can confirm that Jesus existed, had a brother named James, was considered divine by His followers, was crucified, and that something else important happened that caused His disciples to flourish. In other words, the core elements of the gospel message are essentially confirmed by non-Christian writings. And there is more.

This does not mean that these non-Christian writers sounded like Christians defending Christ. Indeed, they were concerned sometimes about what to do with Christians. Given that the movement started by Jesus was relatively limited, confined at first to

---

[4] See the chapter *Using the Bible to Prove the Bible* for more discussion.

[5] See the chapter *What Have Others Said?*

a very small territory, and thought of as just another sect of the Jews, it is significant that anyone paid attention at all in the greater Roman Empire. Yet Christians started making a big impact on that ancient world, and the Romans paid attention. Boyd and Eddy ask, "how are we to plausibly account for a movement arising in Palestine, within a first-century Jewish context, that was centered on the faith that a recent, wonder-working, wise teacher who had been crucified was actually the saving Messiah and, in fact, the very embodiment of Yahweh himself? Saying that this movement was rooted in a legend simply relabels the problem; it does not solve it."[6]

10. *Does archaeology help to shed any light on the recorded events?*

If we are looking for an ancient rock with Jesus' name carved in it, we will be disappointed. Archaeology is not usually going to give us "hard facts." Whatever evidence we have will need to be interpreted and people will work out the implications of those interpretations. The fact is that archaeology in itself will prove little, and it is best not to overstate a case.

Even so, there are some important archaeological discoveries that help shed light on New Testament times. Most of the findings will be in the form of items like pottery, coins, and ruins of buildings. What most of the findings do show is that the world we read about in the New Testament is consistent with what we find in archaeology. Occasionally we find names. For example, a stone containing the name of Pilate confirms that he was in a position of power in Palestine at the time the Gospels indicate. Also, an ossuary (bone box) with the name of Caiaphas has been found, and most believe that this is the same High Priest we find in the Gospels. The point is that the archaeological findings in antiquity are consistent with what we read in the Gospels. This is about all we

---

[6] Gregory A. Boyd, and Paul Rhodes Eddy, *Lord Or Legend? Wrestling With the Jesus Dilemma*, 135.

can expect, so there is nothing here that should cause concern. Many studies are available and they continue to be updated.

What about Opponents?

We've indicated that there were non-Christian writers who had to acknowledge certain aspects of Christianity. Yet another question is raised here. Given the claims of Christianity, one would think that early opponents of Christianity would try to falsify the accounts. Could they do it?

They certainly would have had a motive for trying to disprove Christianity. Sometimes opponents said some malicious things about the disciples (for example, some rumors went around that Christians killed and ate babies in some perverted rituals, as discussed in the late 2nd-early 3rd century work *Octavius of Minucius Felix*). But opponents never could disprove the central claims of Christianity—namely, the death and resurrection of Jesus Christ.

When Peter stood before the Jewish audience on Pentecost, he made a very bold claim that could have easily been falsified if opponents had the means to do it. Yet they could not. "Men of Israel, listen to these words: Jesus the Nazarene, a man attested to you by God with miracles and wonders and signs which God performed through Him in your midst, just as you yourselves know —this *Man*, delivered over by the predetermined plan and foreknowledge of God, you nailed to a cross by the hands of godless men and put *Him* to death. But God raised Him up again, putting an end to the agony of death" (Act 2:22-24). If ever there was a time to falsify Christianity, this was it. Peter indicated that Jesus did His works in their midst, and they knew it. How easy it would have been to say, "What are you talking about Peter? Jesus did no such thing"! But they didn't do it. They couldn't do it. Instead of being stopped, the gospel message went out all over the world.

Can we trust the Bible? If we can trust any documents of antiquity, we can trust the Bible.

Discussion Questions

1. Besides the examples given, can you think of other "self-damaging" material recorded in the Bible? How does this help the Bible's credibility?

2. What is a real contradiction? How does this differ from a difficulty?

3. What is the major issue that affects whether or not someone accepts that the events recorded in Scripture are believable? What would you say to someone who thought the events are not believable at all?

4. How do other sources help establish biblical credibility? How critical is it that other sources are available?

5. What would you expect archaeology to tell you? How can we say that archaeology rarely gives "hard facts"? Do you know of any archaeological finds that support what we read in the Bible?

6. Why do think that early opponents of the Christians had such a

From Original Autographs to Copies **22**

Do we have reason to believe that the biblical documents we possess today are what the writers actually wrote? Skeptics would have us to think that there is so much corruption in the biblical manuscripts that we just cannot have confidence in them. The evidence, however, tells another story. Moreland observed, "Most historians accept the textual accuracy of other ancient works on far less adequate manuscript grounds than is available for the New Testament."[1]

We would love to be able to look at the original autographs of the New Testament—those actual texts penned by the writers—but the fact is that we do not have those originals. This bothers some because it brings up the question of how we can know whether or not the copies and translations that we do have accurately reflect the originals. Perhaps there has been such corruption of the text that we cannot have confidence that we are actually reading the word of God. How do we really know?

Enter the task of textual criticism. "Criticism" may sound bad, but in reality the field of textual criticism is all about getting to the original wording of the text in question. It is the study of copies and manuscripts of a text in order to determine what the originals said. The question here is not, "Is God's word true?" but rather, "What is the actual text of God's word?" This field of study is necessary because of the fact that we lack the original texts and because no two copies agree in every single instance. That may make it sound as though it is a hopeless effort, but bear with me as we see that we really do have solid reason to believe that we have an accurate text today.

---

[1] J.P Moreland, *Scaling The Secular City* (Grand Rapids: Baker Books, 1987), 136.

Textual criticism is applied to both Old and New Testaments, but for our purposes here, and particularly because of our interest in establishing the Gospels as reliable, we are going to focus on the New Testament. How can we be sure that the New Testament we possess today accurately gives us what was originally written?

Number of Manuscripts and Copies

If people pressed the idea that we cannot know what the New Testament really said because we no longer have the originals, "then we must deny that most facts of ancient history can be recovered, because whatever doubts we cast on the text of the New Testament must be cast a hundredfold on virtually any other ancient text."[2] The reason for this is that the New Testament manuscripts are much closer to the originals than any other text of antiquity. Further, there are more New Testament manuscripts than any other ancient work. "The New Testament is far and away the best attested work of Greek or Latin literature in the ancient world."[3] This is not debatable.

"Since the New Testament manuscripts outstrip every other ancient manuscript in sheer number and proximity to the autographs, the New Testament should be regarded as having been accurately transmitted."[4] The numbers are being updated continually, but consider that together there are, roughly, 5,800+ partial and full handwritten Greek Manuscripts that have been found dating between the second and sixteenth centuries AD, and

---

[2] J. Ed Komoszewski, *Reinventing Jesus: How Contemporary Skeptics Miss The Real Jesus and Mislead Popular Culture* (Grand Rapids, MI: Kregel Publications, 2006), 70.

[3] Ibid., 71.

[4] Clay Jones, "The Bibliographical Test Updated." Oct. 1, 2013. http://www.equip.org/article/the-bibliographical-test-updated/. Accessed May 5, 2017. For more continually updated information, see the following websites: New Testament Virtual Manuscript Room (http://ntvmr.uni-muenster.de/home); The Center for the Study of New Testament Manuscripts (http://www.csntm.org).

that number keeps growing as new discoveries are made. In contrast, the average number of extant manuscripts for other classical works is about twenty. For example, for Tacitus (AD 56-120), there are less than 40 surviving manuscripts with the earliest one dating to the ninth century AD. For Livy (59 BC-AD 17), there are about 150, with a time span of 400 plus years to the earliest copies. For Homer's Iliad, there are less than 1,800 manuscripts with the earliest dating about 400 years from the original. Homer's Iliad is the closest work of antiquity to matching the New Testament, but even it doesn't come close. The New Testament has thousands of manuscripts, with the earliest fragments showing up in the 2nd century AD. There is even a fragment of John 18 that appears less than 50 years from the original. Complete copies of the New Testament show up within 350 years. Nothing in antiquity compares.

But wait! There is more. We are talking only about Greek manuscripts so far, which alone exceeds the average classical writings by nearly 300 times. Now add to this Latin, Coptic, Syriac, Armenian, Gothic, Georgian, Arabic, and many other versions of the New Testament that also date to within a few hundred years of the originals. Latin versions were well in production within a couple hundred years of the originals. In fact, Latin manuscripts alone number over ten thousand and date from the third century. "All told, the New Testament is represented by approximately one thousand times as many manuscripts as the average classical author's writings."[5] Skeptics, of course, want to minimize this point, but the sheer force of the evidence speaks for itself.

And there is still more. Did you know that if all of the manuscripts and copies of the New Testament were lost, we could reconstruct virtually the entire New Testament based upon the writings of the early church fathers? They quoted Scripture incessantly and so much that the New Testament stays intact just from them. In fact,

---

[5] Komoszewski, *Reinventing Jesus*, 72.

"The quotations by the church fathers of the New Testament number well over a million—and counting!"[6] Once again, no other ancient classical work has anything like this.

Because of the evidence, F.F. Bruce observed: "The evidence for our New Testament writings is ever so much greater than the evidence for many writings of classical authors, the authenticity of which no one dreams of questioning. And if the New Testament were a collection of secular writings, their authenticity would generally be regarded as beyond all doubt."[7] Notice how Bruce touched on the problem of presuppositions, also. When it comes to the manuscript evidence for the New Testament, we are in great shape.

What about Variants and Differences?

"So who cares if there are lots of manuscripts when all of those copies have thousands of variants and errors in them? That proves they can't be reliable." Skeptics can sound pretty intimidating when they say, "There are thousands and thousands of errors and variants in those manuscripts." How do we respond to this?

First, it is correct to say that there are thousands and thousands of variants in the manuscripts. Is this a huge problem? Not really. There are approximately one hundred thirty-eight thousand words in the Greek New Testament. With the thousands of manuscripts, there are multiple thousands of variants that exist, but just counting the quantity of variants does not consider the whole picture. The question is, what is the quality of those variants? How many of these variants really affect the meaning of the text? Basically, the variants and problems in the manuscripts can be categorized as follows:[8]

---

6 Ibid., 81.

7 F. F. Bruce, *The New Testament Documents: Are They Reliable?* (Grand Rapids, MI: Eerdmans, 1987), 15.

8 Komoszewski, *Reinventing Jesus,* 54-63.

- Spelling differences and nonsense mistakes;
- Minor differences that have no effect on translation, or that involve synonyms.
- Differences that do affect the meaning but are not viable (meaning that they do not have enough support to take seriously); and
- Differences that affect the meaning of the text and are viable.

Spelling and Nonsense. The majority of those thousands and thousands of variants are spelling differences. A name might be spelled differently, but it is clearly the same person. A word might have an extra letter or is missing a letter. Copyists occasionally misspelled a word. Big deal, right? But these spelling differences do not viably affect the meaning of the text in any way. Sometimes the differences are "nonsense," meaning that a tired or inattentive scribe wrote something that makes no sense. This type of error is rarely repeated by the next scribe since it is easy to detect. Again, the meaning of the text remains intact. If there is a question about the reading in one text, there are many other texts to which it can be compared.

Synonyms and Unaffected Translation. Next are differences that do not affect the translation or that involve synonyms. For example, sometimes the Greek uses an article when English does not (as in names—"Mary" or "the Mary"). Sometimes the article in a manuscript is dropped or added, but it makes no difference for translation purposes. There are also transpositions, when the order of words in the Greek is changed (e.g., "Jesus Christ" or "Christ Jesus"). But since Greek meaning is based upon inflection (suffixes and prefixes, etc.) and not word order (as in English), the meaning is the same and the translation is mostly unaffected. Some differences involve the use of synonyms. In that case, the translation might be affected somewhat, but the meaning will typically still be the same.

Meaningful but not viable. Then there are meaningful variants that are *not* viable. This might be a reading that is found in only a single manuscript or a family of manuscripts, but the evidence is clearly against the reading being original. Many of these are found in later manuscripts and probably the result of a scribal addition. "There is little chance that one late manuscript could contain the original wording when the textual tradition is uniformly on the side of another reading."[9] Some scribes were prone to try to harmonize the Gospels, for example, so they might bring a phrase from one Gospel over into another, and usually that is obvious.

Meaningful and viable. Finally, there are the meaningful variants that are also viable. In this case, the meaning is affected to a degree and it changes the reading of the text and translation. There are a few of these, but the two most notable are John 7:53-8:11 and Mark 16:9-20 (most translations have a footnote about these). This is not the place to get into all of the issues about these particular passages, and I would not minimize the importance of the issues raised in those passages, but there are some important matters to note:

1. *No fundamental truth is lost if these passages are not authentic.* For example, the compassion of Jesus is taught in multiple places, and so is baptism. No major doctrine hinges only on these passages. The same is true of the other passages that fall into this category. So if we are discussing this with people who bring the problem up as given in their translation notes, we can simply go to several other places to show the same doctrine. "You don't want to use Mark 16? Okay, let's go over to Acts 2, or Galatians 3, or Colossians 2, or Romans 6, or..." You get the idea. All of those other passages are not in question, so it is easy enough to use them when teaching someone who is uncomfortable with what their marginal notes tell them about a verse. There is no need to get hung up on them.

---

[9] Ibid., 59.

2. This last category is by far the smallest, comprising only *about 1 percent* of variants. These would be the ones that matter the most, but they are found the least. All other variants either do not affect the translation significantly enough to be a problem or they are simply not viable enough to be a real issue.

So, while there are many variants found in the thousands of manuscripts, the bottom line is this: *only about 1 percent are meaningful and viable, and not one of them affects any foundational doctrine or belief!* In other words, "we can be certain that no truth of Scripture or Christian doctrine rests on a doubtful text."[10] In the bigger picture, they are not nearly the problem that skeptics would have us to believe. Christianity is not seriously at stake even in the most problematic of passages.

Between the Greek manuscripts, the versions and early translations, and the writings of the early "church fathers," we truly have been blessed with what some call an "embarrassment of riches." "The wealth of material that is available for determining the wording of the original New Testament is staggering."[11] We believe that God has had a hand in the preservation of His word. Yet the work of textual criticism has been able to successfully demonstrate that the original words of Scripture are available to us. The evidence is overwhelming. Once again, if skeptics doubted what we have with the Bible, they will not be able to trust any ancient work. The Bible surpasses all else, and not just by a little. We can confidently read our biblical text, knowing that what we have is what the authors— and ultimately God—intended to convey.

Greenlee notes: "If twenty manuscripts of a book of the New Testament were selected at random and distributed to twenty people who could read them, any person in the group could read

---

[10] J. Harold Greenlee, *Scribes, Scrolls, and Scripture: A Student's Guide to New Testament Textual Criticism* (Grand Rapids, Mich.: W.B. Eerdmans Pub. Co., 1985), 38.

[11] Komoszewski, *Reinventing Jesus*, 82.

from his manuscript and the others would have no trouble in following him in their manuscripts. Indeed, the verbal agreement between the various New Testament manuscripts is actually closer than the verbal agreement between many English versions of the New Testament."[12] If skeptics wish to fight Scripture, they will need to take their battle elsewhere.

Discussion Questions

1. Why is "textual criticism" important for establishing the text?

2. How much of a problem is it really that we do not have the original manuscripts of the Bible?

3. Can you list the different types of manuscript evidences that we have available for the New Testament? How important are each of these?

4. Why is the fact that there are so many variants not the problem skeptics make it out to be?

5. Discuss passages like John 7:53-8:11 and Mark 16:9-20. If someone said to you, "The notes in my Bible say these passages are not in the earliest manuscripts, so you should not use them," what would you say? Discuss the practical issue of how to deal with the question of Mark 16 and the doctrine of baptism.

6. Exercise suggestion: break up a class into a couple of groups and give each group a different passage (preferably one they might not be familiar with). Have each group (perhaps even each individual in each group) copy the passage by hand and intentionally insert errors (as discussed in the text) into the copy. Then switch the copies between groups and have them figure out together what the original text said. This shows, on a very small scale, what textual critics have to do.

---

[12] Greenlee, 38.

The Canon of Scripture 23

What follows is a brief overview of the canon of Scripture. The issue is a complex one with a great deal of history and debate. So let this serve as a small introduction. The word *canon* really comes to us via the Greek *kanon*, meaning "a rod or ruler." Also, the Hebrew word *kaneh* means "a stalk," "reed," or "rod," and sometimes was used in connection with measurement (Ezek 40:3, 7). The stalk might be taken and used like a measuring stick or ruler today, and so that became a standard by which other items were measured. Paul used the term metaphorically in Galatians 6:16, desiring peace and mercy upon those who walk "by this rule." So the term is used to refer to a standard by which to live our lives.

So, what are we really talking about? Basically, we are talking about the books that belong in Scripture as the rule for our faith. The list of books we know of as the Bible is considered by Christians to be the authoritative writings that came from God and are now a collection of sacred Scriptures. This collection then is the standard or rule by which everything else is judged.[1] In practical terms, this is the Bible from Genesis to Revelation.

That there is a recognized list of authoritative books is one matter. The real question is how that list of books was determined. How do we know we have the right books? Who decided all of this? And, "Didn't I hear that the Church came up with the canon several centuries after Christ?" There is a great deal of confusion. How can we start to make sense of it all? While this issue deserves more space than we can devote here, let's look at a few principles.

---

[1] Norman L. Geisler, and William E. Nix, *From God to Us: How We Got Our Bible* (Chicago: Moody Press, 1974), 62.

Is the Church the Mother of the Canon?

Many argue that the canon was something that a council decided on a few hundred years after Christ. This can make it sound like a bunch of self-authoritative guys arbitrarily voted into the Bible what books they happened to like the best. However it happened, many are under the impression that the canon did not exist until the fourth century and then it was mostly a political decision made by a few very biased people. The "Church" simply invented the canon.

That idea is very misleading. To be sure, there is a relationship between the church and the canon. In fact, it is true to say that the church existed prior to the list of New Testament books. When the church was established, the New Testament books weren't written yet. Paul, who is responsible for thirteen of those books, was not even converted until a few years later. Christianity was already spreading before any of the New Testament books were written. So doesn't this prove that the church invented the canon? Not really.

The underlying principle that determined canonicity of the books is the same principle that stood under the verbal preaching of the apostles while Christianity was in its earliest stages: inspiration. That is, before any of the books or epistles were written, there was still inspired teaching that came from God. This was in oral form until it was put down in writing. So the issue is not whether the church is the mother of the canon, but whether teaching that came from God (whether spoken or put in writing) was what gave birth to the church. That is, the reason the church came into existence was because there were inspired apostles of Jesus who preached the gospel message (Acts 2). Inspired teaching was not the product of the church, but the church was the product of the inspired message. That message just had not yet been written down. So even though the church preceded the written books, the church was not the mother of the books as if those books were produced outside of inspired teaching. Though the fourth century councils spelled out the limits of canonical books, making what we would consider as formal pronouncements, these groups "did not impose any innovation on the churches; they simply endorsed what had become the general consensus of the churches of the west and of the greater part of the east."[2] Again, they recognized what had already been accepted.

Why the Need for a Canon?

There may be several reasons why a list of authoritative books was important. First, it would seem common sense to desire to have the writings of those prophets and apostles who spoke on God's behalf. Those concerned about doing God's will would want to *know* God's will, and if that will had been set down in writing, they would surely want to know about it. The desire to have the will of God seems sufficient.

Another important reason for the canon was the need to differentiate between false claims and truth claims. There were plenty of false teachings being spread by the second century, particularly among Gnostics. Even in the first century, Paul had warned that his readers not be shaken from their composure or disturbed "by a spirit or a message or a letter as if from us" (2 Thess. 2:2). There were letters being passed around that were not from the apostles, so it was important to make those distinctions. Which ones came from the apostles?

By the mid-second century Marcion, a Gnostic heretic, compiled his own canon. This "gave impetus to the need for a set of authoritative (canonical) documents to offset the false teaching" and by the end of the second century, the "apostolic fathers" were frequently quoting the New Testament documents as Holy

---

[2] F.F. Bruce, *The Canon of Scripture* (Downers Grove: InterVarsity Press, 1988), 97.

Scripture.[3] Evidence indicates that by the second century most of the New Testament books were in widespread circulation.[4] By AD 200, lists were already appearing (e.g., the Muratorian Canon) containing a bulk of the New Testament books. We would do well to remember that the New Testament books were written by different authors (some were obviously the same authors) at different places and times. They were then passed around, copied, and re-circulated, so it would be unreasonable to expect that they all be copied and compiled as a complete unit as early as the end of the first century. They were in fact being circulated, just not as one "book" like we have available to us now. That did not stop Christians from recognizing their value and authority.

Principles of Canonicity

The first principle for recognizing the canonical authority of a book has already been mentioned: *inspiration*. But let's think a little more about it. Geisler and Nix state the point well:

> The books of the Bible are not considered God-given because they are found to have value in them; they are valuable because they are given of God—the source of all value. And the process by which God gives His revelation is called inspiration. It is the inspiration of a book which determines its canonicity. God gives the divine authority to a book and men of God receive it. God reveals and His people recognize what He reveals. Canonicity is determined by God and discovered by man.[5]

---

[3] Grant R. Osborne, *3 Crucial Questions About The Bible* (Grand Rapids, Mich.: Baker Books, 1995), 47.

[4] Martin Pickup, "Canonicity of The Bible," in *Reemphasizing Bible Basics in Current Controversies*, ed. Melvin D. Curry (Florida College Annual Lectures, Temple Terrace, FL: Florida College Bookstore, 1990), 174-78.

[5] Geisler and Nix, *From God to Us: How We Got Our Bible*, 66.

Saying that a book belongs in the canon of Scripture is simply to say that it a book that came from God in the first place. In other words, there is a canon in the mind of God and a canon as recognized by men.[6] Ideally, the two are the same. The book doesn't get put in the canon first, then recognized as coming from God. As Witherington noted, "I do not think it is either historically or theologically true to say the church chose and formed the canon, and that it is first and foremost the church's book. No, the church recognized that these books told the apostolic truth, they spoke the word of God, and so they wished to preserve them in a collection."[7] Again, the church does not have the authority over the Scriptures; the Scriptures have the authority over the church. It wasn't the canonization process that bestowed authority upon a book. Rather, it was the understanding that the book already had authority that led to its being recognized as belonging in the canon. "In other words, God had already inspired the books, and the canonical decisions simply recognized that fact. Canon is not the same as Scripture; rather, it simply distinguishes those books God has inspired from those he has not."[8]

How did they recognize a book as being inspired? *Apostolic authority* was primary. That is, a major determining factor of inspiration has to do with a book's association with the apostles of Jesus—not just that an apostle wrote it, but that an apostle is somehow associated with the book or the author. So, for example, evidence indicates that Peter stood behind the Gospel of Mark and Luke had a close tie with Paul. Jesus invested His apostles with authority (John 14:26; 15:26-27; 16:12-14; Matt 18:18; Luke 22:30, etc.). This was done with the expectation that they would teach and

---

[6] James R. White, *Scripture Alone* (Minneapolis, Minn.: Bethany House, 2004), 103.

[7] Ben Witherington III, *The Living Word of God: Rethinking the Theology of the Bible* (Waco, Tex.: Baylor University Press, 2007), 118.

[8] Osborne, *3 Crucial Questions about The Bible*, 49.

deposit the will of God for later generations. "Therefore, the question which Christians have always needed to ask is this: What apostolic, inspired writings are available to us? Whatever apostolic teaching is available would be what Christ said we should follow as our standard, i.e., the New Testament canon."[9]

Another factor for canonicity had to with what the book taught. From the time of the apostles, Christians recognized the difference between orthodox, apostolic teaching from that teaching which strayed. Books that were "accepted by all orthodox churches or by the vast majority of churches" were typically accepted because of the recognition of authority as traced to the apostles.[10] An epistle that contained spurious teaching or that was not universal in its acceptance would be rejected.

Jesus is the Real Key

"In the same way that the integrity of scripture is settled with finality once one accepts the teachings of Jesus on the subject, the canon of the Bible is settled with a similar appeal to the very words of Jesus."[11] This is true of both the Old Testament canon and New Testament canon. Most of what we have been discussing in this overview is connected to the New Testament, but the underlying principles are the same. The Hebrew canon is alluded to by Jesus in Luke 24 when He referenced "all that the prophets have spoken" and "all the Scriptures" (vv. 25-27, 44-45). Though Jesus does not list all the books of the Old Testament, there must have been a corpus of authoritative books that they understood as "all the

---

[9] Pickup, *Reemphasizing Bible Basics in Current Controversies*, 169.

[10] Osborne, *3 Crucial Questions About The Bible*, 48.

[11] Tom Hamilton, "How Can I Be Sure The Bible Includes The Right Books?," in *Challenges of Our Times*, ed. Dan Petty (Temple Terrace, FL: Florida College Bookstore, 2008), 87.

Scriptures." Further, when Jesus referenced "the Law" or "the Law and the prophets," the people would have known what Jesus was talking about—those books that constituted their canon. These books correspond to the same ones we have today (though the groupings and order were likely different).[12]

Perhaps it is easier to see how Jesus gave His approval to the Hebrew Scriptures (the Old Testament), but how did He do this for the New Testament since those books were not yet written? As earlier indicated, Jesus chose the apostles, and in doing so He anticipated the inspired teaching and dissemination of what would become the New Testament. His authority is implicit in the writings of the apostles. So any study of the canon of the New Testament must still find roots in the authority of Jesus Christ. From the beginning, Jesus intended to invest authority in chosen messengers who would spread the gospel to the world. It is from this that the New Testament canon would be born. Scott sums up the process well:

> The 66 books of the Bible were not chosen by any council or synod. They were chosen by God on the basis of their divine inspiration, and this choice was verified by Jesus' endorsement of the Old Testament and His anticipation of the New Testament. The Jews of the Old Testament and the Christians of the first centuries did play an important role in the process of canonization. That role was the collection and recognition of these writings. The criteria for such recognition was not arbitrary or accidental, but was based on the belief that those books were given by inspiration from God.[13]

---

[12] Ibid., 91.

[13] Shane Scott, "The Problem of The Canon," in *A Place to Stand*, ed. Ferrell Jenkins (Temple Terrace, FL: Florida College Bookstore, 1999), 144.

The process of canonization was not without controversy, but that is for further study. Some books were hotly contested (for example, who wrote Hebrews?). But it was that process of debate that can actually give us confidence that they did not treat the matter of God's word lightly or arbitrarily. "God values both the content and the collection and has insured that the canonical books of the Old Testament and New Testament are exactly what He wanted us to have."[14] The process was complex, but the great care exercised by the men involved, coupled with God's divine providence, leads us to conclude by faith that we have what we are supposed to have so that we can properly function as the people of God today.

Discussion Questions

1. Why do you think a list of authoritative books would be important for Christians?

2. Why did we say that the Church was not the "mother" of the canon? What does this mean?

3. What are the most important principles for determining canonicity and why?

4. Why is Jesus the key to the canon of the Old Testament? How can this be established?

5. How does Jesus anticipate the New Testament?

---

[14] Doug Burleson, *Once Delivered Forever Established: The Certainty of the Holy Scriptures* (Vienna, WV: Warren Christian Apologetics Center, 2017), 49.

Issues in the Inspiration of Scripture

24

Paul wrote, "All Scripture is inspired by God and profitable for teaching, for reproof, for correction, for training in righteousness; so that the man of God may be adequate, equipped for every good work" (2 Tim 3:16-17). The word *theopneustos* (inspired) occurs only here in Scripture and literally is "God breathed." In a way, it might be better understood as "expired," that is, God breathed out the Scriptures. The point is that Scripture came from God. Because Scripture came from God, the word is profitable and able to fully equip God's people with what they need to do for Him.

That Scripture affirms inspiration is indisputable. Many places make the claim (see 2 Pet 1:21; Heb 1:1; 1 Cor 2:10-13, etc. along with the numerous times prophets said something like, "Thus says the Lord..."). Here we are considering the *nature* of Scripture. Also, we should keep in mind that when we discuss terms like *inspired* and *inerrant*, we are talking about the original documents, not copies and translations. We believe that we have copies and translations that accurately reflect the originals, but we are careful to distinguish originals from copies and translations.

A Survey of Claims and Arguments

A survey of passages relating to inspiration shows that we can affirm the following:

1. *Verbal inspiration.* The idea is that God guarantees that the words of Scripture convey exactly what He desires. Since God's will is expressed to us in "sound words" (2 Tim 1:13) and "words of the faith" that provide "sound doctrine" (1 Tim 4:6), then we ought to be concerned about the words in Scripture. The concept of verbal inspiration does *not* require the idea that God merely dictated

words and thereby bypassed the personalities and vocabularies of the writers He chose to convey His message. It does, however, mean that the words of Scripture as expressed through the vocabularies and personalities of the writers accurately tell us what God wants us to know.

2. *Plenary inspiration.* "Plenary" refers to "all" Scripture, not just portions of it. This includes direct words from God (such as through the prophets), but also means that the record of what others said or did is accurate (including what the devil said, for example).

3. *Trustworthy.* When God inspires something, it is right. *Inerrancy* is another term that is often used to speak of this. The point is that we can trust that Scripture correctly gives us what God wants without leading us down a false path (see the chapter on inerrancy).

4. *Confluent.* God used human agency and human language to convey His message. There are human elements and personalities so that we have God's message, but in words that can be considered both human and divine (1 Cor 2:10-13). For example, we have the word of God, but also the "words of Isaiah" (Luke 3:4). The human writers were not merely robots, but they operated with their personalities still intact. They had their own styles and vocabularies (as you can see from a basic reading of the Gospels).

Arguments for the proof of inspiration have been many and varied. It is not enough that claims to inspiration are made. God has not asked us to be gullible; He invites a look at the evidence. The Bible provides ample evidence of its inspiration. Some of this evidence includes:

1. *The Uniqueness of the Bible.* The Bible is unique in many ways. Written over a 1500-1600 year period, with 40 plus human authors from various walks of life, cultures, perspectives, and

circumstances, the Bible contains a thematic unity "that defies naturalistic explanations."[1] The main themes throughout the Bible are God's glory and His plan for the salvation of mankind. Such lofty themes with so great a harmony are difficult to explain from a naturalistic worldview.[2]

2. Prophecy. Hundreds of prophecies throughout the Scriptures, with their respective fulfillments, witness to the inspiration of Scripture. Only the true God can infallibly declare "events that are going to take place" (Isa. 44:7). A study of the prophecies of Christ and their fulfillment demonstrate the divine nature of Scripture (see the chapter *The Divine Messiah*).

3. Accuracy. Not only are the prophecies accurate, but so are the historical narratives. The Bible has been attacked both on historical and scientific grounds, and it has been the victim of historical reconstruction. However, these attacks usually come from subjective biases, not objective evidence. Even those of more skeptical persuasion are admitting that the Bible "must be treated seriously as a historical source."[3]

4. The validation of Jesus Christ. Ultimately the validation of Jesus Christ is the most important piece of the puzzle. If Jesus is Lord, then what He says about Scripture should be authoritative. The evidence of Jesus and His views toward Scripture are probably the most significant line of argumentation for both inspiration and inerrancy (see the chapter on inerrancy).

---

[1] Gregory A. Boyd, and Edward K. Boyd, *Letters from a Skeptic* (Wheaton, Ill.: Victor Books, 1994), 130.

[2] For a detailed consideration of the uniqueness of Scripture, see Josh McDowell, and Sean McDowell, *Evidence that Demands a Verdict: Life-Changing Truth for a Skeptical World* (Nashville, TN: Harper Collins, 2017), 3-20.

[3] Hershel Shanks, "The Biblical Minimalists: Expunging Ancient Israel's Past," *Bible Review*: 52.

How Did God Inspire?

The question is how God kept the human personalities intact while inspiring them to write what He wanted. Several theories have been given to help explain this. Geisler and Nix give us a breakdown:[4]

1. Two main theories teach that the Bible *is* the word of God: first is the dictation theory (the men were like mechanical robots) and second is the theory that God inspired only ideas and the men put the ideas down in their words. Some have argued perhaps a combination of the two.

2. Some have argued that the Bible *contains* the word of God: the *illumination* theory is that God granted deep insight to holy men and they wrote with a mix of erroneous ideas and folklore of the day. The *intuition* theory is that there is no divine element to Scripture at all. Men were "inspired" like any modern writer or musician and just used their own intuition and feeling.

3. Some have argued that the Bible *becomes* the word of God through personal encounter. It is not God's word by itself, but only when one "encounters" it and it becomes personal. The more extreme view, as represented by Rudolph Bultmann, is the idea that the Bible was written using the mythology of its day. To understand it, one must "demythologize" it to get to its core message of God's love (without the history meaning anything since it is irrelevant and its history cannot be known).

As readers can probably figure, most of the approaches are pretty subjective in nature and they often make the interpreter the final authority rather than God.

---

[4] Norman L. Geisler, and William E. Nix, *From God to Us: How We Got Our Bible* (Chicago: Moody Press, 1974), 17-21.

So how did God do it exactly? Within the context of believing that the Bible *is* the word of God, the answer is simply this: we don't really know. This is not a cop out. The basic reason for saying this is that the Bible nowhere tells us *how* God did it. The Bible does not give a "systematic theology of inspiration." So anything we say about the "how" will end up being speculative. If we have reason to believe that God "moved men" to speak and write His word (2 Pet 1:21), then we should be content to leave the *how* up to Him.

What Does Inspiration "Look Like"?

Since "we are not given an explanation of how inspiration works," we should recognize that inspiration "looks like what we have in the text, however diverse."[5] We must avoid the danger of taking our modern ideas of what we think inspiration ought to be, and instead let the Bible show us what inspiration looks like. What does that mean?

1. It means that we need to let the text speak for itself. We don't want to place faulty expectations onto the text then complain when it doesn't meet those expectations.

2. It means that any doctrine relative to inspiration must be derived from the text through careful exegesis and study. The problem with any systematic theology is that of creating the paradigm first then superimposing that back onto Scripture.

3. It means accepting the variety and difficulties that are present in the text. We recognize that there are dilemmas and difficulties that we may not always understand or have exact answers for. This doesn't mean there are contradictions, nor does it destroy the overall unity of Scripture, but neither are the texts always so cut and

---

[5] Ben Witherington III, *The Living Word of God: Rethinking the Theology of the Bible* (Waco, Tex.: Baylor University Press, 2007), 10, 48.

dry that we can "pat answer" everything to death. Scripture forces us to grapple with difficulties, and we are better off when we work to understand as opposed to lazily passing over difficult passages.

4. It means recognizing that what the Bible teaches is inspired, but there are statements in the Bible that God did not inspire. There is a difference between recording something said by an actual prophet who is speaking for God on the one hand, and recording something that someone said or did who was not inspired on the other. In the latter case, *the record is inspired* and guarantees an accurate accounting of what was said or done, but certainly doesn't mean that what an uninspired person said is necessarily true. In fact, it may even be an example of something God does *not* want us to believe or practice. It may be a way of God showing us through human frailty how not to act or speak. Maybe God is revealing something about a rebellious nature through the problems that the characters show.

For example, was Satan inspired when he lied? We have the record of it. What of Ananias and Saphira? What of Peter when he denied Christ? Were Eliphaz, Zophar, Bildad, and Job inspired, then rebuked? Clearly they spoke things that were not God's words or message, but inspiration guarantees an accurate record. We need to be careful to interpret within context of who is speaking and under what circumstances.

5. Inspiration involved the author's use of other sources at times. Perhaps we have this superimposed idea that if they were working by inspiration, any use of other sources would somehow nullify that, as if there could be no inspired choosing and editing at all. Read Luke 1:1-4. Doesn't Luke affirm the very point of investigating others, going to eyewitnesses, and recognizing sources already in place? Who says inspiration cannot extend to this process, also? Why couldn't God have moved these men to find the right sources and select the proper materials? Why would we demand otherwise?

Paul quoted from a Greek philosophers (Acts 17:28; Titus 1:2). This shows the principle that all truth is God's truth, even when others speak it or discover it. Epimenides, whom Paul quoted, was not inspired, but Paul's use of the statement was. Ezra (7:11-26) quoted from Persian archives. The fact that they used these sources does not nullify inspiration. Rather, inspiration involved the process of God's oversight as they investigated, learned, and incorporated the right materials into their work. God can guide them to the truth of what others may have said or written. How exactly? Only God knows. But we do know that Paul and Luke both affirm it by inspiration and this is what it looks like.

6. The Scriptures look like documents that belong in the ancient historical context. This is obvious, but the point to make here is that the Bible should not be judged on the grounds of modern standards of historical or scientific precision. The Bible fits well with the nature of ancient historiography and therefore needs to be judged on that basis and not by modern standards.

7. Scriptures show diversity, not contradiction. Sometimes that diversity is difficult to understand, such as some issues in the synoptic gospels. The synoptic problem looks at both similarities and differences between Matthew, Mark, and Luke and tries to understand their relationships to each other. But while we are trying to understand these Gospels together, let's be reminded that they were not all put out together initially. Matthew ought to be studied on its own terms, as well as Mark and Luke. Each had its own purpose and design, and while we want to see them together, we also want to see them independently to understand how they got the message of Christ out to their respective audiences. There is a reason we have four gospel accounts and not just one, so we should respect that level of diversity.

8. The word of God functions through translations. When we talk about something like verbal inspiration, we don't want to leave the

impression that only experts in the original languages will be saved. The Scriptures show that a translation can also be called the word of God so long as it accurately conveys what the original said. For this reason it is important to go to the original for translation purposes, but when that translation is given in another language, the result is still the word of God in written form. How do we know this? The New Testament uses translations (from Greek and Hebrew) when giving Old Testament quotations. Examples of this are throughout the New Testament.

What is the point of all this?

1) Let's not presume to speak for God when He hasn't given us all the information we might like to have. In His wisdom and knowledge He has given us His word in the form of human language and personality, while still retaining His character.

2) Let's be content to let the Bible be what it is, to speak as it is, with those areas that force us to think, fight, and grapple with truth and our own frail understanding. It reminds us of our humanity, our tenuous nature and weaknesses. It reminds us of our need to be modest and humble in our own interpretations and conclusions (cf. Prov 3:5).

3) If the Scriptures are inspired, then they are reliable and we can go to them for faith and practice. Authority is inherent in Scripture because God is the Author of it all. Scripture thus gives us a standard by which to live and measure our lives.

Discussion Questions

1. What do you think when you hear the word "inspiration"? How should it be understood with respect to the Bible?

2. Why should we avoid trying to state exactly *how* God inspired the Bible?

3. Why is it important to affirm the inspiration of Scripture? What would be consequences of not accepting inspiration?

4. Why is it important to distinguish something God said directly from something that is spoken or done by another that is still recorded in Scripture?

5. How can we say that translations can still function as the inspired word of God?

Mistaken Claims

It is easy to claim that the Bible contains inconsistencies and contradictions. Such claims are made on media talk shows, on Internet blogs and websites, in conversations among friends, and in best-selling books. But making such claims is not the same thing as proving them. In fact, many such claims stem solely from the reader's misunderstanding of a writer's purposes; there is no error in what the author is saying. To avoid mistaken claims, readers should attend to the purposes of the biblical authors.

Douglas S. Huffman,
Are the Contradictions in the Bible?
From *In Defense of the Bible, 269*

Issues in Biblical Inerrancy **25**

It would be difficult to overstate the significance of biblical trustworthiness. Eternal matters are at stake, so people cannot be neutral about the Bible. If it is not trustworthy, then it is not God-worthy. If the Bible is true, then those who deny it will reap the eternal consequences for denying God and His revelation. If the Bible is erroneous and untrustworthy, then the hope that the Bible gives for life is forever lost. There can be no hope where there is no ability to trust.

Throughout the history of Christianity, faith in the inerrancy of Scripture has been the common view, but no longer is that the case. The doctrine of inerrancy is subject to many misunderstandings. Primarily, the doctrine needs to be defined within the context of truth. When people spoke or wrote in the name of God, they had to speak or write the truth. If they did not, then they were not considered to be true prophets of God. Truthfulness is what inerrancy is really about. The decision to be made over inerrancy is whether or not the writers of Scripture are "truthful and trustworthy in the various nuanced ways they wanted to present the truth on a variety of subjects, taking into account their intents, limitations, and freedoms."[1] "Trustworthy" is probably the better term because "inerrancy" is open to more misunderstanding.

The historical case for biblical trustworthiness is like the case for inspiration. It would be a mistake to argue that the Bible is inerrant just because the Bible makes spectacular claims. By that logic, imagine how many false prophets and teachers who claim to be inspired should be accepted on those same grounds. No one should

---

[1] Ben Witherington III, *The Living Word of God: Rethinking the Theology of the Bible* (Waco, Tex.: Baylor University Press, 2007), 117.

be so gullible, and God wants people to be more discerning (cf. 1 John 4:1). Even so, the claims of Scripture cannot be ignored or passed off as irrelevant. The case for trustworthiness must be built upon what Scripture claims, but without stumbling over the fallacy of circular reasoning. If Jesus Christ is the basis for both inspiration and inerrancy, then how can the case proceed?

First, the Bible can be approached as a historical record without having to first prove it is inerrant. The basic premise is that the biblical documents reliably convey historical information. This, in itself, is not making a case for inspiration or total inerrancy. Rather, it is recognizing that the documents should be accepted as providing good information. Likely, were it not for the supernatural elements (miracle accounts), most historians would accept the general history of Scripture without much objection.

Second, once the Bible is allowed historical footing, then the information regarding Jesus Christ must be taken seriously. This information is sufficient to lead people to the conclusion that He is Lord. The case for Jesus as Lord finally rests in the resurrection argument. Based upon the claims and works of Jesus, and demonstrated by the resurrection, the historical data leads to this conclusion. Again, if the objection here is based upon a bias against the supernatural, then the unbeliever's philosophy, not actual history, is driving the objection.

Third, once the evidence for Jesus as Lord is established, then so is the evidence for a high view of Scripture. If Jesus really is who He claimed to be, then this provides the grounds for accepting his absolute authority. From here, it is a matter of accepting what Jesus claimed concerning Scripture. Scripture is trustworthy not because we superimpose our own ideas onto the Bible, but because Jesus Christ, the authoritative Lord, says it is. He is the basis for teaching both inspiration and inerrancy, which is, in turn, the basis for biblical authority.

The bottom line is that if people can accept Jesus as Lord based upon the historical evidence for the resurrection, then the case for inspiration and inerrancy of Scripture can be properly presented through His Lordship. History precedes the theology. If Jesus is Lord, with absolute authority, then what He says about Scripture is authoritative and should be adopted as the believer's position.

Is this line of reasoning begging the question? The fallacy of begging the question involves sneaking the conclusion of the argument into the premises. This argument is not begging the question because the conclusion drawn (that the Bible is inspired and inerrant) is not part of the premise (that the Bible contains reliable historical information). Instead, this argument moves from history to the Lordship of Jesus, and from the Lordship of Jesus to a high view of Scripture. Each step, of course, can be developed much more fully, and each point is open to investigation and historical inquiry, which takes the issue out of the realm of subjective whim or an unreasonable dogma. If the history can be accepted, then the conclusion that Scripture is inspired and inerrant (completely trustworthy) can be well-defended on the grounds that this was the position of Jesus.

What did Jesus say about Scripture?

If Jesus is Lord, then His attitude toward Scripture will give us the best insights for how to view Scripture. Since the New Testament had not yet been written while Jesus walked the earth, the Scriptures to which He appealed are the Hebrew (Old Testament) Scriptures, which had been completed by His time. Would Jesus have regarded these Scriptures as holy if they contained error? How did Jesus treat Scripture?

First, Jesus treated the Scriptures as teaching truth about what happened. This includes Creation, Adam and Eve (Matt 19:4-5), Cain and Abel (Luke 11:50-51), Noah (Matt 24:37-39), Sodom and

Gomorrah (Luke 10:12), Lot and his wife (Luke 17:28-32), and Jonah (Matt 12:39-41). Jesus verifies particular events, even details of what happened, including David eating the showbread (Matt 12:3-4), the wilderness serpent (John 3:14), Elijah going to the Sidonian widow (Luke 4:25-26), and Elisha healing Naaman (Luke 4:27). Jesus used the Hebrew Scriptures historically, without calling into question the truth of the accounts.

Second, Jesus used the Scriptures authoritatively for doctrine and ethics. He consistently appealed to what was written in the Scriptures as the standard for action and faith. For example, in His rebuke of the Sadducees, He told them that they were mistaken, "not understanding the Scriptures nor the power of God." He then made His argument on the resurrection by saying, "have you not read what was spoken to you by God" followed by the quote from Exodus 3:6 (Matt 22:29-32). He equated what was written (the Scriptures) with what was spoken by God. The error here was not with the Scriptures, but with the Sadducees' understanding of them. In all of Jesus' dealings with error, He consistently used the Scriptures authoritatively and denounced the false interpretations of them (cf. Matt 15:1-9). The error was always with men's views and never with the Scriptures. Jesus' consistent use of Scripture implies His unreserved acceptance of inspiration and trustworthiness (inerrancy).

Third, Jesus used the Scriptures as the means to overcome temptation. His replies to Satan began with, "It is written," indicating a firm conviction that Scripture is able to do what God desired (Matthew 4:1-11). Note here that both Jesus and Satan used Scripture as the highest court of appeal. Why would Jesus appeal to "what is written" unless He considered it a true standard?

Fourth, Jesus taught that Scripture cannot be broken (John 10:35). He taught that nothing would pass from the law until all was fulfilled (Matt 5:17-20). He also taught that all things written in "the

Law of Moses and the Prophets and the Psalms must be fulfilled" (Luke 24:44). This three-fold designation incorporated the entire Hebrew Scriptures. As He was going to the cross, forbidding His disciples to fight, he asked, "How then will the Scriptures be fulfilled, which say that it must happen this way?" (Matt 26:54) All of these statements help verify the smaller details of Scripture. Even Rudolph Bultmann argued, "Jesus agreed always with the scribes of his time in accepting without question the authority of the (Old Testament) Law."[2]

Though the New Testament had not been written yet, the same basic process of understanding Jesus' view toward the new is in play. Jesus promised His chosen apostles that they would receive all truth when the Spirit came to them (John 16:12-13). The apostles received it and confirmed it. Jesus essentially put His stamp of approval on the New Testament before it came about (see also the chapter on the canon). The point, however, is that Jesus maintained a high view of Scripture as the authoritative, trustworthy word of God. Whatever He believed and taught about Scripture is what Christians today ought to believe and teach because they are following their Lord.

The Synoptic Problem and Alleged Discrepancies

There is a difference between an error and a difficulty; yet these are sometimes confused. Someone reads two passages that, on the surface, seem to be contradictory. The problem is not easily settled as the solution does not become quickly apparent. This is bothersome, and the person lets that struggle stew to the point of questioning whether or the not the Bible is true.

---

[2] Rudolph Bultmann, *Jesus and the Word*, trans. Louise Pettibone Smith and Erminie Huntress Lantero (New York: Scribner, 1958), 61. Bultmann was a 20th century liberal scholar who argued that the Gospels must be "demythologized" and that we cannot really know much about the historical Jesus. Yet even he recognized that Jesus treated the Old Testament Scriptures as authoritative.

The Synoptic Problem is the critic's playground. It has to do with the relationship between Matthew, Mark, and Luke. There are multiple differences and similarities between the Gospels, and there needs to be some way to understand how these work together. Why does one account present a different order of events from another? Why do they give different details? Why do they contain some of the very same material, but then also contain unique material? Superficially, one might look at differences between accounts and charge the Bible with errors. Whether or not that type of charge is fair or accurate is another matter. That there are differences is obvious. That the differences constitute errors is hotly debated. Differences between accounts do not automatically mean they contradict. Witnesses to events can provide completely different, independent accounts, yet not necessarily be in error. They can supply additional details or provide a different perspective, but this is no reason to charge them with contradicting each other.

Ancient writers were not as concerned about chronology as many are in the modern world. Matthew, Mark, and Luke do not always present their information in the same way or in the same order. Those who argue for biblical errors on the basis of the way the ancient writers presented their materials are guilty of forcing a modern assumption back onto an ancient way of thinking. Exact chronology was not an issue for ancient writers like it is for historians in the western academic world.[3] The same event that is given in a chronological order different from other accounts does not constitute a historical error unless it can be shown that the writer did not have other reasons for putting it in the order he did.[4] The writer may have had in mind a topical or a theological ordering for his events. The ancients had no problem with this, and synoptic

---

[3] Paul Rhodes Eddy, and Gregory A. Boyd, *The Jesus Legend: A Case for the Historical Reliability of the Synoptic Jesus Tradition*, 433.

[4] Witherington III, *The Living Word of God*, 117.

differences are expected in a world in which oral presentation was the norm. Differences do not destroy biblical integrity.

The scope of this present study does not permit a full treatment of the Synoptic problem or alleged discrepancies in the Bible as a whole, but a few observations are in order:

First, many alleged discrepancies are settled by studying the given passages in their own context (historically and literary) and letting them speak for themselves (Scripture interprets Scripture). Context often answers the critic who is often too quick to ignore that given context. This includes taking into account the target audience (Jewish, Gentile, Roman, etc.) and the character of the orally dominant culture that allowed for variety in reporting events.

Second, words are often used in differing senses, and sometimes translations fail to bring this out. For example, one might try to press a contradiction between Acts 9:7 (where Paul's co-travelers heard the voice of Christ) and Acts 22:9 (where they didn't "hear"— that is, understand—the voice). The answer should be readily seen in the different ways in which "hear" can be used.

Third, figurative language in the Bible must be recognized for what it is and not pressed too literally. Metaphors, figures, and colloquialisms are common in every language. The goal is to get to the intended meaning of the text, whether expressed figuratively or literally. The interpreter's task is to be discerning and read the text appropriately.

Fourth, some difficulties will come from modern ignorance of the times and culture in which the Bible was written. Trying to understand biblical culture through the eyes of modern culture will be confusing at best. But they knew their own culture back then much better than modern critics can know it, so we need let them speak within their own cultural settings. We should not expect them to think, talk, and tell stories the way 21st century American academics do. We live in a very different world. Imagine going into a foreign country and judging their culture by modern American standards. Would that produce fair judgment?

Fifth, sustaining the charge of contradiction is not an easy task. A contradiction exists only when two statements negate each other because they are mutually exclusive. There is no legitimate way to reconcile them. However, when different senses are intended at different times, there is no contradiction (e.g., Prov 26:4-5).

Putting it All Together

In trying to put together a reasonable apologetic for inerrancy, the following principles should be kept in mind:

1. How people view the question of inerrancy largely depends upon their own perspectives and presuppositions. If people approach the Bible already believing that there must be errors, then they will "find" errors, even when there is no warrant for it. If they approach Scripture with an open mind, however, letting the Bible speak for itself, they will encounter difficulties with an attitude seeking resolution and harmony.

2. Given that the biblical claims are attended by eyewitness testimony, Scripture should be considered reliable until proven otherwise. We generally assume someone is telling the truth until we have good reason to disbelieve what is claimed. Our own courts of law recognize that a defendant in a criminal trial is innocent until proven guilty. If eyewitnesses testify to the innocence of someone, there must be solid, objective evidence presented to overturn the presumption that the eyewitnesses are telling the truth. Our courts also recognize that the evidence in such a case must be "real" and not merely the prejudicial ranting of juries looking to convict no matter what. Given that the writers of Scripture are making claims based upon eyewitness testimony, they

should be considered reliable until solid evidence to the contrary is presented.

3. Copies and translations are not the original documents. Inerrancy, properly speaking, applies to the original documents. While there are copies and translations that accurately reflect the originals, mistakes found in them do not equate to mistakes in the inspired text. Questions of inerrancy should be studied in light of the original intentions of Scripture. This is important because it gives us the target for text criticism, translations, and interpretation.

4. The time in which the Bible was written is very different from today. We should not expect the writings to sound like modern histories or scientific treatises. Studying the Bible with modern presuppositions often results in anachronistic (out of time) fallacies.

5. Jesus is the key to how Scripture should be viewed. Once Jesus is accepted as Lord, then the issue boils down to how Jesus Himself looked at Scripture. If He considered God's word to be infallible and inerrant, then Christians today have the warrant for accepting the same views. This, also, aids in accepting the authority of Scripture as a whole.

Jesus asked His disciples if they were going to quit following Him as others had done. Peter responded, "Lord, to whom shall we go? You have the words of eternal life, and we have believed and have come to know that you are the Holy One of God." (John 6:68-69). Peter's statement was one of faith in the Lordship of Jesus and in His words. We need the same faith today.

What difference does it all make anyway? Since we only have flawed copies and not the original manuscripts, why is inerrancy or trustworthiness important? Believing that the Scriptures are inspired and inerrant is the theological conclusion we can draw after first recognizing the identity of the risen Lord. Once we can accept the Lordship of Jesus, which only requires accepting historical claim (1 Cor 15), then the rest can fall into place. Yet the doctrine does become important for how we view and accept the rest of Scripture.

For further discussion, consider the following chapters.

Discussion Questions

1. Why should "inerrancy" be thought of in terms of "trustworthiness"? What difference does it make whether or not we accept the trustworthiness of Scripture?

2. How does the case for inspiration and inerrancy proceed, based upon the Lordship of Jesus?

3. How did Jesus treat Scripture? Can you think of other passages not in this lesson that show Jesus' respect for Scripture?

4. How should Jesus' view of Scripture affect our view of Scripture?

5. When does a contradiction exist? How should we approach alleged contradictions in Scripture?

Using the Bible to Prove the Bible   26

The charge is sometimes made against Bible believers that they just use the Bible to prove the Bible. The idea is that this is circular reasoning and, therefore, erroneous. They want other sources outside the Bible that verify it, not the Bible itself. Once they set the Bible aside as being unable to testify for itself, they can then argue that there is no evidence for the central events that are the foundation of the Christian's faith—primarily the resurrection and appearances of Jesus after He was confirmed dead. Since such other sources are lacking and the only source we have to use is the Bible itself, the very book that we are supposed to prove in the first place, then our case is said to be non-existent. Therefore, using the Bible to prove the Bible proves nothing, is circular, and should be rejected.

On the surface, that sounds like a convincing point against those who believe the Bible to be true. After all, we would make a similar case against an author who wants to use only his own book to prove his case, and since he is the only one making a particular claim, then his case is built on circular reasoning and therefore unconvincing. It would indeed be circular for someone to say that the proof of his position is that he said so. However, there are some flawed assumptions in this objection that need attention, and much of the problem revolves around a misunderstanding (intentional or not) of the nature and composition of the Bible.

Many Books

First, the Bible is made up of many books, not just one. This is one of the most basic facts about the Bible, but its implications are tremendous, and people tend to forget. Ironically, to argue that the Bible cannot be used to prove itself actually assumes that there is a unity to the Bible as a whole—a unity that critics want to deny.[1] They cannot have it both ways. If Matthew cannot be used to verify anything about Luke, or vice versa, then the assumption must be that they are unified in a way that somehow negates their ability to be used independently. Why would this be assumed? Matthew and Luke did not sit down together and write in unison or collusion. They are separate works. Mark is different from Matthew and Luke, and even if, as is usually assumed, Matthew and Luke used Mark some, that still does not explain their divergences from Mark. Regardless, there is nothing wrong with writers using other sources (as do most modern authors), and Luke even indicates that he did just that. Even so, their works are not clones of each other, as even a casual reading reveals. Even if there were some literary dependence, this would not negate the point. Add to this that "dependence may also be an illusion resulting from 'a natural overlap' in oral tradition or the presence of terms that would be common even if all four Gospels" were independent.[2] In other words, they are telling the same story and using the same terminology that would have naturally grown out of an oral tradition.[3] What we see in the four Gospels is exactly what we would expect from oral traditions that were then written down.

Matthew, Mark, Luke, and John are all first century documents. They were not compiled together into a single entity when they

---

[1] While I have encountered this argument and given responses to it, this particular essay was written after reading the cited article. I am making a couple of the same points, but with some added thoughts. See Michael C. Patton, "You Can't Use the Bible" to Prove the Bible and Other Stupid Statements. Parchment and Pen. Sept. 10, 2013. Web. <http://www.reclaimingthemind.org/blog/2013/09/you-cant-use-the-bible-to-prove-the-bible-and-other-stupid-statements/>

[2] Michael R. Licona, *The Resurrection of Jesus: A New Historiographical Approach*. Downers Grove, IL: IVP, 2010. p. 207.

[3] As Wright says, "It is of course virtually impossible for four sources to tell essentially the same story without using any of the same words." (*The Resurrection of the Son of God*, 589)

were written. Further, Paul and Peter are two more authors who wrote first century documents independently of the Gospel accounts and each other. Their works were not compiled together until later (the canon of Scripture is another issue, but is not a factor for dealing with this objection). Therefore, to argue that these documents cannot be used to help verify or prove each other would be like compiling the works of several different authors today, putting them into one volume, then arguing that they cannot provide any witness for one another because they are all in one book and some of them use the same terminology. The argument is fallacious because it ignores the fact that the Bible is a collection of many books written by many authors over several years, all dating to the first century and earlier. They are not just one book written by the same person.

History and Inspiration

Second, the objection conflates historical claims with claims of inspiration. We aren't using the claims of the Bible's inspiration in order to prove inspiration. That would be a flawed procedure because of the nature of that type of claim. Rather, we start by looking at the historical claims just as we would consider the historical claims of any other ancient works. If the historical claims bear out, then talk of inspiration may later follow. Consider, for example, the opening lines of Luke's Gospel:

> Inasmuch as many have undertaken to compile an account of the things accomplished among us, just as they were handed down to us by those who from the beginning were eyewitnesses and servants of the word, it seemed fitting for me as well, having investigated everything carefully from the beginning, to write it out for you in consecutive order, most excellent Theophilus; so that you may know the exact truth about the things you have been taught.

Notice that there are no claims of inspiration here (which is not the same as saying there are no marks of inspiration in the book or no reason to accept it as inspired). Instead, these are historical claims that need to be taken first with that intent in mind. Further, this opening statement is in no way akin to a fairy tale opening, and to try to turn it into one is disingenuous and an abuse of historical texts. Luke writes of "things accomplished among us" and that which was "handed down to us by those who from the beginning were eyewitness." He speaks of "investigating everything carefully from the beginning" so that "you may know the exact truth" about what happened. Luke's clear intention is to tell the truth based on what really happened in the presence of eyewitnesses. His method was one of careful investigation. For someone to say that we cannot use Luke's account to help verify something in another book assumes that the history must somehow be flawed. To say that we cannot use Luke historically is to call into question every work of ancient history. Why, then, do skeptics call this into question? The answer lies not in counter-evidence of the time, but in a presupposition against the supernatural activities attributed to Jesus. "A major reason some scholars doubted the Gospels to begin with was that they report miracles, which modern Western critics felt could not be attributed to eyewitnesses."[4] If nothing supernatural were being recorded, we suspect that the account would be considered a perfectly good historical source by most historians.

There is a fundamental difference between the claims of history and the claims of inspiration. The claims of history simply speak to what actually happened; the claims of inspiration speak to the character and ultimate origin of a work (i.e., is God ultimately behind it?). We are capable of studying the historical claims without first having to prove inspiration. Studying the historical claims is the same as if we were studying the claims of any other ancient authors. What the

---

[4] Craig S. Keener, "The Historical Reliability of the Gospels," In *Come Let Us Reason: New Essays in Christian Apologetics.* ed. William Lane Craig and Paul Copan. B&H Publishing, 2012 (Kindle Ed. Loc. 2015).

truth of these claims may imply about inspiration is another study that can be taken up after first considering the history. For example, the resurrection claim is a claim about what happened: did Jesus really die and was He later seen alive again? Why or how He was raised can be considered after the first question is answered, and we cannot assess the character of the text until we first know what is being stated. If He was seen alive again, then that historical claim needs to be seen for what it is. The objection that we cannot use the Bible to prove the Bible fails to see the difference between the historical claims and the reasons why the events happened as they did. We must start with the claims (what happened) before we can consider anything else (what those claims mean), and several sources document the same claims. Dismissing them out of hand due to presuppositional biases does not bode well for honest, historical investigation.

Unbelievers in a Better Position?

Third, the objection assumes that unbelievers in the ancient world were in a better position to tell the truth about those events than were believers. Skeptics may argue that bias distorts historical reporting, but they need to recognize that they are defeating their own arguments by this objection, for they, too, fall under the same scrutiny of bias. Even so, their assumption is that since the biblical writers all were passionate and defended Jesus Christ, then somehow their testimony must be flawed. Instead, we need the witness of unbelievers to testify to the very same events. This concept, however, stacks the deck unfairly because if the unbelievers testified to the very same events (e.g., that Jesus was, in fact, seen alive again), then they would be believers in the reality of the events and therefore disqualify themselves from their own witness. Such is absurd. This would be like saying that the only viable historians of an event are those who are opposed to the events in the first place. We recognize that "enemies" can provide important evidence (and they do such even in the documents under question), but requiring that unbelievers be the ones who verify all the details is beyond reasonable.

That said, there are other ancient writers who verify certain aspects of the Gospels.[5] Josephus speaks of James, John the Baptist, Pilate, and Jesus, for example. Other historians and officials spoke of some of the people and referenced certain events like the crucifixion. We cannot expect unbelievers to argue for the resurrection of Jesus. They do speak of certain "mischievous" beliefs of Christians, and clearly the growth of the church was based upon a belief in Jesus' resurrection. They reference enough to infer that the Gospel writers did not just fabricate their accounts, which ought to be enough to promote further investigation into those accounts. Interestingly, the first century documents compiled in the Bible do record how the enemies of Jesus recognized what happened. Would these records count only if they are recorded in another work written by an unbeliever?

If the authors of the Gospels were in a position to know what they were talking about, and if they make clear that their intent was to tell what really happened, then they need to be considered on their own merits as would any ancient author writing about events of their time. To deny the Gospel writers this courtesy is to do so out of presuppositions against what they write about rather than out of the weight of actual evidence. To give the Gospel writers the same courtesy we would give to any other ancient author requires that we take their historical claims for what they are.

Potential Conflicts?

Fourth, as referenced earlier, using one book to help testify about events recorded in another book does not require proof that there are no points of conflict or differences anywhere between the accounts. A study of alleged contradictions and discrepancies can come later, but the initial veracity of well-testified events does not require that all accounts of it agree perfectly and flawlessly in every

---

[5] See the chapter, "What Others Have Said."

detail. If this is made an *a priori* requirement, then, again, nothing in any ancient account can be trusted. Historians do not say, "Before we can believe this event, all accounts of it must be proven flawless and with no differences." Witnesses in a court room might differ on some details, but if they all agree on the primary issue at hand, then a jury can still reach a conclusion beyond a reasonable doubt based on their testimony.

For example, the accounts of the sinking of the Titanic differ in the peripherals. Licona noted,

> The sinking of the Titanic is a good example. Many eyewitnesses claimed that the ship broke in two just prior to sinking, while other eye-witnesses claimed it went down intact. Investigations by both American and British governments immediately after the maritime disaster concluded that the ship went down intact. However, when the Titanic was found and examined in 1985, the team concluded that the ship had indeed split apart and that this had occurred prior to it sinking.[6]

Even though the witnesses differed, no one concluded that the Titanic did not sink. No one thought, prior to finding the actual ship, that the event did not happen simply because eyewitnesses differed in their accounts. The core story was the same and all agreed. It sunk. There was no need to doubt that.

Are we saying that the Bible contains a bunch of contradictions? Not at all, though the skeptics do argue such. We are talking priority of historical reporting, and for the purposes of answering this particular objection, it is not necessary to prove that there are no contradictions in the accounts. If several different documents agree on principle historical events, then we recognize a high probability that those events really happened. In fact, differences in

---

[6] Licona, 67.

peripherals will usually strengthen the evidence for the core events. As William Paley put it, "The usual character of human testimony is substantial truth under circumstantial variety."[7]

When it comes to Scripture, all the Gospel accounts testify to the death and resurrection of Jesus. Paul provides a fifth witness. If they all agree on the same core events (and they do), then we can speak of these events as being historical without being sidetracked by other questions about how much detail they all agree on. Again, the study of those similarities and differences (e.g., the Synoptic Problem) can come later, and we believe that there are reasonable answers that are available. However, this is secondary, for Paul writes that the death, burial, resurrection, and appearances of Jesus are of "first importance" (1 Cor 15:1-4). Even without the Gospel accounts, skeptics must still grapple with Paul, for even they admit that he wrote 1 Corinthians within 25 years of the events in question. Paul wasn't just pulling these ideas out of a hat, but was appealing to what was already well established by eyewitnesses. Since several first century documents all agree that these events occurred, then either we accept these as historical realities or we reject them because of our worldview biases. Yet they cannot be easily or honestly dismissed. If these events did not occur, then whether or not the accounts differ would be irrelevant anyway. Therefore, a skeptic arguing that there are contradictions does not change the principle historical case for the resurrection of Jesus, but is, rather, a diversion that draws attention away from the central case of the Gospels, which involves essential historical claims upon which they all agree.

Conclusion

The objection that we cannot use the Bible to prove the Bible is built upon fallacious assumptions about the nature and composition of

---

[7] William Paley, *A View of the Evidences of Christianity: In Three Parts.* Ed. by Richard Whately (NY: James Miller, 1865), 336.

the Bible. Since the Bible is comprised of many books written by several different authors and not compiled until later, since their central claims are historical in nature, since they were in a position to know what they were talking about, and since the authors agree on the central claims, then there is no reason why these first century texts cannot be used to provide testimony to help verify each other. Such is the way we would use any other ancient sources, whether compiled into one book later or not. After all, there is a reason why these works were compiled as they are. Let's start with their central claims and see what they tell us.

Discussion Questions:

1. Why would skeptics argue that we cannot use the Bible to prove the Bible?

2. Why does the fact that the Bible is comprised of many books important as part of an answer to the challenge?

3. What is the difference in the nature of historical claims compared to the nature of claims about inspiration? Why is this distinction important?

4. Why is it important to begin with the historical claims before assuming inspiration?

5. Why would skeptics argue that we should have other sources outside the Bible? How can we respond to this?

6. What is the central historical issue, and why is this issue so important?

7. Why is is not necessary to prove there are no contradictions before seeing the historical value of the Gospel claims?

Notes of Correspondency

Between the letters which bear the name of Saint Paul in our collection and his history in the Acts of the Apostles there exist many notes of correspondency. The simple perusal of the writings is sufficient to prove that neither the history was taken from the letters, nor the letters from the history. And the undesignedness of the agreements (which undesignedness is gathered from their latency, their minuteness, their obliquity, the suitableness of the circumstances in which they consist to the places in which those circumstances occur, and the circuitous references by which they are traced out) demonstrates that they have not been produced by meditation, or by any fraudulent contrivance. But coincidences, from which these causes are excluded, and which are too close and numerous to be accounted for by accidental concurrences of fiction, must necessarily have truth for their foundation.

William Paley, Evidences of Christianity

Undesigned Coincidences   **27**

In 1851, J. J. Blunt published a work called *Undesigned Coincidences in the Writings Both of the Old and New Testaments: An Argument of Their Veracity.*[1] William Paley, in his *A View of the Evidences of Christianity,* also spoke of undesigned coincidences.[2] I had not looked into this until I heard the argument used by Dr. Tim McGrew, a philosopher and apologist.[3] I owe several of these points to him, particular with respect to the examples in the gospels. I claim no originality here, but am grateful for the attention drawn to these examples. Since my introduction to these, Dr. Lydia McGrew (Tim's wife) published a work in 2017 on undesigned coincidences, entitled *Hidden in Plain View: Undesigned Coincidences in the Gospels and Acts.*[4] For deeper studies, I encourage the reader to consider these works in more detail.

What is meant by "undesigned coincidences"? Tim McGrew writes,

> Sometimes two works by different authors interlock in such a way that would be very unlikely if one of them were copied from the other or both were copied from a common source. For example, one book may mention in passing a detail that answers some question raised by the other. The

---

[1] J.J. Blunt, *Undesigned Coincidences in the Writings Both of the Old and New Testaments: An Argument of their Veracity* (NY: Robert Carter and bros., 1851).

[2] William Paley, *A View of the Evidences of Christianity: In Three Parts.* Ed. by Richard Whately (NY: James Miller, 1865

[3] Tim McGrew, *Internal Evidence for the Truth of the Gospels and Acts* (outline), Feb 2012. <http://apologetics315.s3.amazonaws.com/files/03-internal-evidence-for-the-truth-of-the-gospels.pdf> Accessed July 3, 2017.

[4] Lydia McGrew, *Hidden in Plain View: Undesigned Coincidences in the Gospels and Acts* (Chillicothe, OH: DeWard Publishing Co., 2017).

two records fit together like pieces of a jigsaw puzzle. Fictions and forgeries aren't like this.[5]

Lydia McGrew defines an undesigned coincidence as "a notable connection between two or more accounts or texts that doesn't seem to have been planned by the person or people giving the accounts. Despite their apparent independence, the items fit together like pieces of a puzzle."[6]

"Coincidence without design" is the way Blunt described this phenomenon. It is the idea that there is so much circumstantial "coincidence" that it begins to become incredible to deny the veracity of the accounts. As Blunt says, "It does not require many circumstantial coincidences to determine the mind of a jury as to the credibility of a witness in our courts, even where the life of a fellow creature is at stake."[7]

Blunt points out the fact that coincidence without design "establishes the authors of the several books of Scripture as *independent* witnesses to the facts they relate; and this, whether they consulted each other's writings, or not; for the coincidences, if good for anything, are such as *could not* result from combination, mutual understanding, or arrangement."[8]

The point is that these coincidences demonstrate that the writers did not sit down in collusion with one another or just copy from one another (a claim often made by skeptics). We will see that the evidence of this is in the text itself, and even in what might be considered minor details of the text. This also shows that we are not out of line to take one text (e.g., in Matthew) and use it to show how something is verified in another text (e.g., in Luke).

---

[5] McGrew, Tim.

[6] McGrew, Lydia, 12.

[7] Blunt, 7.

[8] *Ibid.*, 8.

The best way to see this point is to provide examples. While there are examples from the Old Testament (as Blunt shows), here we will focus on a handful examples from the four gospel accounts. We want to provide a taste of what this is about, and perhaps we will discover many more on our own as we are reading the text. Some of these are more significant than others in terms of evidence, but they simply represent a way of putting the pieces of a text together in a way that makes sense of why someone does something a certain way. This is about making connections between various texts, and it happens over and over again throughout Scripture.

New Testament Examples

People wonder why there are four gospels instead of just one. Given that some stories are told in two or more gospels, sometimes in the same words, can we compare them in such a way that we can know they are authentic, historical records?[9] The skeptic says that one of the documents may have just been copied from another. The common idea is that Mark wrote first, then Matthew and Luke copied from Mark, and where Matthew and Luke agree with each other but include material different from Mark, they must have copied from another source called "Q" (which has never been found). This fails to account for these "undesigned coincidences."

There are many examples of this phenomenon, but to demonstrate, we will just give a few (perhaps it will intriguing enough to spark a desire to study this in more depth). Again, I am indebted to the McGrews and Blunt for these. *Hidden in Plain View* demonstrates many more examples in much more detail. This, as we say, is barely scratching the surface, but it introduces the idea.

1. In Matthew 4:18-22, James and John are mending their nets (vs. 21), but why? Then, when Jesus called them, they immediately got up and went with no questions. Why would they do this? Matthew

---

[9] McGrew, Tim.

doesn't tell us. However, in Luke 5, we are told that Jesus already told them to put their nets into the water and that they had caught such a great amount of fish that their nets were breaking (v. 6). That's why their nets needed mending. Further, this great catch of fish caused them to amazed, and were, therefore, willing to follow Jesus (v. 9). Matthew reports what they did without telling us why. Luke tells us why. Luke's account explains what was going on in Matthew.

2. Matthew 9:9-10 tells us of the call of Matthew the tax-collector. Verse 10 says that Jesus was reclining at the table in *the house*, but Matthew doesn't say whose house it was. Mark 2:14-15 clarifies that it was the house of Matthew or Levi. Luke 5:29 specifies further that Levi "gave a reception for Him (Jesus) in his house." Matthew says "the house," but not whose. Mark says it was Levi's house, and Luke says the reason for the event was that Levi gave a reception for Jesus there. All three together gives us a fuller picture.

3. Matthew 26:67-68 records that while Jesus was on trial, "they spat in His face and beat Him with their fists; and others slapped Him, and said, 'Prophesy to us, You Christ; who is the one who hit You.'" If all we read here were Matthew's account, we might find it a bit strange that they were telling Jesus to prophesy who hit Him when the offender is standing right in front of Him. Matthew leaves out some information that Luke provides: "they blindfolded Him and were asking Him, saying, "Prophesy, who is the one who hit You" (Luke 22:64). Luke's information completes the picture.

4. Matt 8:14-16 says that at evening they brought to Jesus many who were oppressed and sick. Why evening, especially if they believed Jesus could heal? Mark 1:21, 29-32 explains that it was the Sabbath (which Matthew doesn't mention). They apparently waited for the Sabbath to end.

5. Following the transfiguration, Luke 9:36 says that Peter, James, and John kept silent and told no one what they had seen. Why

would they not talk about this great event? Luke doesn't say. However, Mark 9:9 records that Jesus had charged them not to tell anyone. Mark tells us of the command, and Luke tells us that they obeyed the command. One gospel informs us about the other.

6. Mark 6:31-44 records the feeding of the 5,000. In Mark, Jesus tells the people to come away to a secluded place because many were coming and going and they didn't have time to eat. Then he has them sit down on the grass. The puzzle here is why there would be so many people at this time. Marks doesn't tell us. However, John 6:4 informs us that it was Passover time. During this time, all of Palestine would be filled with crowds.

7. In Matthew 14:1-2, we read that Herod had heard about Jesus and was saying to his servants that he was John risen from the dead. Why was Herod speaking like this to his servants, and how did Matthew know about this? Luke 8:3 tells us that among those attending to the disciples and providing for their needs was Joanna, the wife of Chuza, Herod's household manager. In other words, there was a direct connection to one of Herod's servants. Would this have been a mere coincidence that Matthew guessed at?

8. Mark 14:58 and 15:29 record the accusations at the cross that Jesus could allegedly rebuild the temple in three days. There is no record in Matthew, Mark, or Luke of Jesus saying anything like that. However, John 2:18-19 shows what Jesus said about destroying and rebuilding the temple (as He was referring to His own body). John gives us the statement of Jesus, but he does not record this as an accusation when Jesus was on trial. Mark gives the accusations but not the original statement of Jesus found in John. This is not what copying from one another looks like.

9. John 13 records Jesus washing the disciples' feet on the night of the Passover before His death. Why exactly did Jesus do this? Was it just on a whim? John doesn't say. However, consider that Luke records a fight between the disciples about who was greatest in the

kingdom (Luke 22:24-27). This happened on the same occasion. Luke mentions the fighting, but not the washing of feet. John records the washing of feet, but not the fighting. "Once this piece of information is in place, it is difficult to doubt that this is the explanation for Jesus' object lesson."[10]

10. Luke 23:2-4 records a strange sequence of events: a) The Jews accuse Jesus; b) Pilate questions Jesus (are you King?); c) Jesus admits to the charge; d) Pilate declares Jesus to be innocent. This by itself might make someone scratch his head. Why does this happen like this? Luke doesn't say. However, John gives more information in John 18:33-38. In John, Pilate's question, "Are you King?" seems to be random. In Luke, Pilate pronouncing Jesus innocent seems to come out of the blue, too. Yet together, they make perfect sense. Luke shows the accusation without explaining, while John gives the answer without recording the accusation.

11. In John 18:10, Peter cuts off the ear of the High Priest's servant, Malchus, and Jesus tells Peter to put the sword away. Then, in verse 36, Jesus tells Pilate that if His kingdom were of this world, His servants would be fighting. Doesn't Peter cutting off Malchus' ear with the sword constitute fighting? Why wasn't Peter arrested for this? John doesn't explain. However, Luke 22:51 tells us, "But Jesus answered and said, 'Stop! No more of this.' And He touched his ear and healed him." Now there was no evidence of the attempt to fight, and what would Peter have been arrested for? If the witnesses tried to explain what happened, they would have had to admit what Jesus did. Jesus' actions in healing and in forbidding Peter further use of the sword shows His claim to be true. There would be no fighting.

12. In Matthew 11:21, Jesus said, "Woe to you, Chorazin! Woe to you, Bethsaida! For if the miracles had occurred in Tyre and Sidon which occurred in you, they would have repented long ago in sackcloth and ashes." What miracles is He talking about? Matthew

---

[10] McGrew, Lydia, 49.

doesn't say. Here's what we learn elsewhere. John 6:5 says, "Therefore Jesus, lifting up His eyes and seeing that a large crowd was coming to Him, said to Philip, "Where are we to buy bread, so that these may eat?" Why specify Philip? Consider Luke 9:10-11: "When the apostles returned, they gave an account to Him of all that they had done. Taking them with Him, He withdrew by Himself to a city called Bethsaida." John 12:21 informs us that Philip was from Bethsaida. What's the point of this? Luke doesn't mention Philip, and John doesn't mention Bethsaida as the backdrop for the miracle. However, by putting them together we can understand that Jesus speaks to Philip in John 6:5 because Philip was from Bethsaida. By comparing Luke's account with these others, we can learn that the feeding of the 5,000 miracle took place prior to Jesus' pronouncing the woes on Bethsaida (Luke 10:13). Taken together, the sequence of events, with the places and people, make sense.

On we could go. Tim McGrew points out that the cumulative force of this is that one undesigned coincidence might be seen purely as accidental—by chance two pieces of a puzzle happened to fit. But once we start discovering numerous examples of "crisscrossing the documents," as he says, "it becomes ridiculous to insist that they are all just accidental."[11] I often say that we need to study the Gospels on their own merits—Matthew for Matthew's sake, Mark for Mark's sake, and so on. Yet it is also important to see that there are indeed four accounts, and though independent, they also fit together in a remarkable way and can indeed help to verify each other. In other words, we can use one book of the Bible to help verify another book of the Bible. Just looking into the gospels themselves, apart from other evidences, can give us confidence in their truthfulness.

---

[11] McGrew, Tim.

Conclusion

Connecting to the previous lesson, the objection that we cannot use the Bible to prove the Bible is built upon fallacious assumptions about the nature and composition of the Bible. Since the Bible is comprised of many books written by several different authors and not compiled until later, since their central claims are historical in nature, since they were in a position to know what they were talking about, and since the authors agree on the central claims, then there is no reason why these first century texts cannot be used to provide testimony to help verify each other. Such is the way we would use any other ancient sources, whether compiled into one book later or not. After all, there is a reason why these works were compiled as they are. Further, "Undesigned coincidences" provide excellent examples of the way these gospels fit together, demonstrating that they weren't just merely copying. They were independent, yet they still provide information helping to verify and explain one another.

Discussion Questions:

1. What is meant by "undesigned coincidence"?

2. How do undesigned coincidences demonstrate that the gospels were not just copied from one another?

3. How do they demonstrate that the gospels can be used to help verify one another?

4. What does the cumulative force of so many examples indicate?

5. Challenge: can you find more examples of undesigned coincidences?

The Gospel as its Own Apologetic 28

While we are concerned with providing proper evidence and reasoning in the support of our faith, it may be easy to overlook one of the best ways to do this: let the message speak for itself. Sometimes we may point out that God doesn't really need our help in His defense, even though He has provided many evidences to which we may rightly appeal. The Gospel message is indeed one of these.

By *Gospel*, in this context, we are speaking of the basic message to which Paul referred:

> Now I make known to you, brethren, the gospel which I preached to you, which also you received, in which also you stand, by which also you are saved, if you hold fast the word which I preached to you, unless you believed in vain. For I delivered to you as of first importance what I also received, that Christ died for our sins according to the Scriptures, and that He was buried, and that He was raised on the third day according to the Scriptures, and that He appeared... (1 Cor 15:1-5a)

How, then, does this message serve as its own defense? In order to answer this, let's go back to the beginning of 1 Corinthians. Read 1 Corinthians 1:18-25:

> For the word of the cross is foolishness to those who are perishing, but to us who are being saved it is the power of God. For it is written, 'I will destroy the wisdom of the wise, and the cleverness of the clever I will set aside.' Where is the wise man? Where is the scribe? Where is the debater of this age? Has not God made foolish the wisdom of the world? For since in the wisdom of God the world through its

wisdom did not come to know God, God was well-pleased through the foolishness of the message preached to save those who believe. For indeed Jews ask for signs and Greeks search for wisdom; but we preach Christ crucified, to Jews a stumbling block and to Gentiles foolishness, but to those who are the called, both Jews and Greeks, Christ the power of God and the wisdom of God. Because the foolishness of God is wiser than men, and the weakness of God is stronger than men.

Notice that the "word of the cross is foolishness to those who are perishing" (v. 18). The Jews were seeking signs and the Gentiles were seeking human wisdom; the cross was a stumbling block to the Jews and folly to the Gentiles. The point Paul makes is that neither the Jew nor the Gentile could make sense of the gospel message based upon their own wisdom and efforts. This is why, a little later, Paul writes that his message focused on Christ and Him crucified, not on persuasive words of human wisdom. Faith was not to rest on these elements that came out of such human wisdom.

The Essence of the Story

Think about the essence of the Gospel message. An uneducated Jewish peasant from a small, obscure town in Galilee claims to be the Son of God, works miracles, and teaches with authority, thereby silencing His opposition. His enemies, prominent Jewish leaders from Jerusalem, manage to get Him arrested, charged, and crucified as a criminal by Roman authorities. Three days later He is risen. His disciples soon after begin to proclaim the death, burial, and resurrection of Jesus, and from this point the group of disciples grows and spreads to the rest of the world.

A crucified Jewish, uneducated peasant from Galilee is the Savior of the world? Many reject the Gospel story precisely because it sounds so foolish to them. They think it is all made up. Again, think about the above account. Even in the first century the Jews stumbled over it and the Gentiles thought it foolish. Detractors will point to the silliness and unlikelihood of the idea that a man who was crucified on a Roman cross could be the savior of the world. After a good laugh at all those fools who believe such a story, unbelievers can then go on their way confident that reason has served them well. Yet it is here that they may fail to think the issue through, and the irony should not be missed.

We should recognize, of course, that if the story is not true, then we really are wasting our time. Paul wrote that if Christ was not raised, "then our preaching is vain, your faith also is vain. Moreover we are even found to be false witnesses of God, because we testified against God that He raised Christ, whom He did not raise, if in fact the dead are not raised. For if the dead are not raised, not even Christ has been raised; and if Christ has not been raised, your faith is worthless; you are still in your sins. Then those also who have fallen asleep in Christ have perished. If we have hoped in Christ in this life only, we are of all men most to be pitied" (1 Cor 15:14-19).

On the one hand, if it is not true, then our faith is vain and anything we do for the Lord is worthless (see v. 58). On the other hand, if it is true, then faith is not vain, and those who oppose it will find themselves in a very precarious situation, lost, and without any hope. The importance of this issue cannot be overstated, so does it not constrain anyone who wants truth to look into it and make sure without dismissing it out of hand?

Where did the Story Originate?

Let's take another look at question of where this story came from, and consider:

1. There is no question but that the Gospel story arose during the early part of the first century. The story is claimed as historical (Luke 1:1-4), based on eyewitnesses, and carries with it the recognition that if it didn't happen, Christianity as a whole is

fallacious (1 Cor 15:12-19). Paul wrote 1 Corinthians within about 20-25 years of when the events are said to have happened (so recognized even by critics), and he argued that everything hinges on its historical truthfulness. The question here is, where did the story originate? This will tell us a great deal about whether the story is true or just a legend bred and grown within an extremely short time period.

2. Would the story have arisen from within the Gentile community? Who could think that the pagan Gentiles of the day would concoct a story about a Jewish peasant who would have condemned their religious practices and whom they killed as a criminal? No, the Gentiles of the day wouldn't have come up with it. Further, the charge that the story of Jesus was mirroring pagan stories falls flat when we consider that early non-Christian writers accused Christians of new, mischievous and superstitious beliefs. When Paul preached at Athens, the heart of ancient philosophy, people listened because it was new and strange (Acts 17:20-21). After hearing it some sneered at it and others wanted to hear more (vs. 32). Why would Greeks and Romans have a problem with a religion doctrine that mirrors their own beliefs and that they had already invented? Why would they invent that kind of story, then kill those who accepted it? No, that line won't work.

3. If it did not arise from within the Gentile community, then it must have arisen from within the Jewish community. But which Jewish community would have invented a story about an uneducated, Galilean Jew from an obscure family who turns out to be the Son of God and long-promised Messiah? Which Jewish community was expecting their Messiah to be crucified on a Roman cross? Why would they invent the story of a man who condemned their attitudes and traditions as well, then lay the blame on Jewish leadership for his death? Keep in mind these points, also: a) to claim to be the Son of God was considered blasphemy, so they condemned Him to die for it; b) to be crucified on a Roman cross was to be cursed; c) He was put to death at the

insistence of His own people while His handful of disciples scattered for fear; and d) the gospel accounts contain a number of embarrassing facts, including the way the disciples acted, making it unlikely that the later disciples just invented these things to the embarrassment of the apostles and early leaders. Something else is going on here.

Critics and legend-theorists have a problem. The story of Jesus would not have come from a typical Jewish community who were expecting their long-awaited Messiah, only to tell a story about His being put to death, cursed, and committing blasphemy. It certainly couldn't have come from the wealthy, ruling classes who despised what Jesus stood for, and the poor, uneducated Jews wouldn't have been able to write about it so eloquently. Jesus was not a Messiah expected by any Jewish group, so which group would have invented Him to be such? They would have to then surmise that the story arose from within a more isolated and unorthodox Jewish community. If that is the case, then what would explain the quick and wide-spread acceptance of it all?

Yet, the story is there, and the irony is that those same details that critics think make the story foolish also make the story that much more unlikely to have arisen from within any typical Gentile or Jewish community, unless it really happened as described. The only alternative is to think that a bunch of uneducated fishermen, in conjunction with a highly educated Jewish Pharisee were able to sell a fable that condemned all of them alike, gave them no cultural advantage, and had no other particular benefit (if untrue) except for false hope. Oh, and they had to be willing to stake their own lives on this lie while knowing all along they are lying about it all. Then this lie became the cornerstone of a new movement that could not have gone anywhere without some reason for both Jews and Gentiles to accept it. It was an unlikely story to begin with, and even more unlikely to develop such a following if it were that devoid of truth. Christianity is not based on the testimony of one or two people who privately claimed to have seen something supernatural; rather, it is based upon the public proclamation of public events in public settings where multiple eyewitnesses were called upon. As Luke said, it was something that could be investigated (Luke 1:1-4). The knowledge of these matters was such that Peter could stand before a Jewish audience on Pentecost and tell them to their faces that they knew what happened (Acts 2:22-23). This is not the way of myth.

What best accounts for the Gospel message? Paul answers in 1 Corinthians 1, again in a work written less than 25 years from the events described. The story of Jesus was a stumbling block to the Jews, and it was foolishness to the Greeks. The answer is that the story ultimately came about by the power of God, and the historical resurrection is the final piece of evidence that gives it its full strength. The details of the Gospel are best explained, not by an appeal to any particularly unorthodox Jewish or Gentile community that just happened to gain a following, but by the simple recognition that it is what actually happened. Sometimes, the simplest explanations are the best. The Gospel is indeed its own apologetic because the one explanation that truly fits its existence is that it is the truth. Paul writes,

> Where is the wise man? Where is the scribe? Where is the debater of this age? Has not God made foolish the wisdom of the world? For since in the wisdom of God the world through its wisdom did not come to know God, God was well- pleased through the foolishness of the message preached to save those who believe. (vv. 20-21)

The Gospel is what it is in part because God didn't want anyone boasting that they could have ever come up with such a plan to save mankind from sin. We won't know God from our own wisdom, but only through His wisdom as displayed through the death and resurrection of the Son of God.

Discussion Questions

1. Why can we say that the Gospel is its own apologetic? What does that mean?

2. Why was the message of the cross foolishness to the Gentiles and a stumbling block to the Jews?

3. Why is Christianity so dependent upon the truth of the resurrection?

4. Why is it difficult to explain the rise of the Gospel story by appealing to typical Gentile or Jewish communities?

5. Why is there irony to the fact that critics find the Gospel story so foolish?

6. What best accounts for the Gospel story and why?

Courage Under Fire

Here is the lesson: Don't retreat in the face of opposition. Too much is at stake. Be the kind soldier who instills respect in others because of your courage under fire. Make your case in the presence of hostile witnesses. Throw your gauntlet into the arena and see what the other side has to say. It's one of the most effective ways to establish your case and to help you cultivate a bullet-proof faith over time.

Gregory Koukl, Tactics, 197

How Shall We Understand the Bible?

Many of the issues associated with whether or not we can believe the Bible centers around questions and problems in Hermeneutics. "Hermeneutics" refers the science of interpretation, and this itself is a huge field of study on its own. Nevertheless, overviewing this arena in relation to trusting the Scriptures is important because there are a number of considerations that will help us understand and alleviate some of the issues associated with the believability of the Bible.

A skeptic just pointing to a passage and arguing that the passage contradicts another passage is not enough, any more than just randomly pointing to a passage from a believer's viewpoint and saying, "This is what the Bible says." If we fail to see literary and historical contexts, to understand how language is used and how communication operates, or to appreciate the over-arching umbrella of what Scripture teaches, we will likely be guilty of fallacies that result in severe misinterpretations and misrepresentations of Scripture. Both believers and unbelievers do this.

Let's consider a few principles, then, that will help us keep some of these matters in perspective, take a look at some difficult texts, then end with a broad appeal for growth.

Two Basic Goals of Biblical Understanding

First, we need to try to understand the Bible based upon the initial context in which it was written, not based upon our context 2,000 years later. This is not to say that we should not make modern applications of Scripture, but meaning and application are not the same. We have two basic goals in our Bible study:[1]

1. To learn what the text means.
2. To make the proper applications.

1. What does the text mean? If we forget about finding the meaning of the text and go straight to application, then we will very likely abuse the text and make it fit whatever we feel at the time. This is how postmodernism reads a text as it jettisons authorial intent in favor of the reader's creative meaning. We can make the Bible "say" whatever we want, and this is often what happens. How many of us have been sitting in a Bible study, only to hear, "What does this mean to you?" without ever addressing what the text first means?

The question here is not, "what does it mean to me?" We cannot properly answer the application question until we first know what the text means. This first question is more objective in nature. We are asking, "What did Paul mean when he wrote...?" What did the author intend to convey to his readers? From a theological perspective, what did God intend to convey in the text?

Our purpose right here is not to go into all the details relative to discovering what the text means, which would take its own course and series of lessons. Rather, we are just drawing attention here to the first principles that can easily be forgotten.

2. How is the text to be applied? Once we understand what the text means, then we can make applications to our situation. This is the "what it means to me" part, and it properly follows "what it means."

---

[1] See, for example, Gordon D. Fee and Douglas Stuart, *How to Read the Bible for All Its Worth* (3rd ed. Grand Rapids, MI: Zondervan, 2003), 17-31. They argue for this two-step process by referring to *exegesis* (getting the meaning out of the text) and *hermeneutics* (which they apply to application, though generally the term is seen as more encompassing).

Again, we need to be careful not to get that out of order, lest we turn the text into our own playground for self-justification.

Learning to See the Beauty and Depth of Scripture

With the two basic goals before us, we want to add some important principles that will help us see the beauty and depth of Scripture.

Learn to understand the text and application through connections. Learn to see the types/antitypes and foreshadowings. I have been a Bible student for the greater part of my life, and I must confess that there are days when, during my Bible study, I think to myself, "Where have I been? Why didn't I see that before? How could I have been so blind?" There are days when I feel like I'm finally waking up to the depth and beauty of Scripture. The more I study, the more I see that.

There is a depth and beauty to Scripture that can easily be missed, depending on how we are reading it and what our goals are when we read. We might have a tendency to read the Bible in some strict linear fashion. We read from Genesis to Revelation and tell the story, and this is necessary. Yet how often do we read while failing to make connections between passages and concepts? We may see a flat-line story without seeing the layers of ideas that are interwoven throughout. The Bible is not just a linear story. It is an interwoven tapestry filled with beautiful patterns. If a written text can be said to be 3D, Scripture is that! We need to put our glasses on so we can see its depth leaping off the pages.

Scripture is filled with conceptual relationships. Types and antitypes, shadows and substance, are staples of understanding the importance of connections. While we need to be careful with our approach to these connections, it is still true that, as Habershon put it, "The precious things of God's Word are not all upon the surface. We must dig in order to find them. Like the first sinking of the shaft, the work may be laborious at the outset, and therefore needs diligence; but when we reach a rich vein of ore we are well rewarded, as we find that we come upon a mine of inexhaustible wealth."[2] If we aren't willing to be diligent, we will rest upon the surface and often find ourself dissatisfied with the results. People tend to blame Scripture for the bad results when in reality it was their own laziness and failure to dig deep.

For example, "For Christ our passover has been sacrificed" (1 Cor 5:7) is a beautiful statement connecting back to the passover and the exodus. The book of Hebrews is filled with such connections and cannot be understood without seeing these. The book of Revelation's connections to the Old Testament are grand, exploding with meaning. The way the New Testament quotes the Old Testament adds a depth that we might easily miss, and this challenges us. Over and over, we find fulfillment of prophecy and concept. The biblical story is told many ways and through many images, from the Garden, to the Exodus, the Temple, the holy city of Jerusalem and more, finding masterful fulfillment in Christ. There is a great joy of discovery when we see these connections and begin understanding the depth at which these connections are made. This is one reason why Bible study should never become cold, lifeless, or boring. If we are bored with Bible study, we haven't turned our minds on yet. We haven't yet seen.

Failing to see some of this depth is part of the reason, I am convinced, that people end up rejecting Scripture. People might take passages, read them flatly, and conclude some kind of contradiction or problem, when, in reality, they are missing the depth of what the passages are teaching because they draw hasty conclusions without putting much thought into it. This is one of the very reasons some of the Jews rejected Jesus as the Messiah. They didn't dig deep enough.

---

[2] Ada R. Habershon, *Study of the Types* (Grand Rapids, MI: Kregel Publications, 1997), 11.

For example, many times I hear a critic, in a somewhat mocking tone, discount the Bible by making some flippant remark about how ridiculous it is to follow the Bible when it contains commands about not mixing fabrics together. If they know where the reference is, they seldom know anything about the context of the passage, the covenants, or the greater issues involved. They see a flat-line order that sounds silly on the surface, and they run with that impression.

"You are to keep My statutes. You shall not breed together two kinds of your cattle; you shall not sow your field with two kinds of seed, nor wear a garment upon you of two kinds of material mixed together." (Lev 19:19)

Reading it flatly, and without further consideration, one can think how senseless this sounds. If we even read Leviticus, how often would we skim over a passage like this and think, "That's weird, but, oh well, that's just part of the Law"? We must think deeper. One of the points that is easily missed is that God was teaching an overall culture of holiness and pure-minded devotion. One of the ways that He got people to think about that was through physical and visible reminders, even in their daily routines and mundane activities. Through engaging in actions that forced their minds toward the ideas of cleanness, holiness, not mixing with the unholy, pagan people of the land, they would be more inclined to remember how important it was to remain faithful always. Not mixing materials was a daily reminder, even in the way they constructed and wore their clothes, to stay pure, unmixed with sin, and faithful to God. It would be like our putting sticky notes on mirrors and refrigerators as reminders that no matter where we are or what we are doing, we are to be holy and pure. People wear rings and jewelry to remind them of important relationships and events. Being a child of God encompasses all areas of life, including how business is conducted, how work is done, and how we do our mundane activities. There may even be more, but the point is that a passage like this, flatly read, is boring and silly. Seen in its greater context and message, it is brilliantly reminding God's people how overarching holiness was to be in their lives. It wasn't so much about the fabric as much as it was about the lesson derived from the process and the action. I find it intriguing that this comes on the heels the second-greatest commandment.

Bible study is to be a careful undertaking, not a hasty effort that requires little thought or sound exegesis. Such hasty efforts lead not only to poor understanding and bad interpretation, they can lead to rejection of Scripture altogether. "I don't understand why this is, so I'm rejecting the whole thing." Flat-line Bible reading contributes to flat-lining spirituality. If people are bored with Scripture, they'll be bored with their religion.

There are cautions. We don't want to overdo it. I'm not saying that one has to be some super intellect to study and understand. Nor am I arguing that we should try to see phantom connections or start allegorizing everything. Not at all. Scripture makes the connections, shows the contexts, and leads us to draw the conclusions. Our task is to see them, not to invent things for the sake of novelty, so be careful about making connections that are not warranted. At the same time, be careful to make the connections that *are* warranted.

Learning through difficult passages and questions

There is no question but that there are difficult passages. I have no magic bullet here to say, "This will take care of every question." No, in fact, I believe some of these difficulties are intentional. We are expected to struggle with meaning and application sometimes. Rather than just give us a list of do's and don'ts, Scripture gives us puzzles that we must work out, work through, and to which we must diligently apply ourselves. Study is not for the lazy. It is not always convenient, but it is challenging and rewarding, which itself seems to suit our needs.

Jesus spoke in parables, pictures of the kingdom (Mark 4:30), which weren't always readily understood by those who heard Him. "Then the disciples came and said to Him, 'Why do you speak to them in parables?' And he answered them, 'To you it has been given to know the secrets of the kingdom of heaven, but to them it has not been given. For to the one who has, more will be given, and he will have an abundance, but from the one who has not, even what he has will be taken away. This is why I speak to them in parables, because seeing they do not see, and hearing they do not hear, nor do they understand'" (Matt 13:10-13).

While this can puzzle us a little, I believe Jesus was indicating that the nature of truth is just this way, and its discovery is suited to the people God has made. If we want to know and understand, if we diligently apply ourselves, then we can learn. If all we want is everything handed to us on a silver-platter without having to put in much effort, then our laziness will blind us. If our interest is in justifying our own will, we will hear but not hear. Digging into Scripture will yield its rewards, but it will also separate between the serious and the not-so-serious.

When the question of difficulties arises, we are often drawn into the question of biblical inerrancy. Inerrancy can be an ill-defined concept in biblical studies. If someone asks me, "Do you believe in the inerrancy of Scripture?" my first question will be, "What do you mean by inerrancy?" I'm not trying to get around the question; I'm trying to understand what people mean by it. I'm not convinced everyone understands it the same way, and it can be a fairly abstract idea unequally grasped by a large number of people. My goal here is not to go into a full-blown discussion of inerrancy, but, again, to point to some principles that may help us with perspective.

Inerrancy means "free from error" or "infallible," but that doesn't really get to the problem I'm addressing. For some, "free from error" may mean "free from difficulties," for why should God ever make anything difficult? Then, when faced with difficulties that aren't readily answered, they feel they must give up "inerrancy." But that's not what it means.

For others, inerrancy may mean "free from contradictions." True enough, but the problem here is that "contradiction" is itself an oft-misunderstood and abused word. Many equate difficulty with contradiction, and others say, "contradiction!" when the issue at hand is a difference in how something is stated or interpreted. Inerrancy to some may also mean that it must coincide with what they deem reasonable. Many others will argue that the Bible nowhere teaches the doctrine of inerrancy anyway, so we need to give it up.

The other problem we have is that we don't have the original autographs of Scripture, and the copies we have are not technically inerrant, as earlier studied. The doctrine of inerrancy was never about the copies or manuscripts. It's always been about the character of God and what He inspired men to say and write. Is Scripture accomplishing what God wants accomplished (cf. Isa 55:8-11)? Did He inspire men to write in such a way that reflects His character, and do we have a reliable record of this message? Inerrancy is more of a theological conclusion we draw based on who God is, and we believe His message is faithfully preserved through the copies and translations we have.

I have concluded that the better, more understandable, term to use is "trustworthy." The question is this: when we read a text of Scripture, can we trust we are getting reliable information?

There are a few reasons I believe this is the better way to talk about this. For instance:

1. Paul makes the point about being a steward of God's mysteries: "Let a man regard us in this manner, as servants of Christ and stewards of the mysteries of God. In this case, moreover, it is required of stewards that one be found trustworthy" (1 Cor 4:1-2). While it is the steward here who is to be trustworthy, the point is that he saw himself as a steward who needed to be faithful in getting the message out properly. If the steward is trustworthy, then

he'll faithfully put the information out there that comes from God. The message will be trustworthy as well.

2. One of Paul's well-used phrases to Timothy and Titus is, "It is a trustworthy statement…" (1 Tim 1:15; 3:1; 4:9; 2 Tim 2:11; Titus 3:8). "Trustworthy" means that these statements are "deserving full acceptance" (1 Tim 4:9). These are matters about which we may "speak confidently" (Titus 3:8).

"Trustworthy" is the biblical term, so that captures the point we are making. The writers state what we can trust as being true. That's really the point, is it not?

Not knowing the Scriptures or the power of God will lead to error on our part (cf. Matt 22:29), but the message itself is trustworthy because it is based on a trustworthy God who entrusted it to trustworthy stewards, who in turn conveyed God's message through writing. As Peter put it:

"Therefore, I will always be ready to remind you of these things, even though you already know them, and have been established in the truth which is present with you. I consider it right, as long as I am in this earthly dwelling, to stir you up by way of reminder, knowing that the laying aside of my earthly dwelling is imminent, as also our Lord Jesus Christ has made clear to me. And I will also be diligent that at any time after my departure you will be able to call these things to mind" (2 Pet 1:12-15).

The purpose of the writing is that we will be able to "call these things to mind," and the expectation from a passage like this is that it will be a trustworthy message faithfully transmitted. The question is, do we trust God, the stewards, and the message? That depends, again, on perspective.

What about unanswered questions, though? One of the principles that seems understated sometimes is this: read the text with giving the benefit of the doubt to the writers when there might be unanswered questions. Perhaps they saw or knew something that we didn't see or know.

Like we would want to treat anyone else we love (1 Cor 13), if there is more than one way to look at something, and one way is negative, while the other is positive, then why not go with the positive view about it? Why would we automatically assume the worst in someone? Why would we automatically assume the worst of a biblical text when it is possible to see it from another angle that gives us a different picture?

Looking at Difficult Texts

To illustrate the point, I want to consider three examples of texts that are difficult, and about which skeptics argue represent contradictions or serious problems. While I'm not saying that I have all the answers to difficulties, and I'm not saying that I absolutely know the final explanation, I do believe we can show legitimate explanations that help us make sense of what's going on, and these will help illustrate how we might approach other difficult passages as well.

1. Matthew 2:14-15. "And he rose and took the child and his mother by night and departed to Egypt and remained there until the death of Herod. This was to fulfill what the Lord had spoken by the prophet, 'Out of Egypt I called my son.'"

This quote comes from Hosea 11:1. The problem is that Matthew appears to pull this completely out of context and just randomly applies it. How can we trust Matthew as an author if he didn't even know the context of Hosea? His misuse of this passage renders him untrustworthy, you see. Not so fast, though.

Granted, who, in Hosea's day, would have really thought that the verse was something that should be applied to the Messiah? There's nothing contextually that would make us think that. Notice, too, that Matthew doesn't explain the context, nor does he even try to justify explicitly why he used that passage the way he did.

Now, we could just say, "Matthew didn't know what he was talking about, and is, therefore, in error." Does this do justice to Matthew and his purposes, and does it give any benefit of the doubt to the text? Do we just assume the mistake? Or is there a better way to approach a passage like this?

I believe Matthew's use of Hosea 11:1 is brilliant. In fact, I believe the passage is a key thesis for Matthew's message in the gospel account. Just consider the fact that Matthew pulls from a context where God was severely chastising the people for idolatry. God's care for them was evident, as expressed by His bringing them out of Egypt as a nation. What greater expression of His care can there be but to come into the world Himself and initiate another great exodus, but this time out of sin? Matthew calls to their minds what God did for them, and it points to something even greater that God does through Jesus as He fulfills the very purpose for which God initially called out a holy nation. It's all about connections. Jesus is the embodiment of Israel. He is the passover lamb connected to the Exodus, and He was about to lead His people on a new exodus out of their sins and into a new life and new covenant. That one statement from Hosea can bring all of this to mind, and more.

The New Testament writers made these types of connections, and if we aren't willing to see them, we may well conclude that they were mistaken, rather than showing the web of concepts that tied together the Messiah with the Old Testament expectations. There is no need to think Matthew was mistaken, but there is every reason to think that Matthew knew exactly what he was doing, carefully choosing a passage that connects to an idea with which the Jews were well familiar. The exodus event was the defining moment for them, as they came out of slavery into a new life. The new defining moment is Jesus.

2. Matthew 27:9-10. When Judas returned the pieces of silver, for which he betrayed Jesus, then went and hanged himself, the counsel took the blood money and purchased the land. Acts 1:18 tells us that Judas' actions provided the occasion for the purchase. That Matthew says Judas hanged himself does not contradict that Judas fell and burst open. Neither account is exclusive of the other, and it is not a stretch to believe that Judas hanged himself, but then fell as Luke describes. When exactly Judas died, we don't know, as neither text says, and it wouldn't change anything. Now the verse I want to focus on is Matthew 27:9-10:

"Then was fulfilled what had been spoken by the prophet Jeremiah, saying, 'And they took the thirty pieces of silver, the price of him on whom a price had been set by some of the sons of Israel, and they gave them for the potter's field, as the Lord directed me.'"

Here's the problem: the reference is made to Jeremiah, but the quote appears to come from Zechariah. How are we to understand this difficulty?

We could just say that Matthew got it wrong, as per the skeptic. Or we could say that this was a copyist error that crept into the text at some point. That's possible. Or we could say that both Jeremiah and Zechariah said it, but only Zechariah recorded it. That's possible, but not likely. One solution offered is that Jeremiah was at the head of the scroll that contained Zechariah, and Matthew was just referencing the scroll from which the prophecy came. Again, that's possible, but I believe there is a better way to think about this, and it involves a deeper process of study and seeing connections.

If you examined the quote carefully, you will notice something pretty significant: it is not an exact quote of either Jeremiah or Zechariah. However, we might note that there are connections between what Zechariah said, what Jeremiah said, and what happened in the case of Judas.

Zechariah 11:12-13 says, "Then I said to them, 'If it seems good to you, give me my wages; but if not, keep them.' And they weighed out as my wages thirty pieces of silver. Then the Lord said to me, 'Throw it to the potter'—the lordly price at which I was priced by them. So I took the thirty pieces of silver and threw them into the house of the Lord, to the potter.'"

We add to this passages from Jeremiah 32:6-9, 18:2, and 19:1-13. In Jeremiah 32, Jeremiah was told to buy a field for the right of redemption. Yet closer to the situation is Jeremiah 19:1-13, where the leaders of the people were told that a calamity was about to strike. They have filled the place with the blood of the innocent and did what was wicked. The field associated with this was Topheth, the valley of Hinnom, which would be known as the valley of slaughter and a place of defilement.

Putting these elements together, we find the concepts of thirty pieces of silver for betrayal, throwing the pieces, utilizing a potter and a field, purchasing land that has been defiled, burial, and the destruction that came from the betrayal of Yahweh by the those who were supposed to be his people. Interestingly, the valley of Hinnom is the very place Jesus used to talk about Hell, a place of defilement and destruction. In Acts 1, Luke describes the field as the field of blood. It was a field of slaughter paid by the price of wickedness (as with the leaders in Jeremiah's day). We might also note that Judas was called the "son of perdition" or destruction (John 17:12), giving us another connection. What Judas did was a microcosm of what Israel had done during the days of Jeremiah.

It takes both Jeremiah and Zechariah to get the pieces of this puzzle into place. What Matthew appears to do is combine information from both, then cite the more prominent prophet, who is Jeremiah. Weber writes, "It is not surprising that the Jewish leaders did not see the similarities between their situation and the prophetic details. The fuller Old Testament picture paralleling Judas's and

Jesus' blood money was only seen when Matthew pulled together the themes of Jeremiah 19:1–13 and the wording of Zechariah 11:12–13."[3]

Blomberg writes, "Matthew mentions the potter's field as if it were well-known. An ancient tradition associates it with a site at the east end of the Valley of Hinnom, just south of Jerusalem (cf. Jer 19:7), a natural place for a cemetery." He continues: "Better still, however, is the interpretation which sees Jer 19:1–13 in Matthew's mind, especially with its references to 'the blood of the innocent' (v. 4), the 'potter' (vv. 1, 11), the renaming of a place in the Valley of Hinnom (v. 6), violence (v. 1), and the judgment and burial by God of the Jewish leaders (v. 11). Matthew is again employing typology and combining allusions to texts in both Jeremiah and Zechariah."[4]

The point is that Matthew was making the connections between Zechariah, Jeremiah, and the circumstances of Judas as one of the leaders and apostles who had fallen deep into wickedness. This is exactly what happened to Israel as a whole.

We should note that what Matthew does here in combining a reference and using the more prominent name is not unique. In Mark 1:2-3, Mark uses a combined reference from Malachi 3:1, Isaiah 40:3, and possibly Exodus 23:20. Yet he only cites Isaiah by name. Matthew 2:5 combines a reference from Micah 5:2 with 2 Samuel 5:2, yet just speaks of "the prophet." They saw this as a legitimate way to reference something, and we have no reason to think they were mistaken in doing this.

---

[3] Stuart K. Weber, *Holman NT Commentary: Matthew* (Nashville, TN: Broadman and Holman, 2000), 459.

[4] Craig Blomberg, *The New American Commentary, Vol. 22: Matthew* (Nashville, TN: Broadman and Holman, 1992), 408-409.

All of this also shows that sometimes the references that we call "quotes" are not intended to be exact word-for-word quotes. Sometimes they paraphrase. Sometimes they allude to a passage or an idea. All of this was completely within acceptable understanding and conventions of the day. Ironically, we err when we make our modern assumptions about how it should be done, then cast our expectations back onto how they did it then only to pronounce that they were mistaken.

3. When the disciples were passing through grainfields on the sabbath and picking grain, Pharisees chastised them for doing this. Jesus responded, "Have you never read what David did when he was in need and he and his companions became hungry; how he entered the house of God in the time of Abiathar the high priest, and ate the consecrated bread, which is not lawful for anyone to eat except the priests, and he also gave it to those who were with him?" (Mark 2:25-26)

The difficulty here is the reference to Abiathar the high priest. However, the account of David doing this in 1 Samuel 21 tells us that the priest David dealt with was Ahimelech. Here, according to skeptics, is a clear mistake. Perhaps the author's memory just slipped. Perhaps this was a copyist error that persisted. Another possibility is that the original text said, "abba Abiathar," which would then tell us that the proper referent here is Abiathar's father, who is Ahimelech. The typical explanation is that Mark was just confused, or that the names just got tangled. Either way, it is a mistake, we are told. However, is there is another way to look at this that provides some lee-way in how this is told?

The solutions that have been offered for this are many and varied. I don't know that I could provide the final solution, but the fact that there are a number of possibilities is sufficient enough that we shouldn't lose faith. Daniel Wallace presents an overview of a number of options, some of which are not so attractive, and some that are certainly possible.[5] Some argue that the Abiathar reference is meant to represent a section of the Old Testament, and would translate it "at Abiathar," because "in the time of" technically isn't there.[6] Let's think through a little of this.

Abiathar was the high priest who officiated at the house of God in Jerusalem (Cf. 1 Sam 22:20–23; 2 Sam 15:24, 35; 17:15; 19:11), not just in Nob where the bread was given to David. Jerusalem is significant since this is where David set up his capital and organized the entire priesthood with Abiathar as the high priest. Interestingly, Matthew, Mark, and Luke all mention the "house of God," which 1 Samuel 21 does not actually mention, and Abiathar was most connected to that in Jerusalem. It's possible that there may be something significant about the house of God connection in Jerusalem that is bigger than just the event taken from 1 Samuel 21, and I believe the clue to this is in Matthew's account: "But I say to you that something greater than the temple is here" (Matt 12:6). Could Jesus have purposefully pulled in Abiathar's name because of his connection to David and the "house of God" at Jerusalem in order make the point that something even greater is here? This would be about connections, which, as we have seen, is common enough through Scripture.

My view is that "the time of Abiathar" is a reference to the period in which Abiathar became most connected to David and David's work with the priesthood and laying the groundwork for the temple in Jerusalem. While Ahimelech was the priest during the specific event referenced, Abiathar became more prominent and traveled with David. He was the priest most associated with David. "The

---

[5] Daniel Wallace, *Mark 2:26 and the Problem of Abiathar*. Web, 2004. <https://bible.org/article/mark-226-and-problem-abiathar> Accessed July 4, 2017.

[6] Robert H. Gundry, *Commentary on Mark* (Baker Publishing Group, Kindle Edition, 2011) loc. 687-688.

time of Abiathar" could be a period reference. After David ate the showbread, the priests of Nob were slaughtered, and Abiathar escaped to tell David. He was the survivor of the priests. He carried the ephod, and David felt a special responsibility to Abiathar, telling him, "I have brought about the death of every person in your father's household. Stay with me; do not be afraid, for he who seeks my life seeks your life, for you are safe with me" (1 Sam 22:22-23). It makes some sense, then, to associate Abiathar with David.

This also means that Jesus' reference to the Pharisees' hypocrisy in accepting David's actions but condemning a lawful act of the disciples was meant to convey, even more, that in rejecting Jesus, they were rejecting not only Him, but everything that David and the house of God stood for. This need not be seen as an insurmountable problem when seen in the context of connections.

Learning to see the Big Picture:

Growing in our faith is vital, but sometimes we may stifle our growth because we haven't learned the bigger principles. When we fail to learn these, we may find ourselves thinking that Scripture isn't that applicable, and that we just don't see the point in trying so hard. We may end up losing our faith. This is not just about answering skeptics. This is about learning to see better so that our hearts will be fortified and our lives enriched by a deeper sense of what Scripture does. Here, let's focus a bit on what we can do to grow in our faith and understanding.

If we zoom in on a flower petal—I mean really got so close that all we could see was a close up view of the veins—we might not have any clue as to what we are looking at (unless we've really studied what that would look like). If we start backing up, we would begin to see the whole petal, then the whole flower. Then we might see that the flower is in a clump of other flowers, which are, in turn, in a garden. As we continue zooming out, we might see trees, a road nearby, mountains in the background, and the sky. Now we have the bigger picture in which sits the flower petal. It all makes sense.

Sometimes our Bible study might miss the bigger picture of God's plans and purposes. We take a phrase in a passage and study it. We look at it word by word, minutely taking it all apart to get to the deeper meaning (so we think). Then we become more puzzled as to its meaning, or we get an idea stuck in our heads based on a very limited and narrow view of a term. While there are difficult phrases and ideas in Scripture, our first step ought to be to zoom out. Back up and take a look at the entire scenery. See the sky, the mountains, and the roads before getting so close to the flower petal that it looks unrecognizable. Once we back out, we may see the simplicity of it. In its context, it makes sense. The flower petal is just that—a petal on a flower in a larger picture, helping bring beauty to the entire scene.

This, it appears to me, is part of what creates difficulties when looking at particular issues. We ask, "Where does the Bible condemn this or that?" "Where does God say not to do that anymore?" "Where does it say to do it this way or that way?" The answer may not be found in a single verse that says, "do this or don't do that." It may be found in understanding the bigger picture where God expects us to discern between right and wrong. God doesn't always spell everything out in detail, but this does not mean that the details don't matter. He expects His people to grow in maturity enough to discern what they should or should not be doing. That can only be done through seeing that bigger picture.

> For though by this time you ought to be teachers, you have need again for someone to teach you the elementary principles of the oracles of God, and you have come to need milk and not solid food. For everyone who partakes only of milk is not accustomed to the word of righteousness, for he is an infant. But solid food is for the mature, who because of practice have their senses trained to discern good and evil. (Heb 5:12-14)

Again, God doesn't spell everything out in detail. He expects us to "get it" through mature observation and application. For example, let's consider the overall practice of Judaism. We often point out that the Jews, who were the first Christians, did not necessarily quit their practices that were entrenched in Judaism. This is true. There was nothing inherently wrong with what was commanded in the Law. The New Testament makes it clear, though, that the Law was not something God intended to continue as a binding practice (read Romans, Galatians, and Hebrews if this is not clear). Where did God ever say, "You shall no longer practice any of this at all?" He didn't need to say that. The Jews could initially continue in their practices, especially those that had become more cultural in nature, but there was certainly no intent to expand the "regulations of divine worship and the earthly sanctuary" (Heb 9:1) out so that more people would be practicing these things. Quite the opposite. Did God really have to say, "Don't do these things" in order to make His intentions known about them, or does the bigger picture help us come to a better understanding and conclusion about these practices?

At least two factors clarify that God's intentions were for His new people under Christ to move beyond those older "regulations of divine worship":

1. Jesus Christ was the fulfillment of the old. "Do not think that I came to abolish the Law or the Prophets; I did not come to abolish but to fulfill" (Matt 5:17). The point was not to destroy what the old represented, but to complete the picture. The old picture is incomplete; Christ finished it. Thus, instead of continuing indefinitely with the Passover, Christ is the Passover (1 Cor 5:7). He is the Temple, the sacrifice, and the High Priest. If we see this picture of completion, why would we argue for going back to these things in some other physical sense? Does God really have to say, "don't have an earthly High Priest" in order for us to get it? Does He have to spell it out if we see the bigger picture of His plans fulfilled?

Likewise, God's people fulfill roles from the old covenant. Christians are a priesthood. Christians are sacrifices. Christians are the instruments of praise. Christ's body is also the Temple. Christ and His people fulfill these roles in a much greater sense. If we understand this picture of God's purposes, why would He need to specify what not to do anymore? When we feel that we need specific "do nots," we are zooming in on the petal too closely and oversimplifying the way God has revealed Himself and His will (in just "do's" and "do nots"). The bottom line is that Christ and His people fulfill and complete the picture that was sketched out in the Old Testament. The beauty of the whole picture is there for us to behold in Christ and His people.

2. God explicitly foretold the destruction of Jerusalem (e.g., Matt 24). This destruction makes one thing quite clear: God intended for the old to end, and the destruction of Jerusalem sent that message loud and clear.

Jerusalem was the seat of Judaism. It was the heart of the "regulations of divine worship." I wonder sometimes if we focus so much on looking for exact wording in order to decide something ("don't do that") that we miss what an event like this may really signify in the bigger picture. It was the destruction of the "system," not just a city and a temple. It was God putting an exclamation point on the end of the old.

"When He said, 'A new covenant,' He has made the first obsolete. But whatever is becoming obsolete and growing old is ready to disappear" (Heb 8:13). Will we continue to argue, after the destruction of the city and temple, and now 2,000 years later, that the old is still not quite yet obsolete? That the practices and rituals under which operated in the old are still viable and in force? The book of Hebrews argues from the lesser to the greater. Christ is better and greater. What we have in Christ is better and greater than the old could ever give. Jesus Christ and His people are the fulfillment of the divine regulations. The city and temple were destroyed, putting a divine end to the system that supported those divine regulations. All has changed under Christ. God made sure that everyone knew it.

The big picture of God's plans makes a difference. Zoom out once in a while and see the beauty of that image. Then we can start to appreciate the details. Don't make it all about what God specifically said not to do. Make it about the beauty of the bigger picture and how we fill our proper role in this plan.

"And coming to Him as to a living stone which has been rejected by men, but is choice and precious in the sight of God, you also, as living stones, are being built up as a spiritual house for a holy priesthood, to offer up spiritual sacrifices acceptable to God through Jesus Christ" (1 Pet 2:4-5).

"But you are A chosen race, A royal priesthood, A holy nation, A people for God's own possession, so that you may proclaim the excellencies of Him who has called you out of darkness into His marvelous light; for you once were not A people, but now you are the people of God; you had not received mercy, but now you have received mercy" (1 Pet 2:9-10).

Conclusion

Bible study can be complex, but it can also be exciting and highly rewarding. When we ask whether or not we can believe the Bible, we have to consider not only the other technical issues about the Bible, like textual criticism, but also the ways in which we approach the Bible, including the way we consider difficult passages.

Let's open our eyes and see the beauty and the depth of God's word, and prepare to be amazed!

Challenging Doubt

Pascal's approach shows us the way: "The hypothesis that the Apostles were knaves is quite absurd. Follow it out to the end." This is the thinking believer's equivalent of Christ's statement, "You will recognize them by their fruits" (Mt. 7:20). What the seed is to the fruit, the premise is to the conclusion. Many of us might never be able to distinguish one variety of seed from another, but we have no trouble in telling an apple from a pear or a cauliflower from a cabbage.

The same is true of presuppositions and conclusions. Find out what the person in doubt is believing wrongly and help him to follow the logic of these presuppositions to their necessary conclusion. Challenge him to check the full-blown consequences of his ideas to see where they lead. He will then see that his views are both wrong and unchristian. Nothing is more nourishing to doubt than hazy mists of vagueness, but clear thinking disperses them and leaves a clear cut choice either to believe or to disbelieve.

Os Guinness, In Two Minds, 95

God and the Slaughter of Innocents

One of the common reasons atheists give for not believing, or questions people have about the Bible, concerns the issue of God slaughtering the nations. Biblical theists are often charged with believing in a barbaric God who, as critics would say, did much worse than abort babies. God committed genocide, commanding His people to completely destroy nations, including innocent women and children. How can we believe in a God like that?

There are aspects of issues like this that go beyond our comprehension, and learning to be content with that lack of understanding or knowledge is as much a part of our trust as is accepting the positive answers that are available for other issues. Here we will simply explore some basic issues that help put a framework around this question.

Let's recognize a basic truth here. How we feel about this or any other difficult question is not what determines whether or not God exists. God's existence is independent of our feelings, so the better approach is to try to understand with what and whom we are working. Feelings don't have the power to determine the reality of God, so whether we like Him or not is irrelevant to His existence.

Acknowledging the Problem

We must acknowledge what Scripture says. It is a difficulty. God told Israel that He would "drive out" or cast out the nations from the land (Exod 34:24; Lev 18:24). God would, according to Balaam, through Israel "devour the nations" who are adversaries of His people and crush their bones in pieces (Num 24:8). The people were told that when they are brought into the land, the Lord would clear away the nations: "and when the Lord your God delivers them before you and you defeat them, then you shall utterly destroy them" (Deut 7:2). Israel was not to make a covenant with the nations, intermarry with them, nor show them any favor. They were to "tear down their altars, and smash their sacred pillars, and hew down their Asherim, and burn their graven images with fire" (v. 5). The reason for this kind of drastic action is also stated. If they didn't utterly destroy the nations, then those same nations would turn the people away from following Yahweh. But these people whom Yahweh called were to be holy, belonging only to Him. In fact, if the people weren't careful, then they would perish "like the nations that the Lord makes to perish before you" (9:1). He did not want them to "imitate the detestable things of those nations" (18:9). Several other passages in Deuteronomy clearly show God's intention to wipe out the nations from before His people. Yet even His own people were warned about being destroyed.

Is it possible that some of the language in Scripture relative to these judgments are hyperbolic in nature? Yes, and I don't believe we can completely dismiss the suggestion. We often hear of one side in a conflict "destroying" or even "annihilating" the other side while recognizing that as an exaggerated emphasis. As we will later see, there is a fluid nature to judgment language. Even if there are some purposefully exaggerated elements, that's probably not fully satisfactory when it comes to understanding all of the passages or answering the objection, for the language still tells us that some awful events occurred, and that included the deaths of many people both young and old. We can't just say, "hyperbole!" and walk away. More needs to be considered.

Others have offered the idea that the accounts are not historical, and therefore they didn't really happen that way at all. That's not very satisfactory, because then we would be dealing with fictions that portray awful events to help give a nation its identity. We would be left to wonder why such fictions would be dreamed up to bolster God's people, so I'm not sure how that helps, for then we be needing to explain that.

Not all of the commands to drive out the nations include total slaughter, but clearly the most disturbing of the commands seem to include genocide. One such clear command is given when king Saul was ordered to annihilate the Amalekites: "Now go and strike Amalek and utterly destroy all that he has, and do not spare him; but put to death both man and woman, child and infant, ox and sheep, camel and donkey" (1 Sam 15:3). Saul found himself in deep trouble when he did not carry this command out completely.

All of the foregoing is just acknowledging the fact that there are orders given by God to His people to destroy particular nations. How, then, do we understand such facts that can indeed be difficult and disturbing?

The Real God of Scripture

Let's start with God Himself. One fundamental problem is that of understanding roles and authority. In order for critics to make the case that God slaughtering the innocents is in any way, shape, or form like humans taking it upon themselves to kill babies (unborn or otherwise), they must bring God down to the same level as humanity or understand Him in a way that is less than what Scripture describes. Therefore, this issue must first be addressed.

A lesser version of God who is prone to ignorance and mistake is not the biblical view of God, and believers should have no interest in defending anything or anyone less than Yahweh with His full authority and glory. To treat God as if He is subject to the same lack of knowledge, the same misunderstandings, the same mistakes, and generally the same limitations as humans is to use the term "God" in a way that does not remotely match the biblical description of Yahweh. If God is somehow amenable to a higher standard of authority or morality than Himself, then He is not the biblical God.

If the god being critiqued is limited and prone to error, then believers would have to agree that such a god taking the lives of the innocent would be egregious, because that would be a god who does not have the wisdom, knowledge, power, and authority over life and death. That being would not be Yahweh.

The God of Scripture cannot be put into such a box, walled in with human limitations. Therefore, before a serious critique of God slaughtering the nations can be undertaken and soberly entertained, critics, to be fair, should first acknowledge the complete biblical descriptions of the God they are trying to critique. It is hardly fair to take one item described in Scripture (e.g., that God orders annihilation), severely critique it, while ignoring another part that is vital for understanding the issue under consideration (e.g., that God is omniscient). Once God is fully acknowledged as Scripture describes, then we might begin to understand why pushing human limitations upon Him winds up with straw men arguments. If the actual, biblical concept of God is not the one truly under consideration, then there is not much else to discuss, for all should agree that a creature who is less than all-wise, all-knowing, and all-authoritative, would have no right to take life in the manner described in Scripture. No one should worship such a god, and this is not what believers defend.

Critics find themselves in an awkward place here, for if they do not acknowledge the full biblical concept of God as they forge their arguments, then they will be guilty of addressing their points against a god that is less than what Scripture describes. In this case, their arguments are straw men and not worthy of consideration because they aren't talking about Yahweh. If, on the other hand, they do acknowledge the biblical descriptions of God, then the critics must believe that they, as critics who are finite and lacking knowledge, have a right to pronounce ultimate judgment on a God described as having infinite knowledge and authority and able to do far more than anyone else is capable of thinking (Eph 3:20). Yet if God is amenable to our finite reason, then He is no longer God.

If the critics think this dichotomy is false, then what other possibilities are there? Let them name the options. Otherwise, either people must accept that God is as described in Scripture or just acknowledge that they won't believe, regardless of who God is. Either option is chosen by faith, but if we start critiquing God, we need to be honest about who God is in His full character and not straw-man Him in order to deny Him.

At this point, one might say, "But you've made an argument about God that cannot be defeated. It is stacking the deck. If what you say about God is true, then there would be no way to deny Him." To this we say that this is indeed the nature of the God of the Bible. He cannot be defeated; if He can be defeated, then He's not God. He cannot ultimately be denied, and in order to deny Him, you really do have to tone Him down somehow and talk about Him in ways that make Him lesser than He is presented in Scripture. If God exists, then all knowledge and wisdom is His, and we will not fully understand all of His ways. We cannot remove His ownership of life and death, then fuss about Him taking life, for again we are no longer really talking about Yahweh.

The real issue, then, is not so much about God taking life, but about whether there really is a God who has all knowledge, wisdom, understanding, and authority. If He exists, then taking life is His prerogative, and whether we like it or not is irrelevant. Denying God based upon human ignorance does not bode well for honest investigation, but speaks highly of human arrogance. If one grants the existence of the God described in the Bible, then the question of whether or not God has a right to take life is already answered. Even if one does not believe such a God can or does exist, to be fair in critiquing the God of Scripture, the critic should still grant the "character" of God the full rights and power that He, as a character in Scripture, is said to possess in the context of that literary work (for the sake of argument). Even characters critiqued in works of fiction deserve to be dealt with as fully described in the target literature.

Biblical Considerations

Following are some considerations based upon seeing God in the total biblical context that need to be kept in mind:

1. God has the inherent, complete, and absolute authority over life and death, and no other life is possible without Him. Yahweh set life and death before the people (Deut 30), and His authority is stated plainly: "See now that I, I am He, and there is no god besides Me; it is I who put to death and give life. I have wounded and it is I who heal, and there is no one who can deliver from My hand" (Deut 32:39). When Hannah was granted a child by the Lord, her thanksgiving included this acknowledgement: "The Lord kills and makes alive; He brings down to Sheol and raises up" (1 Sam 2:6). When Jehoram, the king of Israel was asked to have Naaman the leper healed, he understood his limitations: "Am I God, to kill and to make alive, that this man is sending word to me to cure a man of his leprosy?" (2 Kgs 5:7) The psalmist stated, "Our God is a God of salvation, and to God, the Lord, belong deliverances from death" (Ps 68:20, ESV). The point is that only God has the ultimate authority over life and death issues. To Him belong the "keys of death and hades" (Rev 1:18). Job, who suffered the loss of his own children, acknowledged, "The Lord gave and the Lord has taken away. Blessed be the name of the Lord" (Job 1:21). Later, he recognized that "Sheol is naked before God" (26:6). Because God has such all-encompassing authority, taking life is taking only what belongs to Him in the first place. It is His realm, in His power, and by His will that any human life exists at all (Acts 17:28). If we remove this from God, we are no longer talking about the God of Scripture.

We are reminded of how Paul made a similar point: "The thing molded will not say to the molder, 'Why did you make me like this,' will it? Or does not the potter have a right over the clay, to make from the same lump one vessel for honorable use and another for common use?" (Rom 9:20-21) We must not underestimate God's prerogatives, nor take His prerogatives upon ourselves as if we have His authority.

In contrast, humans have no inherent authority over life and death, but only as God gives it. God, at times, commanded the death penalty, and did allow for particular situations in which killing was permitted (e.g., self-defense under the Law; government bearing the sword, Rom 13). Killing was never allowed generally or just arbitrarily put under the authority of some human. Murder is always wrong in part because it involves people taking the authority of God upon themselves while dishonoring the fact that others are made in God's image. To take life and death issues into one's own hands is to "play God," as we sometimes say, and people have no right either to bring God down to their level or to pull themselves up to His level. Interestingly, the idioms dictionary defines "play God" this way: "to behave as if you have the right to make very important decisions that seriously affect other people's lives."[1] The point is that even popular culture recognizes, at least in principle, that there is a difference between God and the rest of us.

2. God's commands relative to the destruction of nations are given in a particular context concerning one nation, Israel, and those who were dwelling in the land that God had mapped out for Israel's life. Deuteronomy 20:16-18 tells us,

> "*Only in the cities of these peoples that the Lord your God is giving you as an inheritance*, you shall not leave alive anything that breathes. But you shall utterly destroy them, the Hittite and the Amorite, the Canaanite and the Perizzite, the Hivite and the Jebusite, as the Lord your God has commanded you, so that they may not teach you to do according to all their detestable things which they have done for their gods, so that you would sin against the Lord your God."

---

[1] http://idioms.thefreedictionary.com/play+God

The command to destroy is limited to this territory. "The Bible records a command to a specific people for a specific time, not a general command to all people."[2] This is not a universal command, and no one else was expected or authorized to do any of this. It is not a requirement for all military campaigns, even in that period of time. We see this fact in that God prohibited Israel from destroying other surrounding nations. For example, they were not permitted to destroy Edom (Deut 2:4), Moab (v. 9), or Ammon (v. 19). Deuteronomy 23:7 says, "You shall not detest an Edomite, for he is your brother; you shall not detest an Egyptian, because you were an alien in his land." God put boundaries around what and who they were allowed to fight. This was not a willy-nilly "kill them all" type of plan. It was measured, purposeful, and limited.

There is absolutely no warrant for extrapolating the commands to destroy as applying to any other army or situation at any other time or place. God was specific about the contexts and the reasons for such destruction, and this was perfectly within His purview. There is no warrant for a modern army, or modern nation—or any other nation at any time for that matter—to take these commands out of context and use them to justify something like genocide now. These commands give no comfort to such misuse of what we see going on in a specified context in the Bible. Context is critical here, and today, the kingdom of Christ is not about fighting physical warfare. Whatever else we may think about the issue of Israel fighting the nations, Christ brought about a change in how we are to think about the nation of God. Recall that Jesus prohibited His disciples from fighting in order to keep Him away from the cross, and declared to Pilate, an earthly ruler: "My kingdom is not of this world. If My kingdom were of this world, then My servants would be fighting so that I would not be handed over to the Jews; but as it is, My kingdom is not of this realm" (John 18:36).

---

[2] Cowan, Steven B. and Terry L. Wilder, eds. *In Defense of the Bible: A Comprehensive Apologetic for the Authority of Scripture.* Nashville, TN: Broadman and Holman Publishing Group, 2013.

Even if people have a hard time understanding what was happening in the Old Testament context, if we cannot see how Christ brought about renewal and change, then we are failing to see the bigger picture of Scripture, and this will certainly lead to greater misunderstandings.

3. God took life in the context of judgment, not because He is arbitrary and malicious. Judgment and justice came as a result of the nations practicing such sordid evil that there was no hope left, even for the children and their future. Note again that Deuteronomy 20:16-18 says that the judgment on these nations was connected to "all their detestable things." The land became "unclean" because of all the detestable things and abominations committed by the nations (Lev 18:27). Moses said it was "because of the wickedness of these nations that the Lord is dispossessing them" before His people (Deut 9:4). Because of their wicked examples, God wanted those nations gone so that His people would avoid the same wickedness (Deut 12:29-31). One of the evil practices of the nations was burning their sons and daughters in fire to their gods (v. 31). These nations were practicing human sacrifice, taking life and death matters into their own hands. One must not think that these were just some innocent people minding their own business. They were wicked to the core, and God was exercising *His right* to bring judgment down upon them. Justice is, again, God's realm, and to deny Him this is to think that evil has more priority than justice, or that God's holiness and glory are meaningless, or that God should never have a right to initiate judgment when things have gotten so bad that there is no hope left.

God gave Abraham and his seed the promise of the land, but was still giving the people in the land time to repent. Abraham's descendants would have to wait hundreds of years "for the iniquity of the Amorite is not yet complete" (Gen 15:16). That is, their sins had not reached the full measure of when God considered it appropriate to bring judgment. As Scripture consistently teaches, the time for judgment does come. Yet, only God can determine the timing of this. Even so, we actually find that there were those among the gentile nations who did repent. We have the example of Rahab, and the fact that there were other Canaanites who were included in Israel's renewal ceremony in Joshua 8:33-35:

> All Israel with their elders and officers and their judges were standing on both sides of the ark before the Levitical priests who carried the ark of the covenant of the Lord, *the stranger as well as the native.* Half of them stood in front of Mount Gerizim and half of them in front of Mount Ebal, just as Moses the servant of the Lord had given command at first to bless the people of Israel. Then afterward he read all the words of the law, the blessing and the curse, according to all that is written in the book of the law. There was not a word of all that Moses had commanded which Joshua did not read before all the assembly of Israel with the women and the little ones *and the strangers who were living among them.*

What this shows is that the issue was not ethnic or national identity, but rather doing what is right, obedience to God. Repentance of the wickedness and detestable things resulted in being spared from the judgments (cf. also Jonah). What God was eliminating was evil influence, not differing cultures per se (styles of clothes, languages, food choices, etc.). In that sense, the destruction was not always absolute, but conditional, and we need to read these narratives with that context in mind. We might note again that the command was not always to exterminate, but there is more emphasis on "driving out" or dispossessing the Canaanites (Exod 23:28; Lev 18:24; Num 33:52; Deut 6:19; 7:1; 9:4; 18:12; Josh 10:28ff; 11:11, 14). This is not

---

[3] For an alternate view of the meaning of this text, see John H. Walton and J. Harvey Walton, *The Lost World of the Israelite Conquest* (Downer's Grove, IL: IVP Academic, 2017), 50-62.

to mitigate against the harsher statements, but it does show it wasn't always utter annihilation that was in view.

Interestingly, the same term (*charam*, חָרַם, utterly destroy) is used about the destruction of Judah when Babylon came down upon Jerusalem: "I will utterly destroy (*charam*) them and make them a horror and a hissing, and an everlasting desolation" (Jer 25:9). God would "vomit" Judah out of the land (Lev 20:22). Yet, even with that same language in place, God spared a remnant of people, including some of the poor who were left in the land when they were invaded. The point is, "utterly destroy" does not always carry the connotation of complete annihilation, for Judah did live to return once again. The point was more that there would be dispossession. Loss of life was inevitable, but it didn't *always* means that every last person died. The language of judgment in Scripture works this way, as the prophets well demonstrate concerning a number of nations. The bottom line is that God knows the time and extent of any judgment, and we need to allow for the fluid nature of judgment language.

In contrast, people take innocent life, as in abortion, in the context of trying to cover over their own sin, and for selfish reasons. This is more akin to the sacrificing of children to the fire. God has a right to execute justice, and He has full knowledge of the extent of that justice. People are interested in justice, too, but do not have the wisdom and knowledge of God to know how to enact the full extent of justice. A practice like abortion is not about justice. There is no comparison with God's actions here.

4. God took life in the context of a full understanding of the situation at hand. He knew who the people were, what they stood for, and what they would be in the future. God, the great I AM, knows and declares the end from the beginning (Isa 46:10). He would well have known what kind of people these children would grow up to become. He knew their religious culture, the parents, their future, and pagan ways that allowed immorality and evil to

run rampant. In this light, it is not out of the question to think that God was, in fact, sparing these children from becoming the wicked people He knew they would become. There was no hope left for these nations. There would be no salt, and God spared further wickedness and destruction. This admission is no mere cop-out; at its core is the confession of God's full understanding of all that is just and right. The Judge of heaven and earth always does what is just and right (cf. Gen 18:25). He may well have saved them from themselves, but that is within His realm and none other's.

In contrast, people take life in the context of a finite understanding, not knowing fully who the person will become and what he or she will accomplish. People, as finite creatures, have no ability to know the end from the beginning. They cannot know what type of person the child will grow up to become, whether good or bad. They may be destroying the salt of the earth and light of the world rather than sparing great wickedness. There is no way of knowing, so the reasons for taking life this way cannot be with the same understanding and purposes as God.

The knowledge of God is paramount here. If we are not willing to allow an all-knowing, all-wise God who owns life and death, then there can never be a way to answer or come to any kind of conclusion that will provide some peace. If we are not willing to admit our own ignorance and lack of infinite wisdom, then no doubt we will continue to find fault with God, not believing that He truly is the glorious God Scripture shows Him to be.

5. The reason that we are having this discussion is due to the problem of sin. God took life as a consequence of sin, but with a will to redeem people out of sin by using death. The problem of sin needs to be seen for what it really is: a rebellion against God and an effort to enthrone self where God sits. In God's infinite holiness and glory, Scripture shows that He cannot simply overlook the problem. The guilty are often punished with hopeless death, but what of the innocent?

First, any innocent who die are safe in God's hands and will not suffer any more. God redeemed the lives of the innocent by taking them as a consequence of judgment and justice in a wicked world brought about because of sin; the innocent often suffer along with the wicked because of being in a world corrupted by sin. Yet God spared them from their own evil futures (and only He could see their future). Again, this is His, and only His, prerogative as the owner and authority over all life and death, and as all-knowing and all-wise.

Second, the concept of the innocent dying for the sins of others is fulfilled and brought to fruition in Jesus Christ. There is a sense in which the death of the innocents foreshadows the death of God's innocent Son. God Himself entered into suffering and, as an innocent suffering servant, died in order to redeem the guilty through forgiveness (cf. 2 Cor 5:21). The fact that Jesus died as an innocent sufferer shows to us that such is not contrary to God's love, for it was because of His great love that He desired to offer Himself as a sacrifice for sin and redeem us out of our sins back into a fellowship with Him (Rom 5:6-11; 8:31ff). Because of the death that He died for us as sinners, we may now die *to* sin to be raised with Him (Rom 6:3-5).

In contrast, people take the lives of the innocent, not out of redemptive purposes, but for self-designed purposes usurping prerogatives that do not belong to them. Only God can redeem a life, for the soul in eternity is His, and He assigns all eternal outcomes. There is no human comparison to be made here, so trying to equate the actions of God with evil men completely misses the mark. Men who are already tainted with evil, and using their own self-will to take the lives of the innocent, in no way compares with a holy, righteous, just, all-knowing God who has the ability to redeem and glorify a soul eternally. There are worse things than physical death, and if we cannot see this perspective, we'll completely miss God's purposes.

Conclusion

There is no inconsistency in recognizing that God has absolute power over life and death, while people have only the limited authority granted to them by God. If God, in His infinite wisdom and knowledge, knows the exact time and place for the giving or taking of life, whoever that may include, this is no way suggests that humans may take it upon themselves with their own authority to decide such issues of life and death. Again, at the heart of the objection lies the faulty concept that God and humans are in some way on par with each other and subject to the same limitations and failed judgments. Any of these discussions must begin by considering the real God of the Bible, not a tone-down limited god who is prone to error and ignorance.

God's judgment and justice took the lives of the pagan nations, yet the gospel shows an even greater plan in action:

First, death has been overcome through Christ. The resurrection is God's evidence that there will be a final day of judgment (Acts 17:30-31). Second, God's plan through Jesus includes the redemption of the nations. All nations are welcomed in Christ (see Acts 10:34-35). In a way, the judgment upon the nations foreshadowed justice and judgment in the ultimate sense. All temporal judgments point to a greater final judgment. Still, God often spared the nations and showed mercy. His plan in Christ encompasses all the nations, and the offer for salvation is open to all. "This is good and acceptable in the sight of God our Savior, who desires all men to be saved and to come to the knowledge of the truth" (1 Tim 2:3-4).

Let God's will be done on earth as it is in heaven. May God bless us as we continue to study issues like this, and may we be open to seeing His plan come to fruition through Jesus Christ.

The Problem of Slavery

We do not have the space to address this issue fully, but we do want to offer some suggestions and consider principles for thinking about the context and question of slavery in Scripture. A common argument in an effort to discredit the Bible is that since the Bible condoned slavery, and we all know how wrong slavery is, then the Bible must be erroneous. Others who still want to hold on to faith will argue that the condoning of slavery in the Bible shows that the Bible was just wrong about some matters. For that reason, we need to be open to other ways of understanding right and wrong. The prime example now is how open we need to be to same-sex marriage. Since the Bible was wrong about slavery, then it was likely also wrong about its condemnation of homosexual practice. We just need to progress in our thinking (and many will, at that point, attribute the progress to the Holy Spirit). Neither option works.

Was the Bible wrong about this matter? Was God really condoning a practice that is it to be equated with the horrors of racial slavery in 19th century America? We should acknowledge the difficulty of an issue like this. We are treading on difficult turf, so how do we begin to process this?

One of the problems up front is what we mean by "slavery." We must define what we are talking about. Not all forms of what's called "slavery" are the same, and understanding the differences is critical. Otherwise, we see the term "slave" in the Bible, automatically associate that with early American slavery (because that is our modern context), complete with chains and whips, and are thus confused or shaken in our faith. We have seen picture memes depicting African slaves in chains and referencing Bible passages in order to show how ludicrous accepting the Bible is in our enlightened age. This is misinformed argumentation at best.

Slave owners who also claimed to be following the Bible erroneously used the Bible to defend their practices. Isaac Allen, who wrote in the 19th century against slavery, pointed out how slave-owners reasoned that if it's legal in the Bible, then it must have been right.[1] They, like modern unbelievers, failed to understand the bigger picture of Scripture and God's plan to redeem all human beings through Christ. They were using Scripture as a pretense for doing what they wanted, not to find what God wanted.

Such depictions of what we find in Scripture are based on straw men arguments and superficial readings. What can we begin to say about this? Here are some starting principles to consider:

First, once sin came into the world, relationships became distorted. Distorted relationships are the result of sin, not the result of God desiring them or pronouncing them good. This included certain practices involving various nations, including slavery. Now God could have overturned free will, but He has always allowed people the freedom to do as they will while pleading with them to consider their ways. Slavery is a practice because sinful men made it so, not because God wanted it to be so. The fact that God regulated something that came about due to the problem of sin does not mean that this was what He wanted from the beginning.

When we consider Scripture as a whole, we can see that "the Bible does not present the world as a place in which God intended people to be owned by other people or abused because of their sex. God did not make the world for slavers and sexists."[2] Those who focus

---

[1] Isaac Allen, *Is Slavery Sanctioned by the Bible?* (Public Domain Books: Kindle Edition), 1.

[2] James Hamilton, "Does the Bible Condone Slavery and Sexism?" In *In Defense of The Bible: A Comprehensive Apologetic for the Authority of Scripture,* eds. Steven B. Cowan and Terry L. Wilder (Nashville, TN: Broadman and Holman Academic, 2013), 336.

on slavery as a way to discredit Scripture are missing the bigger picture of the problem of sin and how God deals with it. Once we consider the bigger issues, we can see that God never intended human enslavement. It was a distortion.

Slavery was based on a curse. The first mention of slavery is after sin entered the scene, in Genesis 9, where Ham's family (Canaan) is cursed because of sin (v. 25). Sin brings curses into the world, and slavery was one of the curses. Even so, God set into motion his plan for dealing with it. Abraham would be the one through whom all families of the earth would be blessed (Gen 12:1-3). God "promises to overcome the distortion of human relationships" through this blessing, and we ought to think of this "in light of God's purpose to redeem and renew" through Christ.[3]

Second, God allowed certain actions that He later prohibited, modified, or regulated differently. Polygamy and divorce are examples of this along with slavery.

Why did He allow these practices? Perhaps the best answer is found in Jesus' response to the Pharisees when they asked Him about Moses permitting a man to divorce his wife for any cause. Jesus answered, "Because of your hardness of heart Moses permitted you to divorce your wives; but from the beginning it has not been this way" (Matt. 19:8).

Jesus was pointing to what God really wanted from the beginning. That is, how people came to practice marriage and divorce, and even how God regulated the practice under Moses, was not really what God had in mind from the beginning. Relationships were distorted because of sin and God regulated the fall-out for a time in order to help protect those who might be further abused. One of the points to be taken from this is that Jesus came to set matters straight. His standard for behavior was not going to be based upon

---

[3] *Ibid.*, 342.

regulation laws that had to be set into place as a result of hardened hearts. That era was over. Through Christ it's back to the beginning!

There is a difference between the ideal that God made "from the beginning" and what He allowed and regulated after sin and corruption entered the picture. *Permitted and regulated does not equate to condone or desire. Allowance does not equal ideal.* In other words, "God never 'supported' slavery in the sense that it was His ideal. Rather, it was something He tolerated in certain forms, at a particular time, and in a particular place."[4]

Due to hardened hearts and in order to avoid further evil abuses that would come from hardened hearts, God regulated slavery. Under Christ, the concept of slavery moves from the physical to the spiritual. Physically, God would have people be free (see 1 Cor 7:21-24). While that may not always be possible due to the way people still act, the ideal is still given: "if you are able also to become free, rather do that." If that's not possible, and God won't force people to act against their wills (people still divorce against God's will, too), then they are to serve God to the best of their ability no matter what condition they are in. Again, there is a difference between what God permitted to happen subsequent to sin entering the world and what God desired from the beginning and ultimately makes right in Christ. God's intention from the beginning was not that people would own other people.

What we see in Christ is a reversal and renewal process. Jesus' argument in Matthew 19 gets back to the beginning for marriage (one man, one woman, no divorce), and the entire gist of the New Covenant is built around the idea that freedom (primarily from sin, but includes being owned by others) is what God ultimately wants

---

[4] Natasha Crain, *Keeping Your Kids on God's Side: 40 Conversations to Help Them Build a Lasting Faith* (Harvest House Publishers, 2016), Kindle Edition, 182.

(John 8:32; cf. 1 Cor 7:21; Philemon). To see this clearly, though, one needs to study through the contexts and the bigger picture of Scripture from the beginning to the end.

To see what God really wanted, therefore, we go back to the beginning. When sin occurred, we see how the curse of sin changed everything. Then we see how God brings reversal and renewal through Christ. What God desires is what is found "from the beginning" and made anew in Christ. What God permitted and regulated for the hardness of hearts prior to Christ, while now commanding all to repent because of Christ (Acts 17:30-31), is not a fair representation of what God actually desires and sets straight through Jesus Christ.

Third, sometimes God regulates a less-than-desirable practice for the purpose of protecting those who may otherwise be easily abused. It's the way the world was at the time. That doesn't make it right, but it does mean that we need to see such issues in the context of the culture and world at that time. We cannot rightly bring a modern, westernized mindset to the Scriptures and then make accusations about its accuracy and modes of expression based on a perspective thousands of years removed from the times and culture. We invalidate our interpretation by doing so.

God regulated how men were to treat women, and He regulated slavery within the context of a world that regularly abused both. The laws were given as safeguards against further abuse. For example, Deuteronomy 23:15-16 regulates what happens when an Israelite encountered a runaway slave, presumably from another nation. "You shall not hand over to his master a slave who has escaped from his master to you. He shall live with you in your midst, in the place which he shall choose in one of your towns where it pleases him; you shall not mistreat him." Greengus points out that these laws "represent a radical departure from ancient Near

Eastern conventions" in which slaves were expected to be returned.[5] Note especially that just because they had been slaves did not give anyone a right to mistreat them. Abuse was never acceptable.

God's laws regulating slavery were, indeed, different from others. Bear in mind that there is an overarching law against kidnapping: "He who kidnaps a man, whether he sells him or he is found in his possession, shall surely be put to death" (Exod 21:16; cf. Deut 24:7). This coincides with the eighth commandment: "You shall not steal" (Exod 20:15). The type of slavery we are used to hearing about made its mark through kidnapping and stealing. This is not comparable to what we find in the Scriptures.

Further, God provided for ways in which the slave could be redeemed and made free. Deuteronomy 15:12-15 makes this clear:

> If your kinsman, a Hebrew man or woman, is sold to you, then he shall serve you six years, but in the seventh year you shall set him free. When you set him free, you shall not send him away empty-handed. You shall furnish him liberally from your flock and from your threshing floor and from your wine vat; you shall give to him as the Lord your God has blessed you. You shall remember that you were a slave in the land of Egypt, and the Lord your God redeemed you; therefore I command you this today.

Notice, here, that this form of slavery involved their own kinsman, the Hebrews. Freedom was the goal, and God provided for this. This brings us to the next important point:

Fourth, we need to distinguish types of slavery. "The key to understanding the complexity of Old Testament slavery is

---

[5] Samuel Greengus, *Laws in the Bible and in Early Rabbinic Collections: The Legal Legacy of the Ancient Near East* (Eugene, OR: Cascade Books, 2011), 121.

recognizing that there were several different categories of slaves, each under a unique set of laws."[6] Not all forms of slavery are the same, and it is a mistake to lump them all together. We would be mistaken to equate the slavery we read about in Scripture with the type of slavery common in early America. Here is a brief survey:

1. *Indentured servitude* is the more common type of slavery that is regulated (Exod 21; Deut 15). This is where one might, of his own free will, sell himself into a position of slavery in order to pay off a debt. Once the debt is paid, or redemption is made, the slave is set free. God provided for the release of debts and freedom every seventh year. This type of servitude was *voluntary*. It was not a forced kind of slavery that is associated with chattel slavery, in which slaves are not even considered persons, and the masters may do with them whatever they please.[7] Even though rabbinic law spoke of such, the Bible "contains no laws on the sale of chattel slaves."[8] The point is that indentured servitude, though itself not ideal, is not to be equated with chattel slavery. This looks more like a hired hand under contract. "He shall be with you as a hired man, as if he were a sojourner; he shall serve with you until the year of jubilee" (Lev 25:40).

2. *Servant Girls as Future Wives* (Exod 21:7-11). The misunderstanding here is in thinking this is about selling young girls as slaves for sex. That's not the case, and context is key. This passage provides measures to protect females "from sexual exploitation by adding marriage to their condition of bondage." The "creditor is made to act as a kind of guardian" to the female in this situation.[9]

---

[6] Crain, 177.

[7] Allen, 5.

[8] Greengus, 113.

[9] *Ibid.*, 88-89.

Girls were to expect an arranged marriage (again, part of that culture and many others). A man who wishes to marry would normally give the father of the bride some kind of dowry. However, if a man was too poor, he might choose to "sell" his daughter to a future husband while she was young with the intent that the man marry her. Basically, the dowry was paid early. "This was a way for the poverty-stricken father to receive money for his daughter's marriage much earlier, and it allowed his daughter to marry into a higher socioeconomic class than she otherwise would have. These verses regulate this practice to protect the girls who were entering into such arrangements."[10]

Working toward freedom was not the point of these arrangements, but rather working toward marriage. If the potential husband decided he didn't want to marry the girl after all, or give her to his son in marriage, she would be redeemed and returned to the family. He could not just sell her to foreigners. Finally, she was to be treated as family. There simply is nothing in this approaching sex-trade or chattel slavery.[11]

3. *Foreigners as slaves* (Lev 25:44-46). While this is the more troublesome passage, I see at least a couple of possibilities to consider here. Given that the passage doesn't specify the reason for the slavery, we need to be cautious.

First, warfare was "the principle cause of slavery in Mesopotamia."[12] Though not Mesopotamia, the area was near enough, and it's possible that this passage reflects results wherein one was "a captive taken as booty in warfare."[13] Recall that the pagan nations were

---

[10] Crain, 179.

[11] *Ibid.*, 180.

[12] John H. Walton, Victor H. Matthews, and Mark W. Chavalas, *The IVP Bible Background Commentary: Old Testament* (Downers Grove, IL: InterVarsity Press, 2000), 140.

[13] Greengus, 86.

hostile to God and His people. Israel was not to make a covenant with them, nor were the pagans to live among them "because they will make you sin against Me; for if you serve their gods, it will surely be a snare to you" (Exod 23:32-33).

Think about it this way. Even though Israel might rule another nation that would then serve them, this was not based upon skin color or some broader-based ethnicity. This was localized, specific, and temporary, based upon the surrounding pagan nations. It may have been the result of what happened with warring nations at a time in which such wars were common. When pagan nations attacked Israel, there were consequences from their hostility to God's purposes and people. Again, this can be understood in light of the curses (cf. Gen 9:25-27). The pagan nations were immoral and evil. They sacrificed their children to idols. They committed wicked acts of immorality without reservation. They would have readily destroyed Israel if they had the chance. Their wickedness meant that their freedom was removed (I think of it kind of like a prison sentence). The exceptions to this sometimes see a good person who assimilated into Israel (like Uriah the Hittite), but this type of slavery was considered part of the curse and the enmity that existed. Even if a foreigner didn't convert, he was not permitted to bring in his wicked practices.

Second, it's possible that the foreigner may have voluntarily sold himself into servitude if he was too poor to pay debts. Once in this situation, he might have been acquired by someone in Israel then kept in the family. Given the regulations about how Israel was to treat foreigners, they still would have been obligated to treat them humanely. Once again, God regulated the relationship, intending to bring change all along.

In any case, the text indicates that a stranger or sojourner may be redeemed and set free "if the means of a stranger or sojourner with you becomes sufficient" (v. 47). The existence of these regulations do not support slavery outside of this context. This was never meant to be a circumstance that would translate into other nations and cultures, and no modern nation may find comfort in buying and selling slaves. This is no blanket endorsement of slavery, but regulations for circumstances that would pass.

Fifth, the laws were regulatory to deal with relationships distorted by sin, but the ideals were also built into the Law. If everyone acted according to the ideals, then the problems often connected to slavery would have ceased. We should understand that many of the laws given were meant, not to be held up as what everyone should be normally doing, but rather as conditional laws to be followed when the ideal is broken. To see this point, consider what John wrote:

"My little children, I am writing these things to you so that you may not sin. And if anyone sins, we have an Advocate with the Father, Jesus Christ the righteous" (1 John 2:1).

John was not advocating sin. He was, rather, pointing out that the reality of sin, to which all succumb, has been dealt with by Jesus. There is hope for the Christian who sins, not because the sin is acceptable, but because Jesus has provided a way to forgiveness. Thus, if anyone sins, we have an advocate through Jesus.

In the Law, God was not advocating divorce in Deuteronomy 24. However, He provided laws attending to divorce even though divorce was not condoned. Likewise, slavery was the reality of a broken and cursed world, not the result of ideal principles from the beginning. Since the reality of slavery was part of the broken and cursed world, God regulated it in a way that helped to mitigate against further abuses and helped protect those who were on both sides of the situation.

If people had acted toward fellow man the way they ought, what a difference that would have made! Loving neighbor as self (Lev

19:18), and treating the sojourner with respect would have helped mollify against abuses. If the pagan nations would have repented, ceased anger against God's people and purposes, and given up their abject wickedness, perhaps there would been no enslavement. Perhaps there would have been peace.

Prisons are not built in order to condone criminal activity, but rather to keep criminals from causing more harm. While forms of judgment and punishment were given for sin and evil (even as in our own justice system and in every system around the world), nowhere does God indicate that one may acceptably mistreat, abuse, and dehumanize another person just because they come from somewhere else or are another ethnicity. No enslavement was based solely on the notion that the people were foreigners or strangers, the very people they were supposed to treat well.

Consider how Israel was specifically directed to treat strangers: "You shall not wrong a stranger or oppress him, for you were strangers in the land of Egypt" (Exod 22:21; 23:9). Consider, also, Solomon's prayer regarding the temple:

> Also concerning the foreigner who is not from Your people Israel, when he comes from a far country for Your great name's sake and Your mighty hand and Your outstretched arm, when they come and pray toward this house, then hear from heaven, from Your dwelling place, and do according to all for which the foreigner calls to You, in order that all the peoples of the earth may know Your name, and fear You as do Your people Israel, and that they may know that this house which I have built is called by Your name. (2 Chron 6:32-33)

The problem, then, was not just in being a foreigner. It seems more likely that the problem, insofar as pagan enslavement was concerned, was that those who were evil, hostile to God and His people, and who would have destroyed everything associated with

Israel, were still going to suffer the consequences of the curse. They were kept in check by God's regulations.

New Testament Slavery and Silence

Does the New Testament endorse and promote slavery? Bear in mind that Christians were having to adapt and live within a culture that was not Christ-like. Slavery was a Roman practice, and Christians had to grapple with that reality. The whole relationship between slaves and masters would change drastically under Christ if the affected people actually listened to Christ's teachings (Eph 6:5-9; Col 3:22-4:1).

One situation in the New Testament concerns Philemon and his slave Onesimus. We don't know what the exact circumstances were that led to Onesimus' slavery (perhaps an indentured servant), nor what led to his running away. However, when Paul sent Onesimus back, both Onesimus and Philemon were brothers in Christ. Paul pleads with Philemon to do what was right and proper, with the implication that Paul could have forced Philemon's hand under compulsion. Instead, he wanted Philemon to do what was proper out of free will, to forgive and receive Onesimus back as a brother (which would have included all that being a brother in Christ entails; think of those implications in Col 3:12-15). Paul was confident that Philemon would do even more than what was being asked. This letter shows that when both master and slave became Christians, their relationship would indeed change, giving further evidence that those coming under the power of Christ would be renewed and changed. This is not a letter that gives any approval or comfort to the racial slavery of early America or any other time. It shows, rather, that there is an expectation of a changed relationship.

Still, some wonder why the New Testament isn't more explicit about the condemnation of slavery. Though it is a mistake to read into Scripture the racial, chattel slavery of early America, the New Testament is not completely silent about the implications of slavery, and in several ways stands in opposition to the institution of slavery. Most obvious is the condemnation of "slave traders" in 1 Timothy 1:9-10. Some translations say, "kidnappers," but the word indicates those who deal in slaves. It references "those in Biblical times who sold people as slaves (so NRSV 'slave traders'), and specifically to those who used kidnapping as a way of capturing people for the purpose of selling them into slavery."[14] This is explicitly condemned. Copan observes:

> We can confidently say that Paul would have considered antebellum slavery with its slave trade to be an abomination —an utter violation of human dignity and an act of human theft. In Paul's 'vice list' in 1 Tim 1:9-10, he expounds on the fifth through the ninth commandments (Exodus 20/ Deuteronomy 5); there he condemns 'slave traders' (NIV) who steal what isn't rightfully theirs.

Critics wonder why Paul or New Testament writers (cf. 1 Pet 2:18-20) didn't condemn slavery outright and tell masters to release their slaves. Yet we should first separate this question out from other considerations. The New Testament writers' position on the negative status of slavery was clear on various points:

- the repudiation of slave trading (1 Tim 1:9–10);
- the affirmation of the full human dignity and equal spiritual status of slaves;
- the encouragement for slaves to acquire their freedom whenever it is possible (1 Cor 7:20-22);
- the revolutionary Christian affirmations (e.g., Gal 3: 28) which, if taken seriously, would help to tear apart the fabric of the institution of slavery; indeed, this is

---

[14] Daniel C. Arichea and Howard A. Hatton, *A Handbook on Paul's First Letter to Timothy*, UBS Handbook Series (NY: United Bible Societies, 1995), 26.

precisely what took full effect several centuries later—namely, the eventual eradication of slavery in Europe; and

- the condemnation of treating humans as cargo (Rev 18:11-13, where doomed Babylon—the 'city' of God-opposers—stands condemned because she had treated humans as 'cargo,' having trafficked in 'slaves [literally 'bodies'] and human lives,' NASB).[15]

Without question, a true practice of Christianity undermines and destroys the foundations of slavery. If people practiced what Christ and the apostles teach, slavery as we know it would be done.

From Slavery to Freedom

Christ came to bring change and create new relationships. In doing so, He used the relationship of slavery to describe sin. Forgiveness by His grace is freedom from the slavery of sin.

> "God did not create humans to be slaves but to serve him freely. God redeemed slaves, set them free, broke the yoke from upon them, and made them walk erect that they might serve him in dignified freedom. Those who trust in Christ are no longer slaves of sin but slaves of God (Rom 6:18, 22). Even if they are enslaved in the present, their identity is to be found in their union with Christ by faith (Gal 3:28), by which they are sons of God (3:26). This will enable them to rise above the burden of slavery, which they should cast off if they can (1 Cor 7:21).
>
> The distortion of human relations that is slavery will not be perpetuated in the future."[16]

---

[15] Paul Copan and William Lane Craig, eds, *Come Let Us Reason: New Essays in Christian Apologetics* (Nashville, TN: B&H Academic, 2012), 262-263.

[16] Hamilton, 347.

The anticipation of both bringing in the foreigners and bringing freedom from the slavery of sin is prophetically stated by Isaiah:

> Also the foreigners who join themselves to the Lord,
> To minister to Him, and to love the name of the Lord,
> To be His servants, every one who keeps from profaning the sabbath
> And holds fast My covenant;
> Even those I will bring to My holy mountain
> And make them joyful in My house of prayer.
> Their burnt offerings and their sacrifices will be acceptable on My altar;
> For My house will be called a house of prayer for all the peoples. (Isa 56:6-7)

When Jesus began His public ministry, He quoted from Isaiah 61 and made it clear what His purpose was:

> The Spirit of the Lord is upon Me,
> Because He anointed Me to preach the gospel to the poor.
> He has sent Me to proclaim release to the captives,
> And recovery of sight to the blind,
> To set free those who are oppressed,
> To proclaim the favorable year of the Lord. (Luke 4:18-19)

Jesus' purpose was to set free those who are help captive by sin. As Isaiah indicated, this was for all people. Though slavery was part of a cursed and corrupted world, Jesus came to reverse that curse and set people free. Ultimately, though the sin in this world still harms people, Jesus offers rest, peace, and freedom (Matt 11:28-30; Rom 5:1-2; 8:1-2). Physical slavery was symptomatic of what sin itself does to all of us. The only real, ultimate freedom is going to be in Christ. Concerning this, as it related to the Law, Paul wrote, "It was for freedom that Christ set us free; therefore keep standing firm and do not be subject again to a yoke of slavery" (Gal 5:1). Sadly, some may not have escaped physical slavery, but ultimately all can be made spiritually free in Christ. In the end, the freedom found in Christ will be the greatest freedom of all.

Conclusion

The problem of slavery is certainly difficult, but when understood in its context, we can see that the arguments made in trying to equate modern forms of chattel slavery to what the Scriptures say fall apart. God regulated what grew out of the curse of sin. He does not condone the slavery prevalent in early America. This type of slavery of which we are familiar from modern history was based upon an explicit denial that God made all men equal and, one race "not being equal to" another, "that slavery subordination to the superior race is his natural and normal condition."[17] Scripture never justifies or promotes such a view, nor does God condone the abuse of others based on ethnicity. Further, whatever difficulties were involved in regulating matters relative to the curse, Christ came to bring reversal and renewal for all people. Everyone ought to be free from the ravages of human oppression and free the bondage of sin. If we cannot do so physically, we certainly can do so spiritually as look for the city whose Builder and Maker is God.

---

[17] Alexander Stephens, *"Corner Stone" Speech.* 1861. <https://web.archive.org/web/20130822142313/http://teachingamericanhistory.org/library/document/cornerstone-speech/> Accessed August 22, 2017. Stephens was the Vice President of the Confederate States of America through the American Civil War.

Bibliography and Select Resources

GENERAL APOLOGETICS

Baxter, Batsell Barrett. *I Believe Because ...: A Study of the Evidence Supporting Christian Faith.* Grand Rapids: Baker Book House Co, 1971.

Boa, Kenneth D., and Robert M. Bowman Jr. *20 Compelling Evidences That God Exists: Discover Why Believing in God Makes so Much Sense.* Tulsa, OK: RiverOak Pub., 2002.

Boyd, Gregory A., and Edward K. Boyd. *Letters from a Skeptic.* Wheaton, Ill.: Victor Books, 1994.

Burgett, Gene. *Dear Lisa: How to Combat Religious Doubt.* Huntsville, AL: Publishing Designs, 2005.

Bush, L. Russ, ed. *Classical Readings in Christian Apologetics.* Grand Rapids, MI: Academie Books (Zondervan), 1983.

Casteel, Herbert C. *Beyond a Reasonable Doubt,* rev. ed. Joplin, Mo.: College Press, 1992.

Copan, Paul and William Lane Craig, eds. *Come Let Us Reason: New Essays in Christian Apologetics.* Nashville, TN: B&H Academic, 2012.

Craig, William Lane. *Apologetics: An Introduction.* Chicago: Moody Press, 1984.

_____. *On Guard: Defending Your Faith with Reason and Precision.* Colorado Springs, CO: David C. Cook, 2010.

Crain, Natasha. *Keeping Your Kids on God's Side: 40 Conversations to Help Them Build a Lasting Faith.* Harvest House Publishers, Kindle Edition, 2016.

Corduan, Winfried. *No Doubt About It: The Case for Christianity.* Nashville, TN: Broadman and Holman Publishers, 1997.

Cottrell, Jack. *The Faith Once for All: Bible Doctrine for Today.* Joplin, MO: College Press, 2002.

Cowan, Steven B., ed. *Five Views On Apologetics.* Grand Rapids, Mich.: Zondervan Pub. House, 2000.

Cowan, Steven B. and Terry L. Wilder, eds. *In Defense of The Bible: A Comprehensive Apologetic for the Authority of Scripture.* Nashville, TN: Broadman and Holman Academic, 2013.

Craig, William Lane, and Walter Sinnott-Armstrong. *God? a Debate Between a Christian and an Atheist.* NY: Oxford University Press, 2004.

Craig, William Lane. *Hard Questions, Real Answers.* Wheaton, Ill.: Crossway Books, 2003.

_____. *Reasonable Faith: Christian Truth and Apologetics*, 3d ed. Wheaton, Ill.: Crossway Books, 2008.

Dembski, William A., and Jay Wesley Richards, eds. *Unapologetic Apologetics: Meeting the Challenges of Theological Studies.* Downers Grove, Ill.: InterVarsity Press, 2001.

Frame, John M. *Apologetics to the Glory of God: An Introduction.* Phillipsburg, N.J.: P&R Pub., 1994.

Geisler, Norman L. *Christian Apologetics.* Grand Rapids: Baker Book House, 1976.

_____. and Patrick Zukeran. *The Apologetics of Jesus*. Grand Rapids, MI: Baker Books, 2009.

_____. *Baker Encyclopedia of Christian Apologetics*. Grand Rapids, Mich.: Baker Books, 1999.

_____. and Ronald M. Brooks. *When Skeptics Ask*. Wheaton, Ill.: Victor Books, 1990.

_____. and Frank Turek. *I Don't Have Enough Faith to Be an Atheist*. Wheaton, Ill.: Crossway Books, 2004.

Groothuis, Douglas. *Christian Apologetics: A Comprehensive Case for Biblical Faith*. Downers Grove, IL: IVP Academic, 2011.

Guinness, Os. *Fool's Talk: Recovering the Art of Christian Persuasion*. Downer's Grove, IL: InterVarsity Press, 2015.

_____. *God in the Dark: The Assurance of Faith Beyond a Shadow of Doubt*. Wheaton, IL: Crossway Books, 1996.

_____. *In Two Minds: The Dilemma of Doubt and How to Resolve it*. Downers Grove, IL: InterVarsity Press, 1976.

Hoover A. J. *The Case for Christian Theism*, Grand Rapids, MI: Baker Book House, 1980. Rpt. of *Dear Agnos*. 1976.

House, H. Wayne, and Joseph M. Holden. *Charts of Apologetics and Christian Evidences*. Zondervan Charts series. Grand Rapids, Mich.: Zondervan, 2006.

Keller, Timothy. *The Reason for God: Belief in an Age of Skepticism*. New York: Dutton, 2008.

Koukl, Gregory. *Tactics*. Grand Rapids, MI: Zondervan, 2009.

Kreeft, Peter, and Ronald K. Tacelli. *Handbook of Christian Apologetics*. Downers Grove, IL: InterVarsity Press, 1994.

Kumar, Steve. *Christianity for Skeptics.* Peabody, MA: Hendrickson Publishers, 2000.

Lewis, C.S. *Miracles.* NY: Macmillan Publishing Co., 1960.

Little, Paul E. *Know Why You Believe.* 4th ed. Downers Grove, IL: InterVarsity Press, 2000.

McDowell, Josh and Sean McDowell. *Evidence that Demands a Verdict: Life-Changing Truth for a Skeptical World.* Nashville, TN: Harper Collins, 2017.

McGrath, Alister E. *Doubting: Growing through the Uncertainties of Faith.* Downers Grove, IL: InterVarsity Press, 2007.

_____. *Intellectuals Don't Need God and Other Modern Myths.* Grand Rapids, MI: Zondervan, 1993.

_____. *Mere Apologetics: How to Help Seekers and Skeptics Find Faith.* Grand Rapids, MI: BakerBooks, 2012.

Montgomery, John Warwick. *History and Christianity.* Minneapolis, MN:: Bethany House Publishers, 1965.

Moreland, J. P., and Kai Nielsen. *Does God Exist? The Debate Between Theists and Atheists.* Buffalo, NY: Prometheus Books, 1993.

Moreland, J.P. *Scaling the Secular City.* Grand Rapids: Baker Books, 1987.

Morrow, Jonathan. *Think Christianly: Looking at the Intersection of Faith and Culture.* Grand Rapids, MI: Zondervan, 2011.

Murray, Michael J., ed. *Reason for the Hope Within.* Grand Rapids, MI.: W.B. Eerdmans, 1999.

Nash, Ronald H. *Christian Faith and Historical Understanding.* Grand Rapids, MI: Zondervan, 1984.

Schaeffer, Francis A. *Escape from Reason.* Downers Grove, IL: InterVarsity Press, 1968.

_____. *The God Who Is There.* Downers Grove, Illinois: Intervarsity Press, 1998.

_____. *He Is There and He Is Not Silent.* Wheaton, IL: Tyndale House, 1972.

Sire, James W. *Why Good Arguments Often Fail: Making a More Persuasive Case for Christ.* Downers Grove, Ill.: IVP Books/ InterVarsity Press, 2006.

Sproul, R.C. *Reason to Believe.* Grand Rapids, MI: Zondervan Publishing House, 1978.

Sproul, R.C., John Gerstner, and Arthur Lindsley. *Classical Apologetics: A Rational Defense of The Christian Faith and a Critique of Presuppositional Apologetics.* Grand Rapids, Mich.: Zondervan, 1984.

Strobel Lee. *The Case for Faith: The Film.* Santa Monica, CA: La Miranda Films, 2008, DVD.

_____. *The Case for Faith: A Journalist Investigates the Toughest Objections to Christianity.* Grand Rapids, MI: Zondervan, 2000.

Taylor, James E. *Introducing Apologetics: Cultivating Christian Commitment.* Grand Rapids, Mich.: Baker Academic, 2006.

Vos, Howard F. *Can I Really Believe?* Iowa Falls, IA: World Pub., 1995.

Wallace, J. Warner. *Cold Case Christianity: A Homicide Detective Investigates the Claims of the Gospels.* Colorado Springs, CO: David C. Cook, 2013.

Zuck, Roy B., and general, eds. *Vital Apologetic Issues: Examining Reason and Revelation in Biblical Perspective.* Grand Rapids, MI: Kregel Resources, 1995.

BIBLICAL TRUSTWORTHINESS, INSPIRATION, INERRANCY, AND CANON

Arndt, William. *Bible Difficulties and Seeming Contradictions.* Rev. ed. St. Louis: Concordia Pub. House, 1987.

Barnett, Paul. *Is the New Testament Reliable? A Look at the Historical Evidence.* Downers Grove, Ill.: InterVarsity Press, 1986.

Blomberg, Craig L. *Can We Still Believe the Bible? An Evangelical Engagement with Contemporary Questions.* Grand Rapids, MI: Brazos Press, 2014.

_____. *The Historical Reliability of the Gospels.* Leicester, England. Reprint, Downers Grove, Ill., USA: Varsity Press, Inter, 1987.

Blunt, J.J. *Undesigned Coincidences in the Writings Both of the Old and New Testaments: An Argument of their Veracity.* NY: Robert Carter and bros., 1851. (available as a pdf on http://historicalapologetics.org/blunt-john-james/)

Boyd, Gregory A. and Paul Rhodes Eddy. *Lord or Legend? Wrestling With the Jesus Dilemma.* Grand Rapids, MI: BakerBooks, 2007.

Brake, Donald L. *A Visual History of the English Bible: The Tumultuous Tale of the World's Bestselling Book.* Grand Rapids, MI: Baker Books, 2008.

Bruce, F.F. *The Canon of Scripture.* Downers Grove: InterVarsity Press, 1988.

———. *The New Testament Documents: Are They Reliable?* Grand Rapids, MI: Eerdmans, 1987.

Burleson, Doug. *Once Delivered Forever Established: The Certainty of the Holy Scriptures.* Vienna, WV: Warren Christian Apologetics Center, 2017.

Center for the Study of New Testament Manuscripts, The. http://www.csntm.org. Accessed May 5, 2017.

Geisler, Norman L., and William E. Nix. *From God to Us: How We Got Our Bible.* Chicago: Moody Press, 1974.

———. ed. *Inerrancy.* Grand Rapids, Mich.: Zondervan Pub. House, 1980.

———. and Thomas Howe. *The Big Book of Bible Difficulties,* reprint ed. Grand Rapids, MI: BakerBooks, 2008.

Gerstner, John H. *A Bible Inerrancy Primer.* Baker Book House, 1965. Reprint, Winona Lake, IN: Alpha Publications, 1980.

Greenlee J. Harold. *Scribes, Scrolls, and Scripture: A Student's Guide to New Testament Textual Criticism.* Grand Rapids, Mich.: W.B. Eerdmans Pub. Co., 1985.

Haley, John. *Alleged Discrepancies of the Bible.* Grand Rapids, MI: Baker Book House, 1977.

Hamilton, Tom. "How Can I Be Sure The Bible Includes The Right Books?" In *Challenges of Our Times*. Edited by Dan Petty. Temple Terrace, FL: Florida College Bookstore, 2008.

Jones, Clay. "The Bibliographical Test Updated." Oct. 1, 2013. http://www.equip.org/article/the-bibliographical-test-updated/. Accessed May 5, 2017.

Keener, Craig S. "The Historical Reliability of the Gospels," In *Come Let Us Reason: New Essays in Christian Apologetics*. ed. William Lane Craig and Paul Copan. B&H Publishing, 2012.

Ladd, George Eldon. *The New Testament and Criticism*. Grand Rapids, MI: Eerdmans Publishing Co., 1967.

Lightfoot, Neil R. *How We Got The Bible*. 3d ed. Grand Rapids, Michigan: Baker Books, 2003.

Madrigal, Ray. "Dealing with Discrepanices." In *A Tribute to Melvin Curry, Jr.* ed. Ferrell Jenkins, 196-205. Temple Terrace, FL: Florida College Bookstore, 1997.

McDonald, Lee Martin and Stanley E. Porter. *Early Christianity and its Sacred Literature*. Peabody, MA: Hendrickson Publishers, 2000.

McGrew, Lydia. *Hidden in Plain View: Undesigned Coincidences in the Gospels and Acts*. Chillicothe, OH: DeWard Publishing Co., 2017.

McGrew, Tim. *Internal Evidence for the Truth of the Gospels and Acts,*. Feb. 2012. Web. Accessed July 3, 2017, <http://www.apologetics315.com/2012/03/internal-evidence-for-gospels-by.html>

Montgomery, John Warwick, ed. *God's Inerrant Word: An International Symposium on the Trustworthiness of Scripture.* Minneapolis, MN: Bethany House, 1974.

Muncaster, Ralph O. *Can You Trust the Bible?* Eugene, OR: Harvest House Publishers, 2000.

New Testament Virtual Manuscript Room. http://ntvmr.uni-muenster.de/home. Accessed May 5< 2017.

Osborne, Grant R. *3 Crucial Questions about the Bible.* Grand Rapids, Mich.: Baker Books, 1995.

Paley, William. *A View of the Evidences of Christianity: In Three Parts.* Edited by Richard Whately. NY: James Miller, 1865. (available as a pdf on http://historicalapologetics.org/paley-william/)

Pickup, Martin. "Canonicity of The Bible." In *Reemphasizing Bible Basics in Current Controversies.* Edited by Melvin D. Curry. Florida College Annual Lectures. Reprint, Temple Terrace, FL: Florida College Bookstore, 1990.

Pinnock, Clark H. *Biblical Revelation: The Foundation of Christian Theology.* Phillipsburg, NJ: Presbyterian and Reformed Publishing Co., 1971.

_____. *A Defense of Biblical Infallibility.* Phillipsburg, NJ: Presbyterian and Reformed Publishing Co., 1967.

Pryor, Neale. *You Can Trust Your Bible.* Abilene, TX: Quality Publications, 1980.

Roberts, Mark D. *Can We Trust the Gospels? Investigating the Reliability of Matthew, Mark, Luke, and John.* Wheaton, Ill.: Crossway Books, 2007.

Robinson, John A. T. *Can We Trust the New Testament.* Grand Rapids, MI: Eerdmans, 1977.

Scott, Shane. "The Problem of The Canon." In *A Place to Stand.* Edited by Ferrell Jenkins. Temple Terrace, FL: Florida College Bookstore, 1999.

Stein, Robert H.. *Difficult Sayings in the Gospels.* Grand Rapids, MI: Baker Book House, 1985.

_____. *The Synoptic Problem: An Introduction.* Grand Rapids, MI: Baker Book House, 1987.

Stewart, Robert B., ed. *The Reliability of the New Testament: Bart D. Ehrman and Daniel B. Wallace in Dialogue.* Minneapolis, MN: Augsburg Press, 2011.

Stott, John R.W. *You Can Trust the Bible,* Discovery House Publishers ed. Grand Rapids, MI: Discovery House, 1991.

Warfield, Benjamin B. *The Inspiration and Authority of the Bible.* Phillipsburg, NJ: The Presbyterian and Reformed Publishing Company, 1948.

Witherington, Ben, III. *The Living Word of God: Rethinking the Theology of the Bible.* Waco, Tex.: Baylor University Press, 2007.

White, James R. *Scripture Alone.* Minneapolis, Minn.: Bethany House, 2004.

Young, Edward J. *Thy Word Is Truth.* Grand Rapids, MI: Eerdmans, 1957.

THE HISTORICAL JESUS CHRIST, MIRACLES, AND THE RESURRECTION

Bauckham, Richard. *Jesus and the Eyewitnesses: The Gospels as Eyewitness Testimony*. Grand Rapids, Mich.: William B. Eerdmans Pub. Co., 2006.

Bock, Darrell L. *The Missing Gospels: Unearthing the Truth Behind Alternative Christianities*. Nashville: Nelson Books, 2006.

_____. *Studying The Historical Jesus: A Guide to Sources and Methods*. Grand Rapids, MI: Baker Academic, 2002.

Bowman, Robert M., Jr., and J. Ed Komoszewski. *Putting Jesus in His Place: The Case for the Deity of Christ*. Grand Rapids, MI: Kregel Publications, 2007.

Boyd, Gregory A. *Cynic Sage or Son of God*. Wheaton, Ill: BridgePoint, 1995.

_____. *Jesus Under Siege*. Wheaton, Ill.: Victor Books, 1995.

Copan, Paul, and Ronald K. Tacelli, eds. *Jesus' Resurrection: Fact or Figment? A Debate Between William Lane Craig & Gerd Ludemann*. Downers Grove, Ill.: InterVarsity Press, 2000.

Copan, Paul, ed. *Will The Real Jesus Please Stand Up? A Debate Between William Lane Craig and John Dominic Crossan*. Grand Rapids, Mich.: Baker Books, 1998.

Craig, William Lane, and Ehrman Bart. "The Craig-Ehrman Debate: Is there Historical Evidence for the Resurrection of Jesus?" March 28, 2006. *Reasonable Faith*. http://www.reasonablefaith.org

Day of Discovery Productions. "Jesus: Man, Messiah, or More? An 8 part Video Series," http://dod.org/Products/DOD2121.aspx.

Eddy, Paul Rhodes, and Gregory A. Boyd. *The Jesus Legend: A Case for the Historical Reliability of the Synoptic Jesus Tradition.* Grand Rapids, MI: Baker Academic, 2007.

Evans, Craig A. *Fabricating Jesus: How Modern Scholars Distort the Gospels.* Downers Grove, Ill.: IVP Books, 2006.

Groothuis, Douglas. *Jesus in an Age of Controversy.* Eugene, Or.: Harvest House Publishers, 1996.

Habermas, Gary R. *The Verdict of History: Conclusive Evidence for the Life of Jesus.* Nashville: T. Nelson, 1988.

_____. *The Historical Jesus: Ancient Evidence for the Life of Christ.* Joplin, MO: College Press, 1996.

_____ and Antony G.N. Flew. *Did Jesus Rise From the Dead? The Resurrection Debate.* San Francisco: Harper & Row, 1987.

_____. *Resurrected? An Atheist and Theist Dialogue.* Lanham, MD: Rowman & Littlefield Publishers, 2005.

_____ and Michael R. Licona. *The Case for the Resurrection of Jesus.* Grand Rapids: Kregel Publications, 2004.

Harris, Murray J. *3 Crucial Questions about Jesus.* Grand Rapids, MI: Baker Books, 1994.

Haygood, Atticus G. *The Man of Galilee.* Heritage of Faith. Reprint. Chillocothe, OH: DeWard Publishing Co., 2007.

Johnson, Luke Timothy. *The Real Jesus: The Misguided Quest for the Historical Jesus and the Truth of the Traditional Gospels.* San Francisco: HarperSanFrancisco, 1996.

Komoszewski, J. Ed, M. James Sawyer, and Daniel B. Wallace. *Reinventing Jesus: How Contemporary Skeptics Miss the Real Jesus and Mislead Popular Culture.* Grand Rapids, MI: Kregel Publications, 2006.

Ladd, George Eldon. *I Believe in The Resurrection of Jesus.* Grand Rapids, MI: Eerdmans Publishing Co., 1975.

Licona, Michael R. *The Resurrection of Jesus: A New Historiographical Approach.* Downers Grove, IL: IVP Academic, 2010.

Licona, Michael R. *Why Are There Differences in the Gospels?: What We Can Learn from Ancient Biography.* Oxford University Press. Kindle Edition, 2016.

Morison, Frank. *Who Moved the Stone?* Grand Rapids, MI: Lamplighter Books, 1958.

Patton, Michael C. "You Can't Use the Bible" to Prove the Bible and Other Stupid Statements.   Parchment and Pen. Sept. 10, 2013. Web. Accessed Sept. 28, 2013. <http://www.reclaimingthemind.org/blog/2013/09/you-cant-use-the-bible-to-prove-the-bible-and-other-stupid-statements/>

Reymond, Robert L. *Jesus Divine Messiah.* Phillipsburg, NJ: Presbyterian and Reformed Publishing Co., 1990.

Strobel, Lee. *The Case for Christ: A Journalist's Personal Investigation of the Evidence for Jesus.* Grand Rapids, MI: Zondervan, 1998.

_____. *The Case for the Real Jesus: A Journalist Investigates Current Attacks on the Identity of Christ.* Grand Rapids, MI: Zondervan, 2007.

Witherington, Ben, III. *What Have They Done With Jesus? Beyond Strange Theories and Bad History -- Why We Can Trust the Bible*. New York: HarperOne, 2006.

Wright, N.T. *The Resurrection of the Son of God*. Minneapolis: Fortress Press, 2003.

SCIENCE AND EVOLUTION

Axe, Douglas. *Undeniable: How Biology Confirms our Intuition that Life is Designed*. New York: HarperOne, 2016.

Behe, Michael J. *Darwin's Black Box: The Biochemical Challenge to Evolution*. NY: Free Press, 2006.

Berlinski, David. *The Deniable Darwin and Other Essays*. Edited by David Klinghoffer. Seattle, WA: Discovery Institute, 2009.

_____. *The Devil's Delusion: Atheism and Its Scientific Pretensions*. NY: Basic Books, 2009.

Dembski, William A., ed. *Darwin's Nemesis: Phillip Johnson and the Intelligent Design Movement*. Downers Grove, Ill.: IVP Academic, 2006.

_____. and James M. Kushiner. *Signs of Intelligence*. Grand Rapids, MI: Brazos Press, 2001.

Denton, Michael. *Evolution: a Theory in Crisis*. 3rd ed. MD: Adler and Adler, 1986.

Denton, Michael. *Evolution: Still a Theory in Crisis*. Seattle, WA: Discovery Institute, 2016.

_____. *Nature's Destiny: How the Laws of Biology Reveal Purpose in the Universe*. NY: Free Press, 2002.

Flew, Antony. *There Is a God: How The World's Most Notorious Atheist Changed His Mind.* San Francisco: HarperOne, 2007.

Gills, James P. and Tom Woodward. *Darwinism Under The Microscope: How Recent Scientific Evidence Points to Divine Design.* Lake Mary, Fla.: Charisma House, 2002.

Hunter, Cornelius G. *Darwin's God: Evolution and The Problem of Evil.* Grand Rapids, Mich.: Brazos Press, 2001.

Huse, Scott M. *The Collapse of Evolution.* 3d ed. Grand Rapids, Mich.: Baker Books, 1997.

Jastrow, Robert. *God and the Astronomers.* New York: W.W. Norton, 1992.

Johnson, Phillip E. *Darwin On Trial.* 2d ed. Downers Grove, Ill.: InterVarsity Press, 1993.

_____. *Defeating Darwinism By Opening Minds.* Downers Grove, IL: InterVarsity Press, 1997.

_____. *The Wedge of Truth: Splitting the Foundations of Naturalism.* Downers Grove, Ill.: InterVarsity Press, 2000.

_____. *Reason in The Balance: The Case Against Naturalism in Science, Law & Education.* Downers Grove, Ill.: InterVarsity Press, 1995.

Meyer, Stephen C. *Darwin's Doubt: The Explosive Origin of Animal Life and the Case for Intelligent Design.* New York: HarperCollins, 2013.

Meyer, Stephen C. *Signature in the Cell: DNA and the Evidence for Intelligent Design.* New York: HarperOne, 2010.

Moreland, J.P. *Christianity and the Nature of Science.* Grand Rapids, Mich.: Baker Book House, 1989.

Paley, William. *Natural Theology.* Heritage of Faith. 12th ed. Reprint. Chillicothe, OH: DeWard Publishing Co., 2010.

Ratzsch, Del. *Science & Its Limits: The Natural Sciences in Christian Perspective,* 2d ed. Downers Grove, IL: InterVarsity Press, 2000.

Sproul, R.C. *Not a Chance: The Myth of Chance in Modern Science and Cosmology.* Grand Rapids, Mich.: Baker Books, 1994.

Strobel, Lee. *The Case for a Creator: A Journalist Investigates Scientific Evidence That Points Toward God.* Grand Rapids, Mich.: Zondervan, 2004.

Woodward, Thomas. *Doubts about Darwin: A History of Intelligent Design.* Grand Rapids, Mich.: Baker Books, 2003.

PHILOSOPHY (Worldviews, Postmodernism, the Problem of Evil, Moral Relativism, Logic)

Aquinas, Thomas. *Summa Theologica.* Coyote Canyon Press. Kindle Edition.

Augustine, Aurelius. *The Works of Saint Augustine.* Kindle Edition, 2015.

Bahnsen, Greg L. *Pushing the Antithesis: The Apologetic Methodology of Greg L. Bahnsen.* Edited by Gary DeMar. Powder Springs, GA: American Vision, 2007.

Beckwith, Francis J. and Gregory Koukl. *Relativism.* Grand Rapids, MI: Baker Books, 1998.

Bloom Allan. *The Closing of the American Mind.* NY: Simon and Schuster, 1987.

Copan, Paul. *Is God a Moral Monster?* Grand Rapids, MI: BakerBooks, 2011.

_____. *"True for You but Not for Me": Overcoming Objections to Christian Faith,* rev. ed. Minneapolis, MN: Bethany House, 2009.

_____ and William Lane Craig, eds. *Contending with Christianity's Critics: Answering New Atheists and Other Objectors.* Nashville, TN: B&H Publishing Group, 2009.

Eagleton, Terry. *On Evil.* New Haven: Yale University Press, 2010.

Evans, C. Stephen. *Philosophy of Religion: Thinking About Faith.* Downers Grove, Ill., U.S.A.: InterVarsity Press, 1985.

_____. *Pocket Dictionary of Apologetics and Philosophy of Religion.* Downers Grove, IL: InterVarsity Press, 2002.

Feser, Edward. *Five Proofs of the Existence of God.* San Francisco, CA: Ignatius Press, 2017.

Geisler, Norman L. *The Roots of Evil.* Grand Rapids, MI: Zondervan Publishing House, 1978.

Groothuis, Douglas R. *Truth Decay: Defending Christianity against the Challenges of Postmodernism.* Downers Grove, IL: InterVarsity Press, 2000.

Hick, John. "Religious Pluralism." In *Philosophy of Religion: Selected Readings.* Edited by Peterson, Michael, et al, 607-617. 3d ed. New York: Oxford University Press, 2007.

Kreeft, Peter. *Socratic Logic.* 3rd ed. Ed. Trent Dougherty. South Bend, IN: St. Augustine Press, 2008.

Johnson, Phillip E. *The Right Questions: Truth, Meaning & Public Debate.* Downers Grove, IL: InterVarsity Press, 2002.

Johnson, Phillip E. And John Mark Reynolds. *Against All Gods: What's Right and Wrong about the New Atheism.* Downers Grove, IL: InterVarsity Press, 2010.

Lewis, C.S. *Mere Christianity.* NY: Macmillan, 1952.

_____. *The Problem of Pain.* NY: Macmillan Publishing Co., Inc, 1962.

McCallum, Dennis, ed. *The Death of Truth.* Minneapolis, Minn.: Bethany House Publishers, 1996.

Moreland, J.P., and William Lane Craig. *Philosophical Foundations for a Christian Worldview.* Downers Grove, Ill.: InterVarsity Press, 2003.

Myers, Edward P. *The Problem of Evil and Suffering.* Revised. LA: Howard Publishing Co., 1992.

Nash, Ronald H. *Faith & Reason: Searching for a Rational Faith.* Grand Rapids, Mich.: Academie Books, 1988.

_____. *Life's Ultimate Questions.* Grand Rapids, MI: Zondervan, 1999.

Paley, William. *Natural Theology.* 12th ed. Reprint. Chillicothe, OH: DeWard Publishing Co., 2010.

Pascal, Blaise. *Pascal's Pensées.* NY: E.P. Dutton & Co, 1958. Public Domain. Kindle Edition.

Pearcey, Nancy. *Total Truth: Liberating Christianity from its Cultural Captivity.* Wheaton, IL: Crossway Books, 2004.

Philip, Johnson C. and Saneesh Cherian. *Logic and Apologetics: The Key to Identification of Right and Wrong Deduction.* 15th Rev. Philip Communications. Kindle Edition, 2015.

Plantinga, Alvin. *God, Freedom, and Evil.* Grand Rapids, MI: Eerdmans, 1977.

Sire, James W. *Naming The Elephant: Worldview As a Concept.* Downers Grove, IL: InterVarsity Press, 2004.

Wells, David F. *God in the Wasteland: The Reality of Truth in a World of Fading Dreams.* Grand Rapids, MI.: W.B. Eerdmans, 1994.

Zacharias, Ravi. *Can Man Live Without God?* Dallas: Word Publishing, 1994.

CITED SOURCES (not listed elsewhere)

Allen, Isaac. *Is Slavery Sanctioned by the Bible?* Public Domain Books: Kindle Edition, nd.

Arichea, Daniel C. and Howard A. Hatton. *A Handbook on Paul's First Letter to Timothy.* UBS Handbook Series. NY: United Bible Societies, 1995.

Beard, Mary, and Simon Price John North. *Religions of Rome.* 2 vol. Cambridge, UK: Cambridge University Press, 1998.

Blomberg, Craig. *The New American Commentary, Vol. 22: Matthew.* Nashville, TN: Broadman and Holman, 1992.

Borg, Marcus J. *Meeting Jesus Again for the First Time: The Historical Jesus & the Heart of Contemporary Faith.* San Francisco: HarperSanFrancisco, 1994.

Bultmann, Rudolph. *Jesus and the Word.* Translated by Louise Pettibone Smith and Erminie Huntress Lantero. New York: Scribner, 1958.

Crossan, John Dominic. *The Historical Jesus: The Life of a Mediterranean Jewish Peasant.* San Francisco: HarperSanFrancisco, 1991.

_____. *Jesus: A Revolutionary Biography.* San Francisco: HarperSanFrancisco, 1989.

Dawkins, Richard. "The Illusion of Design" in *Natural History Magazine*, November 2005.

Edwards, Jonathan. *The Works of Jonathan Edwards.* Kindle Edition.

Ehrman Bart D. *The New Testament: A Historical Introduction to the Early Christian Writings*, 4th ed. New York: Oxford University Press, 2008.

Fee, Gordon D. and Douglas Stuart, *How to Read the Bible for All Its Worth.* 3rd ed. Grand Rapids, MI: Zondervan, 2003.

Ferguson, Everett. *Early Christians Speak*, rev. ed. Abilene: ACU Press, 1987.

Funk, Robert W. *Honest to Jesus: Jesus for a New Millennium.* San Francisco: HarperSanFrancisco, 1996.

Greengus, Samuel. *Laws in the Bible and in Early Rabbinic Collections: The Legal Legacy of the Ancient Near East.* Eugene, OR: Cascade Books, 2011.

Gundry, Robert H. *Commentary on Mark* (Baker Publishing Group) Kindle Edition, 2011.

Guthrie, Donald, and Alec Motyer, eds. *The New Bible Commentary: Revised.* Grand Rapids, MI: Eerdmans, 1970.

Habershon, Ada R. *Study of the Types.* Grand Rapids, MI: Kregel Publications, 1997.

Hick, John, and et al. *Four Views on Salvation in a Pluralistic World.* Counterpoints. Grand Rapids, Mich.: Zondervan Pub. House, 1996.

Huxley, Julian. *Evolution in Action.* New York, NY: Mentor Books, 1953.

Ingersoll, Robert. "Tribute at His Brother's Grave," in *Wit, Wisdom, and Eloquence,* ed. R.L. Gray, 4th ed. Atlanta, GA: The Harrison Co., 1930.

James, William. "The Will to Believe," in *Essays in Pragmatism,* ed. Alburey Castell. New York: Hafner Publishing Co., 1948.

Jeffers, James S. *The Greco-Roman World of the New Testament Era: Exploring the Background of Early Christianity.* Downers Grove, Ill.: InterVarsity Press, 1999.

Lynch, Joseph H. *Early Christianity: A Brief History.* New York: Oxford University Press, 2010.

Niebuhr, Richard R. *Resurrection and Historical Reason.* New York: Charles Scribner's Sons, 1957.

Origen, "Contra Celsum," in *Ante-Nicene Fathers,* eds, Alexander Roberts, and James Donaldson. Peabody, MA: Hendrickson Publishers, 1994.

Pannenberg, Wolfhart. *Jesus--God and Man.* Translated by Lewis L. Wilkins and Duane A. Priebe. Philadelphia: Westminster Press, 1975.

Raven, Peter H., and George B. Johnson, *Biology,* 2d ed. St. Louis: Times Mirror/Mosby College Publishing, 1989.

Ruse, Michael. "What Darwin's Doubters Get Wrong," *The Chronicle Review.* March 12, 2010.

Russell, Bertrand. *Why I Am Not a Christian, and Other Essays on Religion and Related Subjects.* New York: Simon and Schuster, 1957.

Sartre Jean-Paul. "Existentialism," in *Existentialism from Dostoevsky to Sartre,* ed. Walter Kaufmann. NY: Meridian, 1975.

Shanks, Hershel. "The Biblical Minimalists: Expunging Ancient Israel's Past." *Bible Review* 13, no. 3 (July 1997), 32-39, 50-52.

Thiessen, Henry. *Introduction to the New Testament.* Grand Rapids, MI: Eerdmans, 1943.

Tomlinson, Hugh. "After Truth: Postmodernism and The Rhetoric of Science," in *Philosophy: A Text with Readings,* ed. Manuel Velasquez, 9th ed. Belmont, CA: Thomson and Wadsworth, 2005.

Walton, John H., Victor H. Matthews, and Mark W. Chavalas. *The IVP Bible Background Commentary: Old Testament.* Downers Grove, IL: InterVarsity Press, 2000.

_____ and J. Harvey Walton, *The Lost World of the Israelite Conquest* (Downer's Grove, IL: IVP Academic, 2017.

Weber, Stuart K. *Holman NT Commentary: Matthew.* Nashville, TN: Broadman and Holman, 2000.

Wallace, Daniel. *Mark 2:26 and the Problem of Abiathar.* Web, 2004. <https://bible.org/article/mark-226-and-problem-abiathar> Accessed July 4, 2017.

Wilson, Ian. *Jesus: The Evidence.* Cambridge: Harper & Row, 1984.

Made in the USA
Columbia, SC
21 July 2019